Writing the natural way

Also by Gabriele Lusser Rico

Western Literature: Themes and Writers (with G. Robert Carlson)
Living Literature: Beginnings (with Hans P. Guth)
*Balancing the Hemispheres: Brain Research and
    the Teaching of Writing* (with Mary Frances Claggett)

Writing the natural way

Using Right-Brain Techniques
to Release Your Expressive Powers

Gabriele Lusser Rico

J. P. TARCHER, INC.
Los Angeles
Distributed by Houghton Mifflin Company
Boston

Library of Congress Cataloging in Publication Data

Rico, Gabriele L.
　Writing the natural way.

　Bibliography: p. 280
　Includes index.
　1. English language—Rhetoric. 2. Creative writing.
I. Title.
PE1408.R566　1983　808'.042　82–16927
ISBN 0–87477–186–2
ISBN 0–87477–236–2 (ppbk.)

Requests for such permissions should be addressed to:
J. P. Tarcher, Inc.
9110 Sunset Blvd.
Los Angeles, CA 90069

Design by Cynthia Eyring
Layout by Michael Bass
Cluster illustrations by Terrie Lester

MANUFACTURED IN THE UNITED STATES OF AMERICA

V　10　9　8　7　6　5

First Edition

The author would like to thank the following for permission to reprint.

Antonio Canova, sculpture of Napoleon. By permission of Wellington Museum, London. Raymond Chandler, from *The Little Sister*. Copyright © renewed 1976 by Helga Greene. Reprinted by permission of Houghton Mifflin Company. e. e. cummings, "Buffalo Bill's" is reprinted from *Tulips & Chimneys* with permission of Liveright Publishing Corporation. Copyright 1923, 1925 and renewed 1951, 1953 by e. e. cummings. Copyright © 1973, 1976 by the Trustees for the e. e. cummings Trust. Copyright © 1973, 1976 by George James Firmage. T. S. Eliot, "The Hollow Men." From *T. S. Eliot, Collected Poems: 1909–1935*. Copyright 1936, Harcourt Brace & Co., Inc. Reprinted by permission. William Faulkner, *The Hamlet*, Copyright 1964 by William Faulkner. Reprinted by permission of Random House. Donald Finkel, "The Great Wave: Hokusai." From *The Clothing's New Emperor and Other Poems* by Donald Finkel. Copyright 1959 by Donald Finkel. Reprinted by permission of the author and Charles Scribner's Sons. F. Scott Fitzgerald, *The Great Gatsby*. Copyright 1925 by Charles Scribner's Sons. Reprinted by their permission. William Golding, *Lord of the Flies*. Copyright 1955 by Coward-McCann. Reprinted by permission from G. P. Putnam's Sons. Robert Hass, "Song." Reprinted by permission of the author. John Hawkes, *Second Skin*. Copyright 1964 by New Directions. Reprinted by their permission. Ernest Hemingway, *For Whom the Bell Tolls*. Copyright 1940 by Ernest Hemingway. Reprinted by permission of Charles Scribner's Sons. Greg Hill, *Homochronos* (sculpture). By permission of the sculptor. Hiroshige, *Evening Snow at Kambara*. By permission of Heibonsha, Ltd., Tokyo. Katsushika Hokusai, *The Great Wave at Kanagawa*. Reprinted by permission of The Metropolitan Museum of Art, The Howard Mansfield Collection, Rogers Fund, 1936. James Joyce, *Ulysses*. Copyright 1946 by Nora Joseph Joyce. Reprinted by permission from Random House, Inc. Stanley Kunitz, "portrait." From *The Testing Tree*, © 1971, Little Brown and Co. Ole Langerhorst, three wood sculptures, each untitled. By permission of the artist. D. H. Lawrence, "Bavarian Gentians." From *The Complete Poems of D. H. Lawrence*. Copyright 1964, Viking Press. Reprinted by permission. D. H. Lawrence, *Sons and Lovers*. Copyright 1957 by Viking Press. Reprinted by permission. Doris Lessing, *The Golden Notebook*. Copyright 1962, Simon & Schuster, Inc. Reprinted by their permission. Philip Lopate, "photograph." From *Being with Children*, copyright 1975 by Doubleday & Co. Reprinted by their permission. Archibald MacLeish, "The End of the World." From *New and Collected Poems 1917–1976*, by Archibald MacLeish. Copyright © 1976 by Archibald MacLeish. Reprinted by permission of Houghton Mifflin Company. Louis MacNeice, "Prayer Before Birth." From *The Collected Poems of Louis MacNeice*, ed. by E. R. Dodds. Copyright The Estate of Louis MacNeice 1966. Reprinted by permission of Oxford University Press, Inc. Peter Meinke, untitled poem. From *The Night Train and the Golden Bird*. Copyright 1977 by the University of Pittsburgh Press. W. S. Merwin, untitled. From *Green with Beasts*. Reprinted by permission of Harold Ober Associates Incorporated. Copyright © 1956 by W. S. Merwin. Michelangelo, *David* (sculpture). By permission of Accademia, Florence. Diane Wood Middlebrook, "Writing a Poem in Syllabics." *Worlds Into Words*. W. W. Norton & Co., New York, 1980. Flannery O'Conner, "The Displaced Person." From *A Good Man Is Hard to Find*. Copyright 1953, Harcourt Brace & World. Reprinted by permission. Robert Peck, *A Day No Pigs Would Die*. Copyright 1972 by Robert Newton Peck. Reprinted by permission of Alfred A. Knopf, Inc. Nils Peterson, "Bedtime." Unpublished ms. Reprinted by permission of the author. Pablo Picasso, *Tête de tareau*. Height 41 cm, bronze, 1943. By permission of Martin Bressler, V.A.G.A. John Crowe Ransom, "Parting, Without a Sequel." From *Selected Poems*. Copyright 1927 by Alfred A. Knopf, Inc.; renewed 1955 by John Crowe. Alastair Reid, "A Lesson in Music." From *Weathering*, copyright 1978 by Alastair Reid and reprinted by his permission. Alastair Reid, "In Such a Pose Is Love." From *Weathering*, copyright 1978 by Alastair Reid and reprinted by his permission. Theodore Roethke, "The Dying Man." From *Words for the Wind, The Collected Verse of Theodore Roethke*. Copyright 1969 by Indiana University Press. Reprinted by their permission. Theodore Roethke, "The Far Field." From *The Far Field*. Copyright 1964 by Doubleday & Co. Reprinted by their permission. Theodore Roethke, "In a Dark Time." From *The Far Field*. Copyright 1964 by Doubleday & Co. Reprinted by their permission. Anne Sexton, "Ringing the Bells." From *To Bedlam and Part Way Back*. Copyright © 1960 by Anne Sexton. Reprinted by permission of Houghton Mifflin Company. Jon Stallworthy, "Lament." From *Astronomy of Love*, Oxford University Press, reprinted by their permission. Mark Strand, "Elegy for My Father." From *The Story of Our Lives* © 1973 by Mark Strand. Used by permission of Atheneum Publishers. Gertrude Stein, *The World Is Round*. Copyright 1967 by Gertrude Stein. Reprinted by permission of Addison-Wesley Publishing Co. May Swenson, "Question." From *New and Selected Things Taking Place*. Copyright 1954 by May Swenson. By permission of Little, Brown and Company in association with the Atlantic Monthly Press. D. M. Thomas, *The White Hotel*. Copyright 1981, The Viking Press. Reprinted by their permission. John Updike, *The Centaur*. Copyright 1963 by John Updike. Reprinted by permission of Alfred A. Knopf, Inc. John Updike, "Wife-Wooing." From *Pigeon Feathers and Other Stories*. Copyright 1960 by John Updike. Reprinted by permission of Alfred A. Knopf, Inc. Opal Whitely, *Opal*. Copyright 1976 by The Macmillan Co. Reprinted by their permission. Grand Wood, *American Gothic*. Courtesy of The Art Institute of Chicago. Virginia Woolf, *To the Lighthouse*. Copyright 1927 by Harcourt, Brace & Company. Reprinted by their permission. William Butler Yeats, "A Deep-Sworn Vow." From Collected Poems. Copyright 1919 by The Macmillan Company. Used by their permission. Al Young, "There Is a Sadness." From *The Song Turning Back into Itself*. Copyright 1971 by Al Young. Reprinted by permission of Holt, Rinehart, Winston, Inc.

Contents

For P. N.,
without whom,
   naught

Knowing anything in its deepest sense
means knowing how to be creative with it.
   Elliot Eisner,
   Professor of Art and Education
   Stanford University

Preface

Writing the Natural Way has been designed to inform and inspire all writers—beginning or advanced—to call upon and enhance their own creative powers.

The course I present in this book came about because I wondered, as I was teaching more or less in line with traditional composition methods, why so many students had such intense distaste, fear, even loathing for writing. I also noticed that despite my experimenting with a wide variety of techniques, my students left my class just as they had entered: good, mediocre, or poor writers.

Then, during my doctoral work at Stanford in 1973, I stumbled across the exciting frontier of recent brain research through an article by Dr. Joseph Bogen on hemispheric specialization and creativity. The more I read about the two different modes of knowing available to us through the specialized hemispheres of the brain, the more convinced I became that this way of looking at how the mind works had much to tell me about what was wrong with the way we teach writing. I discovered that what I term "natural writing" begins with wholeness, specifically with the innate human drive to shape personally meaningful, coherent wholes. Thus, what was likely to be missing from the traditional teaching of writing was a deliberate right-hemisphere involvement in this complex symbolic activity.

At the same time I was reading psychiatrist Anton Ehrenzweig's *The Hidden Order of Art,* in which appeared a complex diagram, looking very much like a roadmap—his view of what happens in a creative

9

search. As I experimented with what a creative search might look like on paper, the process I have termed "clustering" was born. Seizing the word uppermost in my mind as I looked at Ehrenzweig's diagram, I circled (MAZE) in the center of a blank page and clustered, electrified by the connections in my head that spilled and radiated outward from its center (Figure 1). As I continued to cluster, I suddenly experienced a shift from a sense of randomness to a sense of direction in all this welter, and I began to write.

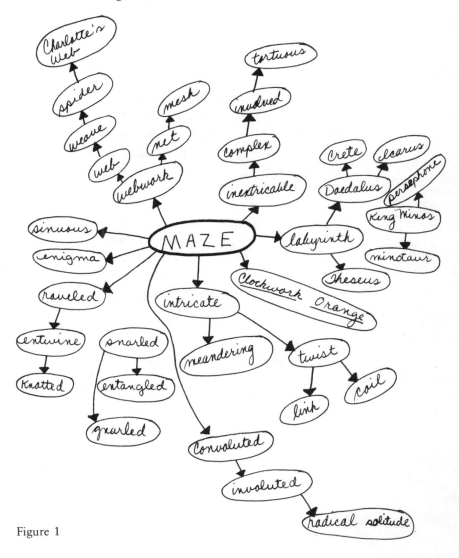

Figure 1

Eagerly I appeared before my freshman composition class the next day and told my students about a new creative-search process that would tap a part of their brain they rarely channeled in writing, a process that might dramatically change their approach to writing. Although they looked at me somewhat skeptically, they complied. From that day on, through the use of the nonlinear brainstorming process of clustering, my students' writing made a dramatic turnabout, and it has been my approach to teaching writing ever since.

In time, I began to examine the brief daily ten-minute writings that resulted from the clusters. Almost all demonstrated a coherence, unity, and sense of wholeness; a recurrence of words and phrases, ideas, or images that reflected pattern sensitivity; an awareness of the nuances of language rhythms; a significant and natural use of images and metaphors; and a powerful "creative tension."

Another by-product of clustering seemed to be a significant drop in errors of punctuation, awkward phrasing, even spelling. At first I was puzzled, but it soon became clear that, once students discover something to write about or at least a sense of direction, they become so involved in expressing this direction, they worry less about *how* the parts fit together or what errors they might be making than about communicating the whole thought.

Concurrently, I was doing considerable reading on the creative process and exploring young children's writing and early storytelling. Much to my surprise I found that many of the same qualities I had discovered in my students' clustered writing also appeared in children's early writing: a sense of wholeness, a sensitivity to language rhythms and recurrences, a heavy dependence on images and metaphor, and so forth.

Exhilarated by all these discoveries and their interconnectedness, I wrote a dissertation in which my background in literature, my abiding interest in writing and the creative process, and my new exposure to the mysteries of the brain all came together in a new synthesis.

In 1976, five months after completing my dissertation, I was both startled and encouraged to discover that, a continent away, someone else had developed a process akin to clustering. That someone was Englishman Tony Buzan whose book *Use Both Sides of the Brain* was published in 1976. He called his process "mapping." Although clustering and mapping are put to different uses and look different on the page, it seemed that two people an ocean apart had arrived independently at an idea whose time had come.

We . . . write to heighten our own awareness of life. . . . We write to taste life twice, in the moment and in retrospection. . . . We write to be able to transcend our life, to reach beyond it . . . to teach ourselves to speak with others, to record the journey into the labyrinth . . . to expand our world, when we feel strangled, constricted, lonely. . . . When I don't write I feel my world shrinking. I feel I lose my fire, my color.

Anaïs Nin,
The Diary of Anaïs Nin, V.5.

My experimentation with the techniques of natural writing over the past seven years in the classroom, workshops, and seminars has culminated in this book. Its thesis, quite simply, is that writing is inherently a much more natural process if we learn to flow with, rather than fight, the natural cooperative rhythms of the hemispheres of our brain. I refer to "natural" in the sense of "inborn," "native." We all have the potential to develop our natural expressive powers.

As the book gradually took shape there came the dawning realization that the natural qualities I had identified in the clustered vignettes of my students and in the writing of young children were the very qualities poets and great writers in general have exhibited for centuries. And those qualities depend heavily on one's ability to tap the right hemisphere's sensitivity to wholeness, image, and the unforced rhythms of language.

Thus, the chapters that follow present my course of proven processes for releasing your natural writer by involving the right hemisphere of your brain. In making its talents accessible to the left hemisphere, you can realize your potential as a creative individual of considerable expressive power. In this course you will rediscover your natural ability for writing by experimenting creatively with different aspects of your long-dormant language capabilities. In so doing, you will discover and develop your own unique means of expression and you will draw on memories, emotions, experiences, and images you may never have thought within reach. And that is only half the benefit. Beyond learning to write naturally, you will learn to exercise your right-brain potential for hearing, seeing, and, ultimately, living more creatively.

Acknowledgments

This book reflects years of input from others. I owe a 20-year debt to Tobias Grether, whose philosophical development of *homochronos*, time-conscious man, has long influenced my thinking; to Dr. Joseph Bogen, who not only served on my dissertation committee as an expert on the split brain but has since become a highly valued friend and an unending source of solid information on brain functions; to Professor Elliot Eisner of Stanford, who almost a decade ago gave me free rein to embark on new ways of seeing; and to Professor Hans P. Guth of San José State University, who many years ago introduced me to the world of publishing.

I also thank my incisive editors, Janice Gallagher and Victoria Pasternack, who, with their uncanny "feel" of what is good (and what is not good), unerringly steered me in the most productive direction; my office mate Scott Rice, who was ever willing to look up the sources for quotations; and Val Williams, who typed a fine manuscript.

Finally, there are my three wonderfully supportive children, Stephanie, Suzanne, and Simone, whose childhood writings long ago became the objects of my scrutiny; the many writing teachers in my workshops and seminars who have provided me with valuable feedback; and my thousands of students whose willingness to try one natural strategy after another allowed me to evaluate the power of each—and whose natural writing is at the heart of this book.

CHAPTER 1/ *Releasing Your Inner Writer*

If you can speak, form letters on the page, know the rudiments of sentence structure, take a telephone message, or write a thank-you note, you have sufficient language skills to learn to write the natural way. Formal knowledge of grammar is not a prerequisite. Just as a flawless piano-playing technique may not deliver a moving performance, a thorough training in the mechanics of writing does not necessarily produce good writing—and it rarely produces writing from within. Fortunately, the potential for natural writing is already within all of us; it is not too late for any of us to learn.

Central to natural writing is an attitude of wonder. If you recall wondering about things as a child, if you daydream occasionally, if you find yourself creating a story out of something that happened to you for the entertainment of your listener, you can develop—through the exercises in this book—the ability to generate written words more easily, to express your ideas more authentically, to develop your own "voice"—that manner of expression unique to you.

We all have heard the saying that so-and-so is a "born writer." This fallacy puts the born writer in a different category from most of us—or so we think—since *we* have to struggle so hard with writing. And we are so dissatisfied with the results. In truth, the innate human need that underlies all writing, the need to give shape to your experience, is a gift we all possess from earliest childhood. Yet only a few of us keep on expressing this need through a sustained relationship with language, our natural urge for self-expression inhibited by the weight of rules and prescriptions. This is sad because children's writing naturally has an expressive power, an authenticity that inherently captures the sound of an individual on the page, an ability we seem to lose the more we learn about writing.

Our loss begins in school, when the process of writing is taught to us in fragments: mechanics, grammar, and vocabulary. Writing becomes fearful and loathsome, a workbook activity. Students write as little as possible and, once out of school, they tend to avoid the entire process whenever possible. As a result, few people turn to writing as a natural source of pleasure and gratification.

Let us begin with the whole, with the fundamental human desire for giving shape to experience, for expressiveness, for creating form and structure out of the confusion that constitutes both our inner and outer worlds. Natural writing is first of all an act of self-definition of what you know, what you discover, what you wonder about, what you feel, see, hear, touch, taste—all of which reflects the many-faceted crystal that you are. The result of expressing your experience is a unique voice: yours. Your voice is expressed in storytelling, in pictures, in sound, in feelings, and above all in the focus you discover each time you write. Each of these characteristics of natural writing forms one of the chapters of this book, ultimately enabling you to achieve connectedness and coherence, texture and rhythm, authenticity and emotional intensity in your striving toward expressive power.

If you have tried writing but found your products dull, or if you have found the process itself painful and all too often frustrating, this book is for you. *Writing the Natural Way* is designed to take you from wherever you are as a writer, be you beginner or professional, fluent or blocked, old or young, and to rekindle your creative expressive powers that began when you first learned to speak—in the uninhibited delight you had in using words long before formal rules and painful criticism blocked your natural drive for self-expression. Learning to write naturally does not depend on literary terminology and grammatical classifications. Instead, natural writing depends on gaining access to a part of your mind we normally do not associate with writing skills. Contacting that part of your mind enables you to discover your own unique and natural voice, which is your primary source of expressive power.

*People often lack any voice at all in
their writing because they stop so
often in the act of writing a sentence and worry and change their
minds about which words to use.
They have none of the natural
breath in their writing that they
have in speaking. . . . We have so
little practice in writing, but so
much more time to stop and fiddle
as we write each sentence.*

Peter Elbow,
Writing with Power

*Most of the methods of training
the conscious side of the writer—
the craftsman and the critic in
him—are actually hostile to the
good of the artist's side; and the
converse of this proposition is likewise true. But it is possible to train
both sides of the character to work
in harmony, and the first step in
that education is to consider that
you must teach yourself not as
though you were one person, but
two.*

Dorothea Brande,
Becoming a Writer

Two Modes of Knowing: Sign and Design

Just as two heads are better than one for solving problems, so two brains are better than one when it comes to writing naturally.

The first step toward gaining originality and freedom of expression is to become aware of the two-sided nature of your mental makeup: one thinks in terms of the connectedness of things and events, the other thinks in terms of parts and sequences. Once we become aware of these different ways of processing our thoughts, we can not only learn to channel each one appropriately toward different phases of the writing process, but we can also learn to ensure that they work cooperatively for the greatest possible creative interaction.

Most teachers of writing, and certainly all investigators of the creative process, tend to agree that there are at least two distinctly different aspects of any creative act that sometimes come into conflict: the productive, generative, or "unconscious" phase; and the highly conscious, critical phase, which edits, refines, and revises what has been produced. Call it unconscious and conscious, artist and critic (I call it the Sign and Design minds, for reasons explained below), but whatever the nomenclature the task is to reserve these functions for their appropriate phases and to have them work harmoniously rather than conflict with one another.

In *Becoming a Writer,* an insightful 1934 book, novelist Dorothea Brande recognized these two conflicting sides of the writer's personality and the necessity for cultivating what she called the unconscious.

I have adopted the terms Sign mind and Design mind for these two aspects of creative thought because they characterize one of the most fundamental distinctions between the workings of the left and right hemispheres of the brain. Recent discoveries in brain research have shown that the left hemisphere, or Sign mind, is largely occupied with the rational, logical representation of reality and with parts and logical sequences. It has the capacity of ordering thought into communicable syntactic form—the way words are put together to form sentences. It acts as critic, censor, and error corrector. It splits the world into clearly definable units and classifies them by giving them clear-cut definitions—such as "woman: a female human being"—composed of unambiguous words used to denote meaning.

*What soul took thought and knew
that adding "wo" to man would
make a woman? The difference exactly. The wide w. The receptive o.
Womb. . . . Seven years since I
wed wide warm woman, white-
thighed. Wooed and wed. Wife. A
knife of a word that for all its final
bite did not end the wooing. To my
wonderment.*

*John Updike,
"Wife Wooing"*

Words used as signs have a precise and narrow scope. "Woman," for example, is a linguistic sign de*sign*ating a particular kind of human being that none of us confuse with children or men.

By contrast, the right hemisphere, or Design mind, constantly thinks in complex images; it patterns to make designs of whatever it encounters, including language, which, instead of clearcut signs, become *designs* of nonliteral meaning. If the Sign mind defines woman as a female human being, the Design mind gives us a "feel" of womanness through patterning, as John Updike does in his story "Wife Wooing."

Although each is a distinct way of expressing the same idea, only one has richness, depth, and originality, the qualities that permit us to understand something profound: Updike's perception of "womanness."

These are the qualities achieved by natural writing—not the stark, conventional, dull expression of a familiar idea, but all the nuances of meaning implicit in the language design that evokes emotion through its sensory images. And these sensory, evocative, unconventional capacities for expression seem to reside in the right hemisphere of the brain.

In writing naturally, participation of both sides is crucial, the one to give you access to the explanatory sign qualities of clear and unambiguous language as well as the sequencing powers necessary to writing; the other to perceive and express the more evocative design qualities of language as word images, rhythm, recurring pattern, and metaphor, all of which charge a passage emotionally.

Moreover, the thought pattern characteristic of the right brain lends itself to the formation of original ideas, insights, discoveries. We might describe it as the kind of thought prevalent in early childhood, when everything is new and everything has meaning. If you have ever walked along a beach and suddenly stopped to pick up a piece of driftwood because it looked to you like a leaping impala or a troll, you know the feeling of pleasure that comes from the sudden recognition of a form. Your Design mind has perceived connections and has made a pattern of meaning. It takes the logical, rational acts and facts of the world you know, the snippets of your experience, the bits and pieces of your language capabilities, and perceives connections, patterns, and relationships in them. While the right brain does this naturally, it is often overpowered by the logical, critical processes of the left brain ("That's not a leaping impala, it's just a piece of driftwood!"). We are going to learn how to cultivate and gain easy access to the right brain's creative potential for expressive power.

Risking an analogy, I might say that your Design mind attends to the melody of life, whereas your Sign mind attends to the notes that compose the melodies. And here is the key to natural writing: the melodies must come first.

Unfortunately, most of us have learned to write not in a state of release but by rule, with the result generally being flat, dull, turgid—most certainly not original, natural, free. The most fundamental difference between writing by rule and natural writing is that the former is imposed from without, whereas natural writing emerges from within. Our almost exclusive exposure to Sign-mind skills in writing courses from elementary school through graduate school has all too often resulted in an intense dislike of writing, even fear. Such one-sidedness has blocked us from—or failed to make use of—our creative, image-seeking mode, sadly limiting our natural potential for satisfying creative expression.

For these reasons, this course focuses on awakening and developing our much neglected Design mind in writing. Our right brain has been a stepchild in education—and in our lives. Much of the excitement of tapping your inner writer comes from restoring it to full function.

Interplay for Creative Power

Ultimately, a finished piece of writing or a painting or a sculpture—in short, any creative product—is the result of the collaboration between the talents of the two hemispheres, but in their proper sequence and in their proper interplay. During the generative phase of the writing process, while we are forming new ideas intuitively, we want to turn off the critical/logical/censoring Sign mind to be free of analytic reasoning. Once we begin to record and structure these ideas, the sequencing Sign mind comes into interplay with the envisioning Design mind. The continuous oscillation between a sense of the whole

*When each [self] has found its
place, when each is performing the
functions which are proper to it,
they play endlessly back and forth
into each others' hands, strength-
ening, inciting, relieving each other
in such a way that the resulting
personality, the integral character,
is made more balanced, mellow,
energetic, and profound.*
                    Dorothea Brande,
                    Becoming a Writer

you have envisioned and the parts with which you sequence that
vision into a more clearly delineated whole enables you to get your
vision onto paper. Finally, when you reread what you have written
and analyze it for structure, word choice, and appropriateness of detail, you are depending almost exclusively on your Sign mind's predilection for correctness. Working together in complementary fashion instead of tripping each other with inappropriate signals, your
two minds can produce a whole symphony of talents.

How to Use This Book

Throughout this book, "Directing Your Hand" is an invitation to
develop your natural writing skills by writing brief vignettes—short,
compressed, evocative pieces that are self-contained wholes. The book
is structured in such a way that you will start with a Design-mind
search for something to say, build on that newly acquired Design-
mind skill by learning seven writing techniques developed to tap the
creative abilities of your Design mind, and finally achieve the cooperation of both Sign and Design minds in producing vignette after
vignette that will be written naturally, spontaneously, pleasurably.

In the beginning you will relearn the fresh, childlike attitude of
wonder through clustering; later you will develop your inborn receptivity to pattern making through the trial web, regain the playfulness
of language rhythms and recurrences, draw on your natural imaging
powers, reclaim the ability to think metaphorically, reconcile opposites to build creative tension, and balance original vision with revision. The culminating chapter leads you into a sustained piece of
natural writing, combining all of the techniques presented throughout the book.

The techniques, each an aspect of natural writing, build on each
other. Each helps you develop originality, authenticity, and expressive power. With the addition of each new technique, you will also
be practicing what you have learned in the previous chapters. Do the
chapters in sequence, but feel free to go back for more experience
with any element that you found appealing or wanted to practice
more. The techniques can be used with any subject of your choosing.
Use your imagination and enjoy the results.

The Writer's Notebook: Your Track Record

In order to chart your own writing progress, keep your writing together in a spiral-bound notebook or loose-leaf binder, on lined or unlined paper, according to your preference. Should you elect to type, keep your writing in a manila folder. Date each writing experience and begin a fresh page for each new assignment. Each chapter will suggest several writing experiences, so by the end of the course you will have compiled a thick folder recording your progress.

Reread whenever you wish. In the course of your writing you will become your own best critic if you allow yourself to be guided by the degree of satisfaction you feel each time you read over what you have written. Pleasure, satisfaction, even amazement at your products are not uncommon responses. You will become immersed in the creative process as you learn to write comfortably and naturally; it will enrich your perceptions of, and reactions to, many aspects of your life, for the creative attitude affects all you do and see.

Writing Tools

A writing tool is an extension of your hand that is in turn directed by your brain. Of necessity I have learned—since I do much writing—to compose directly on a typewriter. For my purposes, it is far more efficient than longhand, just as electronic word processors are more efficient than typewriters. However, for exploratory stages or for trying to untangle a fuzzy thought, I have found that I invariably return to pen and writing pad. Experiment with various writing tools until you find the medium that helps your thoughts flow most freely. In the end, you must do what feels right for you. Some people are not at all intimidated by machinery. Others think even a typewriter is positively diabolical.

Time and Place: Creators As Creatures of Habit

Choose a time of day for writing and stick with it until it becomes a habit. If you are an early riser, get out of bed fifteen minutes before it is "officially" time to start your day and do an exercise in your writer's notebook. If you are a night owl, reserve some time before you customarily go to bed to write every night, or at least every weeknight. Should you be so lucky as to have some time to yourself before or after lunch, take these moments to fill your notebook.

Then find your place: the warm kitchen at 5 A.M. when everyone else is asleep, an extra bedroom, your bed, a corner of the local library, even your car parked along the beach or at a lookout post above the city. Like jogging or brushing teeth, make it happen every day, and sooner or later you will look forward to this time for exploring your own creative potential. If fifteen minutes is not enough time—and soon it won't be because you'll want more time to write—you can extend it or pick up your writer's notebook at other, less predictable times.

Sound and Design: Reading Aloud

"Heard melodies are sweet," wrote Keats. Language is meant to be heard as well as read. Think about it: Research shows that infants respond powerfully to the sound of the human voice, so learning language begins with our ears. Our earliest childhood is filled with sounds of stories being read to us, with skipping rhymes and riddles. Our brains are attuned to the subtleties of voice intonation and pauses. According to Joseph C. Pearce, a student of brain processes, sound—and particularly vocal sound—stimulates the brain into attention, as he explained in *The Bond of Power*.

Read your writing aloud—to yourself or to someone else, if you wish. Listening to the sound of your language will make you aware of its stylistic rhythms as well as the design of its content. The qualities of natural writing, such as wholeness, recurrences, language rhythms, image power, metaphoric connection, and creative tension, which were sadly overlooked during most of your schooling, come to the foreground when read aloud.

Directing Your Hand

Let yourself know where you are as a writer right now, before going on to Chapter 2. For many of you, a blank page generates feelings ranging from mild uneasiness to sheer terror. Don't expect

Sound proves one of the major sources of brain stimulus by which dynamic mental vitality is maintained. Vocal sounds directly resonate through the skull, chest, and body. Our personally produced resonances can charge and revitalize our body and brain.

Joseph C. Pearce,
The Bond of Power

to write a masterpiece yet. You simply want an indicator of your present level of skill to let you see how far you've come by the end of the course.

Try to write quickly and without censoring yourself or worrying about proper grammar or form. Don't worry about how you start or end. In Chapter 2 you'll discover a liberating technique that will erase the anxiety of the blank page, give you focus, help you know where to start, and tell you what you want to say. But for now, it's important to have a point of reference to come back to.

Limit yourself to ten minutes of writing for each of the four entries suggested below. If you cannot muster that much writing, don't worry. Your minimum should be a few sentences and your maximum a page, at most, for each entry. These parameters give you plenty of leeway.

Writing 1
Write something about yourself. Do so from any perspective you wish.
Writing 2
Describe a feeling, such as fear, love, sadness, or joy.
Writing 3
Write about someone you care for.
Writing 4
Write anything you can think of about the word "write."

After Writing

It is quite likely that for one entry or another you chewed the proverbial pencil for some moments, whereas another flowed relatively smoothly once you got started. It is also likely that writing about yourself gave you more trouble than writing about someone you care for, and that describing a feeling left you frustrated. Writing about "write" probably became a chronicle of the feelings you experienced while you were writing the other three entries. As you progress through the chapters, it will be interesting to see how your perceptions about writing will change.

Before and After: Writing Samples from My Students

I have included two "before" and "after" writing samples from beginning writers with diverse backgrounds who have taken my course. The first set lets you see the change from a constricted, fearful writer to a natural writer in three and a half months of instruction with the class meeting twice a week. This writer was a graduate student who had enrolled in a lower-division creative-writing course because, she said, "I never learned how to write." The "before" sample was written on the first day of class before any instruction took place; the "after" sample was part of the final assignment. Both writings focus on the self. Judge the changes in insight, originality, and expressive power for yourself.

Before: January 28, 1981

> *Myself*
>
> My image is developing in the public eye. Growing into a career position where I face hundreds of persons a day, I can feel my confidence stretching; my character demands a more polished self-esteem.
>
> I search for a method to evaluate this change of presence. How do I appear to the crowds of small children I teach? When I open my mind to my new image, a stranger walks about. I strain as I stand before the variety of faces, to reach everyone of them in some way, so they might reach back. I could be mirrored in each personal response and catch a glimpse of my new image reflected in the honesty of a child's eyes.
>
> Jillian Milligan

It is well to understand as early as possible in one's writing life that there is just one contribution which every one of us can make; we can give into the common pool of experience some comprehension of the world as it looks to each of us.
    Dorothea Brande,
    Becoming a Writer

After: May 15, 1981

And Me
In my small heart it is always winter
and my dinner is always cold.
Freezing tears pour in loneliness as I quietly
absorb dinnertable differences.
I pain for my sister's determination.
She succeeds by will at great cost
to her emotional fiber.
She is eternally mature.
   I will never reach her.
I yearn for a motherly soul,
while mommy rushes aimlessly about
in a profusion of feelings belonging
to another family named Humanity.
She is strapped to a raft,
lost in an emotional sea.
   I will never find her.
I hope for fatherly comfort
when his hands squeeze mine too tightly.
I scream fear at the angle of his sailboat,
and he abruptly rights the vessel, sending me
into fits of capsized agony and anger.
There was no calm with daddy at the helm.
His bold uniqueness constantly threatened,
all questions were followed by question
after question, after question.
I never received a simple, reliable answer.
   I will never trust him.
Like wood shrinking in the drying cold,
we have shrunk from each other,
carefully hiding our lives' memories away
in a warm safe deposit box of emotion
and swallowing the key.
My dinner is cold; there is a
great winter storm of
bitter flurries in me, even today.

Jillian Milligan

The second before-and-after set was written by an advanced writer of considerable sophistication—when it came to letters. Writing letters posed no problem for her because, she said, "I just let go and write what comes out without thinking too much about it." But when it came to an assignment, this writer's critical Sign-mind censor totally inhibited the free flow of ideas. In the "before" sample, I asked her to write about someone she cared for. In the "after" sample, only two weeks later, the same subject matter elicited a totally different and richly modulated vignette, specifically focused on one emotional moment. Again, judge for yourself.

Before: February 18, 1981

My Mother
My mother was a caring person, but she was also a person who had many problems, so she didn't pay as much attention to me as I wanted her to. She would stare in front of her a lot worrying about things I was too young to understand, but it made me feel sad and even a little bit rejected. I guess every kid needs to believe she is the center of her mother's universe.

Heide Kingsbury

After: March 2, 1981

I remember wanting to tell my mother what happened. "Mama, listen, Mama, listen to me, I want to tell you . . ." I remember that she only sat there, staring straight ahead. I wanted her to turn her head and look at me, so I would know definitively she was listening to me alone, not to some other voice inside, a voice louder than mine, more insistent than mine. I put my hand under her chin to turn her head to me. I remember the soft, warm skin, and I remember the pull of her chin away from me, until she finally turned her head. I remember my joy as I felt her turn— and I remember panic as her eyes, unfocused, looked past me. "What is it, child?" she asked, but I could not remember what it was I wanted to tell her.

Heide Kingsbury

A Last Word and Heading On

Expressive power in the form of storytelling is a basic human impulse rooted in our Design mind's desire to give form to our experience, to create meaning out of a world that all too often appears chaotic and fragmented. Although we tell stories long before we learn to print the simplest words on paper, the record of our self-definition takes on permanence only when we write it down, a potent tool in the process of growth, insight, and self-awareness. In so doing, we begin to express our own unique perception of our world.

As you read and work through the chapters to come, writing will once more become a natural expressive form rather than drudgery, a source of enormous satisfaction rather than an irritant, a means of expansion rather than fearful contraction. The enormous potential of language is accessible to all of us.

The first step is to immerse yourself in the prewriting process called *clustering,* the subject of Chapter 2. By tapping into the right brain, clustering not only frees your expressive power but also helps you discover what you have to say, encouraging a flow instead of a mere trickle. Let's go on to experience this doorway into your Design mind.

CHAPTER 2/ *Clustering: Doorway to Your Design Mind*

Nature operates by profusion. Think of the nearly infinite number of seeds that fall to earth, only a fraction of which take root to become trees; of those five thousand or so drones that exist solely to ensure the fertilization of one queen bee; of the millions of sperm competing so fiercely to fertilize one small egg.

Similarly, human beings engaged in the creative process explore an astronomical number of possible patterns before settling on an idea. In the preface to *Becoming a Writer* by Dorothea Brande, novelist John Gardner suggests that writers need some magic key for getting in touch with these secret reserves of imaginative power. What we lack is not ideas but a direct means of getting in touch with them.

Clustering is that magic key. In fact, it is the master key to natural writing. It is the crucial first step for bypassing our logical, orderly Sign-mind consciousness to touch the mental life of daydream, random thought, remembered incident, image, or sensation.

Clustering is a nonlinear brainstorming process akin to free association. It makes an invisible Design-mind process visible through a nonlinear spilling out of lightning associations that allows patterns to emerge. Through clustering we naturally come up with a multitude of choices from a part of our mind where the experiences of a lifetime mill and mingle. It is the writing tool that accepts wondering,

not-knowing, seeming chaos, gradually mapping an interior land-
scape as ideas begin to emerge. It is an openness to the unknown, an
attitude that says "I wonder where this is taking me?" Clustering
acknowledges that it's okay to start writing not knowing exactly what,
where, who, when, and how. Most writers acknowledge that this is
how it inevitably is anyway.

Too many of us get stuck because we *think* we should know
where to start and which ideas to develop. When we find we don't,
we become anxious and either force things or quit. We forget to
wonder, leaving ourselves open to what might come. Wondering
means it's acceptable not to know, and it is the natural state at the
beginning of all creative acts, as recent brain research shows.

Though we cannot force the birth of an idea, we can do the next
best thing: we can cluster, thus calling on the pattern-seeking Design
mind and bypassing the critical censorship of the Sign mind, which
relieves the familiar anxiety about what to say and where to start
and opens us to the freedom of expression we knew in childhood.

Letting Design Happen in Clustering

Clustering, as already suggested, is a Design-mind function. It marks
the first step for all the techniques described in this book and for all
the writing tasks you will engage in from now on. Just as many
natural forms come in clusters—grapes, lilacs, spider eggs, cherries—
so thoughts and images, when given free rein, seem to come in clusters of associations.

During all the months of my own wondering about the creative
process and how to facilitate it in writing, two quotations, one by
novelist Henry James, the other by literary critic Northrop Frye,
hummed in my head. James wrote, "The whole of anything cannot
be told; we can take only what groups together." And Frye, observ-
ing that words need never be frozen, wrote that any word can become "a storm center of meanings, sounds, and associations, radiating out indefinitely like ripples in a pool." In a moment of insight,
the word "clustering" popped into my head to describe this radiating
phenomenon of nonlinear connections around a "storm center of
meanings," which I call the "nucleus." And clustering it has been
ever since, the term I use to express the primary technique of natural

writing. A nucleus word or short phrase acts as the stimulus for recording all the associations that spring to mind in a very brief period of time.

Figure 2–1 shows you a student sample of clustering spilled onto paper around the nucleus phrase ⟨LETTING GO⟩ . The clustering was accomplished in a minute or two, the resulting writing in about eight minutes, as a direct result of the ideas that came to mind during the clustering process.

Figure 2–1

Letting go of one's children happens inch by inch over the years so that when it finally happens, that last quarter inch is not hard. Letting go of anger is a giant rebounding from the intensity of my anger, lifting me up with the air, weightless, rocking me softly as feathers sprung loose, rushing me along like blossoms in the spring wind, dropping me as gently as snowflakes falling. Letting go of past dreams and hopes requires more effort, but I can do it, and once I've taken that icy plunge, there's nothing like the invigoration of it, and nothing like pushing off from shore into the deeper waters, slowly rolling over on one's back and getting that sun-slanted view of mountains and arching sky. But letting go of pain is a mirror image of *me.* I look at pain, and I see me at three years old sitting in a closet hunched with knees drawn up, scowling, brows furrowed into an angry slash across the face. When I feel pain, I turn to hold and comfort that child. But she is voracious, comfortless, and all my holding on does no good. She is the worm in the center of my universe.

Shelia Sapir

The cluster around the nucleus "letting go" reflects this writer's emotional interests—of children, of anger, of the past, of pain. It also reflects her images of "letting go"—a "weightless floating in air" and the coolness of a mountain-lake swim. The vignette itself focuses on degrees of "letting go" with a progressive intensification of difficulty: children are the easiest because it is done "inch by inch," and pain the most difficult; when she feels pain, the writer tells us, she becomes a "comfortless child" who is the "worm in the center of my universe."

Note that not everything from the cluster is used: "balloons" and "holding onto the balloon" are left out. Other things are slightly changed. It is important to understand that clustering is the Design mind's shorthand and offers options, not all of which need find their way into the finished product.

Yet clustering is not merely the spilling of words and phrases at random, but something much more complex: for the Design mind, each association leads inexorably to the next with a logic of its own even though the Sign mind does not perceive the connection. Making connections has much more to do with the complexity of images and emotional qualities associated and held fast on paper until we suddenly—or gradually—perceive them as having a pattern or meaning.

The Nucleus: Finding Your Voice

Clustering always unfolds from a center, like ripples generated by a rock thrown into a pond. That center can be a nucleus word or phrase, or it can be a dominant impression, as we shall see later.

Nucleus comes from the Latin *nucula,* meaning "kernel" or "little nut"; it is the seed that contains all potential growth. If a nucleus word is allowed to filter through your personal experiential sieve, it will always generate writing expressive of your unique consciousness. That is the essence of natural writing: expression that is unique and authentic to you, your own "voice" heard in words written on the page.

Any word or phrase has the potential for getting the attention of your Design mind. Although you may not know its precise Sign-mind dictionary definition, as the word echoes through your Design mind it is like a magnet, picking up images, certain feelings and emotional nuances, lines of songs or poems, similar rhythms, whatever your pattern-seeking right brain perceives as related.

Figure 2–2, for example, is the first-time clustering experience of a professor of English, a published poet and clearly a lover of literature. When confronted with the nucleus word TIME , he complained that all he could think of to cluster were lines of poems having to do with time. But these reflect his rich reading background,

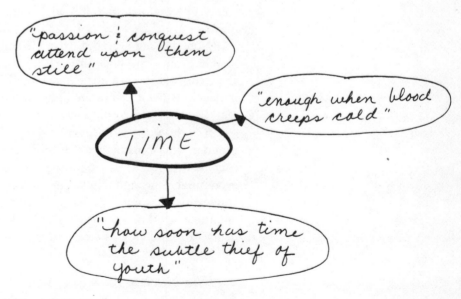

Figure 2–2

and one also gets the feeling that the sound of these lines were resonating in his Design mind just waiting to be tapped. Following the cluster is the vignette generated by these lines that helped him to discover a focus.

> How deeply aware of time are the poets—the quickness of its passing, the fragility of the now, the terror of its going. Dylan Thomas sings: "Time enough when the blood creeps cold and I lie down but to sleep in bed," pissing in his pants with the terror of it. Yeats, sick now and having proposed to Maude Gonne for 30 years and been said no to and thinking that it's all over for him and looking at the swans wheeling up from the dark waters of Coole and seeing them fly away lover by lover, writes out of the barren sadness of his soul: "Passion and conquest attend upon them still." It's all over for him, he feels. And Milton, a mere boy to my middle-aged sight, writes: "How soon hath time, the subtle thief of youth, stolen in truth my three and twentieth year." I may have the figures wrong, but I know the feeling— for I am 48, I am 48, I am 48.
>
> Nils Peterson

A nucleus word tends to evoke clusters of associations unique to each individual responding to it. For Nils Peterson, "time" became far more than the literal Sign-mind definition of "a nonspatial continuum in which events occur in apparently irreversible succession from the past through the present to the future," as the dictionary gives it. The word for him became emotionally charged through all his association with the emotional nuances expressed by other poets long dead.

As noted in Chapter 1, the Sign mind's use of language is largely explanatory whereas the Design mind's use of language is largely evocative. The former pigeonholes, conceptualizes, discriminates, analyzes, defines, constricts, and specifies, whereas the latter, in complementary fashion, connects, associates, suggests, and evokes. Let me illustrate how a nucleus word can evoke Design-mind associations that are initially out of the range of awareness of the Sign mind. Figure 2–3 is the work of a freshman composition student who was clustering for the first time. This student's Design mind clustered the nucleus (NARROW) readily enough, as you can see. It triggered a number of associations primarily derived from images: "tubes," "channels," "openings," "bridges." But here is the interesting thing: as he began to write, this student's Sign mind was still insisting that "narrow" had no meaning for him at all. Then see what happened as he used the Design-mind images made accessible through clustering.

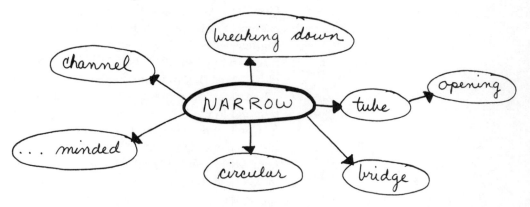

Figure 2–3

Narrow is a word that has no particular meaning to me. It's not that I don't want to write, it's just that, when I think of narrow, I associate it with narrow bridges, narrow channels, generally just narrow openings. For example, a narrow-minded person does not seem like a well-rounded person. Narrowing down to something is a tunneling down or reducing down. Narrowing the chances or narrowing down the competition is like breaking down the resistance, which is what this clustering exercise just did to me. I realize I was wrong about what I said in the first sentence. The word, narrow, does have meanings to me, after all.

Although far from deathless prose, this vignette illustrates the extent to which the Design mind can exercise its powers of associations without the direct awareness of the more logical Sign mind. In his writing, this student moved from insisting that "narrow" had no meaning for him to the realization that "I was wrong about what I said in the first sentence. The word, narrow, does have meanings to me, after all." He also brings us back to the beginning of his vignette, showing us where his thinking started. Interestingly, this technique of referring back to the beginning and thus coming full circle seems to develop naturally out of clustering and Design-mind thinking.

It is like fishing. But I do not wait very long, for there is always a nibble—and this is where receptivity comes in. To get started, I will accept anything that occurs to me. Something always occurs, of course, to any of us. We can't keep from thinking.

*William Stafford,
"A Way of Writing"*

*In most lives insight has been acci-
dental. We wait for it as primitive
man awaited lightning for a fire.
But making mental connections is
our most crucial learning tool, the
essence of human intelligence: to
forge links; to go beyond the given;
to see patterns, relationship, context.*

Marilyn Ferguson,
The Aquarian Conspiracy

Since clustering, which appeals to the information-processing style
of the Design mind, blocks the critical censorship of the Sign mind,
it undercuts tension, anxiety, and resistance. The receptive Design
mind is programmed to deal with novelty, ambiguity, and the unknown. If we are receptive, ideas come of their own accord.

Clustering not only unblocks and releases Design-mind knowings, it also generates inspiration and insight. For centuries we have
assumed that inspiration leaps at us out of nowhere and that we have
no choice but to wait for it to happen. Marilyn Ferguson, in *The
Aquarian Conspiracy,* observes that inspiration, once thought to be
the province of only a chosen few, is available to all of us if only we
learn to develop our innate capacities.

Finally, clustering is a self-organizing process. As you spill out
seemingly random words and phrases around a center, you will be
surprised to see patterns forming until a moment comes—characterized by an "aha!" feeling—when you suddenly sense a focus for writing. This moment is similar to watching clouds, and seeing just clouds;
then, in a sudden moment of recognition you see a horse or a duck
or Lincoln's profile. It is a moment of pattern recognition. The emotional surge of good feeling that accompanies this moment allows
you to begin writing. I have never seen it fail. (The emotionally
charged "aha!" will be discussed in detail in Chapter 5.)

General Principles of Clustering

To create a cluster, you begin with a nucleus word, circled, on a fresh
page. Now you simply let go and begin to flow with any current of
connections that come into your head. Write these down rapidly,
each in its own circle, radiating outward from the center in any direction they want to go. Connect each new word or phrase with a
line to the preceding circle. When something new and different strikes
you, begin again at the central nucleus and radiate outward until
those associations are exhausted.

As you cluster, you may experience a sense of randomness or, if
you are somewhat skeptical, an uneasy sense that it isn't leading anywhere. That is your logical Sign mind wanting to get into the act to

let you know how foolish you are being by not setting thoughts down in logical sequences. Trust this natural process, though. We all cluster mentally throughout our lives without knowing it; we have simply never made these clusterings visible on paper.

Since you are not responsible for any particular order of ideas or any special information, your initial anxiety will soon disappear, and in its place will be a certain playfulness. Continue to cluster, drawing lines and even arrows to associations that seem to go together, but don't dwell on what goes where. Let each association find its own place. If you momentarily run out of associations, doodle a bit by filling in arrows or making lines darker. This relaxed receptivity to ideas usually generates another spurt of associations until at some point you experience a sudden sense of what you are going to write about. At that point, simply stop clustering and begin writing. It's as easy as that.

There is no right or wrong way to cluster. It is your Design mind's shorthand and it knows where it is headed, even if you don't. Trust it. It has a wisdom of its own, shaping ends you can't really evaluate yet. This wisdom has nothing to do with logic; should you try to apply logic to what you have just clustered, this sense of knowing where you're headed will be destroyed. Then you simply begin to write. The words will come; the writing takes over and writes itself.

Directing Your Hand

Find a quiet, uninterrupted time and place to write. Plan on clustering and writing for about ten minutes in the writer's notebook in which you made the first four entries in Chapter 1. On the next blank page at the top left corner, write Vignette #1.

1. Write the word (AFRAID) in the upper third of the page, leaving the lower two-thirds of the page for writing, and circle it. We'll start with this word because even the most hesitant of us will discover many associations triggered by it.
2. Now get comfortable with the process of clustering by letting your playful, creative Design mind make connections. Keep the childlike attitude of newness and wonder and spill whatever associations come to you onto paper. What comes to mind when you think of the word? Avoid judging or choosing. Simply let go and write. Let the words or phrases radiate outward from

the nucleus word, and draw a circle around each of them. Connect those associations that seem related with lines. Add arrows to indicate direction, if you wish, but don't think too long or analyze. There is an "unthinking" quality to this process that suspends time.

This process is for you alone, your Design mind's shorthand made accessible to you so that you can develop it in your vignette. No one will be judging it. At first, your Sign mind may want to interfere, scolding that this is foolish, or illogical, or chaotic. Reassure yourself that this seeming chaos is an important first stage of the creative process you are engaged in.

3. Continue jotting down associations and ideas triggered by the word "afraid" for a minute or two, immersing yourself in the process. Since there is no *one* way to let the cluster spill onto the page, let yourself be guided by the patterning Design mind, connecting each association as you see fit without worrying about it. Let clustering happen naturally. It will, if you don't inhibit it with objections from your censoring Sign mind. If you reach a plateau where nothing spills out, "doodle" a bit by putting arrows on your existing cluster.

4. You will know when to stop clustering through a sudden, strong urge to write, usually after one to two minutes, when you feel a shift that says "Aha! I think I know what I want to say." If it doesn't happen suddenly, this awareness of a direction will creep up on you more gradually, as though someone were slowly unveiling a sculpture. (We will deal more thoroughly with this shift in Chapter 5, on trial webs.) For now, just know you will experience a mental shift characterized by the certain, satisfying feeling that you have something to write about.

5. You're ready to write. Scan the clustered perceptions and insights of your Design mind for a moment. Something therein will suggest your first sentence to you, and you're off. Students rarely, if ever, report difficulty writing that first sentence; on the contrary, they report it as being effortless. Should you feel stuck, however, write about anything from the cluster to get you started. The next thing and the next thing after that will come because your Design mind has already perceived a pattern of meaning. Trust it.

Write for about eight minutes and no more than half to three-quarters of a page, since your aim is to produce a self-contained vignette triggered by the word "afraid." As you write, you will shift from Design-mind vision or pattern to Sign-mind sequencing, the vision guiding the sequencing and the sequencing articulating the vision. You are now in an oscillating process from Design to Sign and back to Design.

Choose only what seems to fit the whole from your cluster. You have given yourself a profusion of choices. There is no need to force everything from the cluster into your vignette. Use what feels comfortable, what seems to relate and make sense. Ignore the rest.

6. Once you have "storied" your thinking on "afraid," bring your writing full circle by referring to what started your thinking in the first place, so that you have a fully formed, self-contained piece. (We will talk more about this in Chapter 6, on recurrences.) You can accomplish this wholeness by looking at your beginning and hooking your ending into the beginning by repeating a word, a phrase, a dominant thought, or an emotion that was also present in your opening line or two.

7. Read aloud what you have written. Spend a minute or two making any changes you think will improve the whole. Rework your vignette for anywhere from one to five minutes until you have a strong sense that everything in it belongs there.

After Writing

You have just accomplished your first cluster with full participation of your Design mind and the resulting vignette with full cooperation of both Sign and Design minds. You allowed yourself to experience the temporary chaos without which natural writing cannot occur. You may have felt somewhat silly to begin with, making circles and scattering words about on the page, but very likely the associations came anyway.

Let me share with you some very brief vignettes of first-time clusterers who more often than not expressed surprise at what they produced. Figure 2–4 is the cluster and vignette of a seasoned teacher.

Figure 2–5 is the writing of a college freshman after being introduced to clustering.

Old man, you bend in time like
tree limbs in the wind.
Your truth lies deep,
Unchanged by aging limbs
Or bending back.

Dee Dickinson

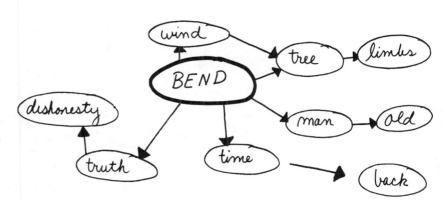

Figure 2–4

Splinter is a terrible word. Its
sound is synonymous with the
sensation: jagged, sharp, piercing,
like the nagging voice of a
dissatisfied wife. I remember
vacationing in Tahoe. The pier
was old, worn, and wooden; the
boards as rough as a face full of
scabs. Running along it, my foot
caught the attention of an angry
spike of wood, injecting itself
cleanly and deeply into the ball of
my foot. If I screamed it was not
from the pain initially felt, but
from anticipated sensations. It's
not the hole the shot makes but
the length of the slim sword that
brings pain.

Laurie Welte

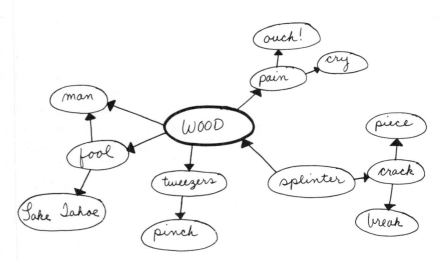

Figure 2–5

Figure 2–6 is the writing of a mature woman just returning to
college who believed she couldn't write.

The technique of clustering gives you access to the patterns and
associations of your Design mind. It provides you with essentially

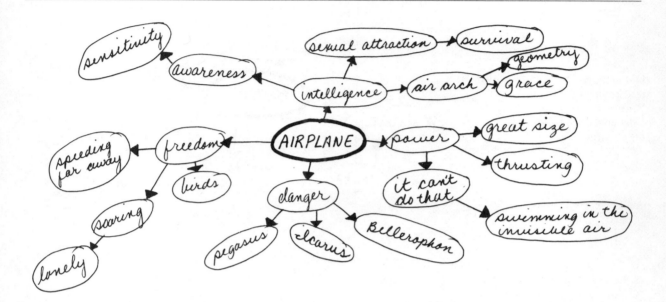

Figure 2–6

A huge silver jet airplane is making a graceful arch in the light blue morning sky, material evidence, to me, of the human mind. It is intelligence and courage thrusting above environment, at home with the impossible, powerful proof of the attraction of intellect in natural selection, as sensual as a strip tease.

Lavelle Leahey

two things: *choices* from which to formulate and develop your thought, and a *focus* meaningful enough to impel you to write. Facts or words in isolation are meaningless until they are brought into relationship by a consciousness that can create relationships. A word, filtered through the sieve of your unique consciousness, allows you to create something from nothing through the medium of words, and here you have the beginning of reawakening your natural writing powers.

Here are some typical comments of first-time clusterers: "It was so easy!" and "I normally have a terrible time getting started, but after I clustered, I wrote without a moment's pause" and "I was so absorbed it was as though I was in another space" and "It's funny—when I circled that last cluster word, I knew exactly what I would write about." Perhaps one of these responses is similar to yours. First-time clusterers express amazement, delight, wonder, surprise at the discovery of their latent creative drive.

Clustering is effective because it seems to be a reflection of the way the Design mind naturally works—that is, it clusters for patterns meaningful to it all the time as it scans its universe. Thus, if you are one of the rare clusterers who experience some frustration, it is not your Design mind but your Sign mind that is likely to be the culprit.

In the beginning your Sign mind may try to take over because it likes to take command of anything to do with language (we'll see why this is true in Chapter 3). But, since clustering is random and nonlinear, your Sign mind begins to retreat from the challenge. You may experience its resistance as "I can't do this" or "this is stupid" or "how childish." One of my students, a teacher in a retraining workshop on writing who had taught German for years according to the traditional grammar-first method, experienced this resistance to the extent that he broke into a sweat and could neither cluster nor write!

But such instances are almost nonexistent. Should you experience resistance to the novelty of clustering, go through the motions of drawing circles and lines around a stimulus word, as in Figure 2–7.

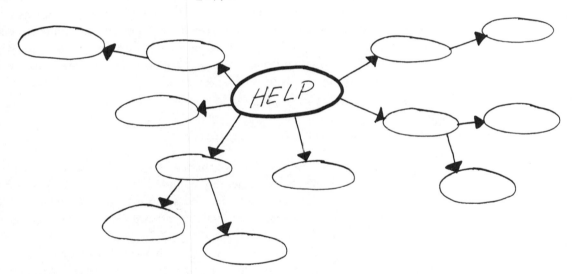

Figure 2–7

Simply relax and doodle, letting the circles and lines shape a pleasing pattern. That very nonlinear act will break down your resistance and you will find yourself filling in those inviting empty circles with the associations that are inevitably triggered by the nucleus word.

I first developed the clustering process, I followed an impulse to circle the words as they spilled out onto paper, for each word and phrase seemed to be a complex, self-contained mini-whole in my mind, like an image. As I explored this impulse further, I recalled learning that circles are the first intelligible shapes to appear in children's drawings

To me a cluster is an expanding universe with each word a potential galaxy capable at each moment of throwing out universes of its own.
      A Reno teacher after a workshop

Clustering brings to my mind truths I may have lost sight of.
                    A student

in all cultures. I also recalled learning that the circle is primary in all human ritual, having its beginnings in human circles around story-tellers, dancers, or priests.

The circle, unlike the man-made squares and rectangles of cribs and coffins, walls and windows that "box" us in, is a natural, flowing, organic shape.

By its very nature the circle centers, focuses. For this reason, circling my mind-spills and connecting them to make webs seemed a natural act. As the cluster expanded before my eyes, each encirlced mini-whole gradually became part of a larger whole, a pattern of meaning that took shape when I began to write.

Circle forms spilled on a page visually and physically—in the movement of your arm, your hand, your pen on the page—reinforce the nonlinearity of Design-mind thought. The circle implicitly suggests bringing into being, activating, animating the pattern-making forces of the creative process. A circle is beginning and birth, womb and egg. It is wholeness. You will see how the cluster's circled words contain the seeds of a whole thought.

Clustering and Vignettes

Clustering virtually always generates writing that possesses the quality of wholeness, of something completed, requiring neither subtraction nor addition, like a finished sculpture or a painting. The two prime characteristics of aesthetic experience are wholeness and a sense of pleasure.

To achieve wholeness, whether on a small scale or large, we will concentrate on "vignette" writing. A vignette, unlike a paragraph, is a whole, a complete thought or statement on a subject, a fully expressed idea, even a very short story with a fully developed plot. When you write a "paragraph" the unspoken assumption is that it is unfinished, that it won't be complete until something comes before or after it. A paragraph, we learned in school, is a unit in a composition having a beginning, a middle, and an end. Until we learned about paragraphs and topic sentences, we had no trouble with natural expression.

But clustering and its resulting vignettes take us back to the un-fettered ability we had in childhood to express a complete thought naturally. A vignette leaves no unfinished business; it stands as an aesthetic whole, and it develops naturally from clustering. You won't have to work at it. Moreover, a vignette can be the length of one paragraph or several, or it can be a free-verse poem or a dialogue. In fact, the writing of longer pieces is actually a natural process of writing a series of self-contained vignettes, mini-wholes, which then become entwined into a larger, more comprehensive whole. (Most professional writers work this way.) We shall explore the how of this phenomenon in the final chapter of this book. The important point now is that a vignette is a self-contained whole, complete in itself.

Capturing this sense of wholeness is best achieved through brief writing experiences deliberately limited to time spans of no more than ten minutes, as you have just seen. This emphasis on the vignette not only propels the Design mind into action but gives the critical censor of the Sign mind no time to intrude with its "yes, but . . ." objections. And from these brief spurts you will experience almost immediate writing success and see dramatic improvement as you begin to incorporate further techniques of natural writing.

Coming Full Circle: Closure

Just as clustering tends to beget wholeness of design without effort on your part, so does it influence your vignettes in such a way that your writing can't help but come full circle. The reasons for this phenomenon will be discussed in detail in Chapter 4. For now, you should know that "closure," or coming full circle, is the result of active Design-mind participation that brings to the writing process an awareness of having grouped together, connected, and related relevant elements of an idea out of the infinite possibilities available to our brain. Through clustering we make a pattern around a given nucleus word, and, as we write, that clustered pattern exerts its power to such an extent that we are largely incapable of leaving the writing "hanging."

Such cohesiveness was rarely the case in my earlier years of teaching before I developed the techniques of this book. Like many writing teachers, I required my students to do journal writing, ostensibly to stimulate the flow of ideas. The results were largely disappointing, often degenerating into mundane, diarylike entries without beginning or end, such as "I wish I were at the beach today instead of school. I'm hungry. After school is out I have to go to work, ugh . . ." and so on. Clustering, because it taps associations that generate patterns of ideas rather than such sequential thinking, does not produce this shallow, uninteresting rattling off of events. Instead, clustering naturally stimulates coming full circle, producing an inner unity out of a multiplicity of associations because the cluster itself is already a Design-mind pattern, an organic whole.

Modeling: Learning from the Masters

Modeling, the use of a master's work for your own expressive purposes, also operates from our ongoing emphasis on wholeness. The culminating exercise for each chapter will be to model your own writing on that of a professional writer's, using your newly acquired tools for tapping your Design mind. Modeling uses a professional's writing for inspiration to do one's own. Its purpose is to give you a structure, an aesthetic pattern to follow, within which to treat your own discovered content. Modeling relieves you of the anxiety of having to think of everything at once, allowing your writing to flow more naturally. Artists learn their skills through modeling established works of art. Children learn language by imitating their parents' speech patterns. It makes sense that the qualities of good writing can be learned by taking cues from the masters.

Modeling appeals to your Design mind because it makes you aware of language rhythms and a spatial arrangement of words on which you will pattern your own writing. Modeling a professional piece of writing is simply one more way of contacting your inner writer to re-create your own unique inner world. It will also lead you to a better understanding of what a writer's "voice" is—his or her unique style and content of expression—which in turn will help you become more conscious of the shape of your own writing and, ultimately, of your own emerging voice.

Untitled
*this is a poem to my son Peter
whom I have hurt a thousand
    times
whose large and vulnerable eyes
have glazed in pain at my ragings
thin wrists and fingers hung
boneless in despair, pale freckled
    back
bent in defeat, pillow soaked
by my failure to understand.
I have scarred through weakness
and impatience your frail confi-
    dence forever
because when I needed to strike
you were there to be hurt and be-
    cause
I thought you knew
you were beautiful and fair
your bright eyes and hair
but now I see that no one knows
    that
about himself, but must be told
and retold until it takes hold
because I think anything can be
    killed
after a while, especially beauty
so I write this for life, for love, for
you, my oldest son Peter, age 10,
going on 11.*

Peter Meinke,
American Poet

In each chapter we will be modeling a brief selection of prose or poetry to reinforce the Design-mind techniques presented in the chapters: wholeness, recurrences, language rhythms, images, metaphors, and creative tension. I frequently use brief poems in these modeling exercises because poems are vignettes, total patterns to which we respond first and foremost as a whole. We tend to fear writing poems only because we have preconceived notions of their difficulty. Yet my students continually discover that poetry is a natural vehicle for their expressive purposes because of its compression and brevity.

Let's experience the process of expressing your own thoughts within a given shape.

Directing Your Hand

Model American poet Peter Meinke's untitled poem by writing a tribute to someone you deeply care for: a teacher, relative, friend, lover—you might even choose someone you don't know, such as an author who has had a significant impact on your outlook on life.

1. Read Peter Meinke's poem aloud, preferably more than once, so that your Design mind can absorb its rhythms and images.
2. In your writer's notebook write the name of the person who is the subject of your tribute in the center of a page and circle it. This is your nucleus. Cluster anything that comes to mind about that person: feelings, personality, idiosyncrasies, failings, strengths, attitudes, associations with objects or places, physical attributes, your attitude toward that person, lines of poems or songs, whatever surfaces.
3. Continue to cluster for two to three minutes or until you suddenly experience a shift from randomness to a sense that you have something to write about, the sense of a tentative whole that you want to put into words.
4. Now begin your vignette with "This is a poem to my _____, _____." Glance at the Meinke poem from time to time for a sense of its phrasing and rhythm and, as you write, draw on your cluster for details.

5. Meinke's poem momentarily moves beyond the intensely personal to make a point that can apply to all human beings when he suggests that we must tell people we care for that they are "beautiful and fair" because "no one knows that/about himself, but must be told/and retold until it takes hold." In your own tribute, make a point that is both particular and universal.

6. The Meinke poem comes full circle with "so I write this for life, for love, for/you, my oldest son Peter," hooking it back to its beginning ("This is a poem to my son Peter"). Bring your own tribute full circle, too.

7. You may wish to spend an hour or more on this modeling exercise, although some people find their ideas flowing so readily that they are surprised to discover they have spent only fifteen to thirty minutes. Whatever time you spend, be open to the flow and enjoy the process of giving shape to your unique perceptions reflected in your cluster.

8. When you finish, read your vignette aloud, and then reread Peter Meinke's poem aloud. You will notice that, although you have written about a different person under different circumstances, there will be a rhythmic similarity between the two. This similarity is the result of your Design mind's sensitivity to created patterns—in this case, Meinke's poem—enabling you to transfer his pattern to your own writing.

After Writing

Now that you have written a poem using clustering, go back to your earlier writing in your writer's notebook, the before-instruction writing in which you described someone you cared for. Reread it and reread the vignette you just completed. Chances are your clustered and modeled version is richer in detail, more concise, more evocative, more polished, more rhythmic. Your words seem to have woven a noticeable pattern. And chances are, too, that you felt greater satisfaction when you were finished than you usually do after writing.

However great or small your sense of pattern or your feeling of satisfaction, your inner writer is beginning to surface. Gradually you will become aware of certain feelings that characterize a surge of creative activity: a sense of ease, increased confidence, pleasure, exhilaration, sometimes amazement that what flows from your pen seems so effortless.

Since each writer's response to modeling is unique, in Figure 2–8 I have included a modeled version of the Meinke poem by a student writer, a university freshman, written after four instructional sessions.

The following is a beginning poem by a beginning writer, but it has an authentic ring; she means what she says. It uses considerable detail to support the picture of a woman facing the debilitation of age and the prospect of death with dignity. It implies, in calling her grandmother "brave," that many people do not grow old gracefully. On the other hand, the cluster indicates that the tribute could be made more poignant by including that this woman was a "highly successful" doctor during an age when most women were house-wives. The writer could have ironed out some awkward rhythms by paring down excess verbiage, but it is a good beginning toward natural expression.

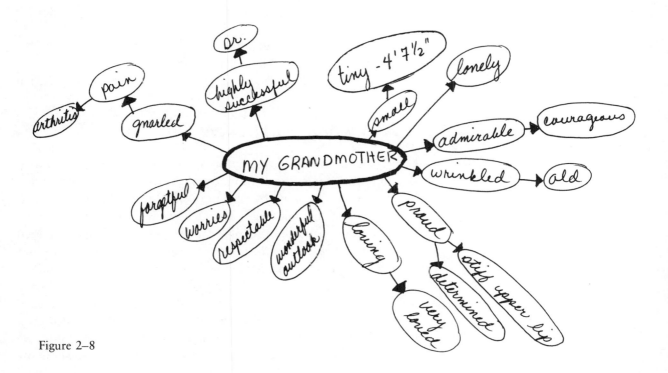

Figure 2–8

For You
This is a poem for you, grandmother
whose eyes have seen the world for ninety years.
This is for your gnarled hands and crippled back,
your failing memory and lasting confusion
that frustrates you again and again.
And this is for all the times you've hidden your pain
and laughed at yourself
when we were ugly and impatient with you.
And this is for your strength and courage
that keeps you going day on day,
letting you ignore the fact that you have lost all
the brilliance that once was yours,
letting you push aside the humiliation
your progressive dependence brings to you.
This is for your determination and stamina,
keeping you from placing blame and becoming embittered.
This is a poem for you,
my sweet, brave grandmother,
because you are all I hope I can ever be.

—Marina Michaelian

A Last Word and Heading On

Clustering, the basic technique of natural writing, can be used to generate ideas for writing of any form: essays, poems, short stories, business reports, song lyrics, even novels. I have used it with students in a business-communication course to ease the inhibitions common to letter writing and the fear of writing reports. Students have used clustering to write songs, to generate insights for their essay exams, to prepare for a verbal confrontation with a friend; one student showed me clusters that had generated ideas for a piece of ad copy for his journalism class. Clustering, with its access to the pattern-making Design mind, is a powerful inspirational/organizational tool; it always reassures us that we have something to say. Best of all, we don't have to worry about the sequence or syntax of ideas; we simply create connections and relationships as the cluster unfolds effortlessly.

Although it is human nature to resist the unfamiliar, the unconventional, give clustering a chance. Don't prematurely ring down the curtain on a process that is certain to produce enormous changes in your writing, your attitude toward writing, and your assessment of your own creative powers. In making the invisible process of your Design mind visible through clustering, you avail yourself of the rich array of choices on which natural writing thrives.

Surprisingly, this storehouse of choices is much more accessible to young children than it is to adults, for reasons we will explore briefly in the following chapter on the childhood origins of natural writing. An understanding of your untutored childhood creative powers, in turn illuminated by an understanding of the development of the two sides of your brain in Chapter 4, will afford you new insights for tapping your own creative potential in general and for enhancing your natural expressive powers in particular.

CHAPTER 3/ *The Childhood Origins of Natural Writing*

The playfulness, the willingness to take risks, the spontaneity that are characteristic of creative behavior in general and natural writing in particular depend on two fundamental acts you engaged in from the moment you began to talk: wonder and storying. "Whazzat, Daddy? Whazzat, Mommy?" was your insistent cry. You wondered about everything because everything was new to you. "Twinkle, twinkle, little star/How I wonder what you are" captures the curiosity and the sense of delight that seem to be the rule of childhood existence. Wonder is so crucial to creative behavior that D. H. Lawrence elevated it to the status of a sixth sense.

Wonder and Storying

Theologian/philosopher Sam Keen has written about the importance of wonder in our lives in *Apology for Wonder*: "To wonder is to live in the world of novelty rather than law (or habit), of delight rather than obligation, and of the present rather than the future." Wonder, Keen continues, requires a relaxed attitude, receptivity, an intuitive sense, a delight in juxtaposing and savoring particulars, sensuousness, openness, and participation. These are also, we now know, the characteristics inherent in Design-mind thought and the sine qua non of natural writing. We possess these qualities in childhood. We need to recapture them as adults.

Children make sense of their world by wondering, and as a result create their own realities in answer to that wonder. The Russian linguistic scholar Kornei Chukovsky writes that the child from two to five is the most inquisitive creature on earth in the service of comprehending its world. In his book *From Two to Five* he cites the example of five-year-old Volik:

> After swallowing each bit, Volik would stop and listen to what was happening inside of him. Then he would smile gaily and say: "It just ran down the little ladder to the stomach."
>
> "What do you mean—down the little ladder?"
>
> "I have a little ladder there (and he pointed from the neck to the stomach); everything I eat runs down this ladder . . . and then there are other little ladders in my arms and legs . . . all over what I eat runs down little ladders to my body. . . ."
>
> "Did someone tell you all this?"
>
> "No, I saw it myself."
>
> "Where?"
>
> "Oh, when I was in your tummy, I saw the kind of ladders you had there . . . and that means that I, too, have the same kind. . . ."

Wondering, as you can see from Volik's virtuoso performance, leads naturally to the second fundamental act of early childhood: "storying."

Storying is a term created by psychologist Renée Fuller, who maintains that this act is so fundamental to intellectual development that we underestimate its importance. The child's ability to create wholeness out of his or her manifold experience, in the form of stories, occurs at the most formative stage of intellectual development according to Fuller, and it occurs in all cultures. As soon as children learn to talk, words and ideas tumble forth in an uninhibited flow, limited only by the boundaries of their vocabulary. Storying expresses an innate human need to make mental connections, to perceive patterns, to create relationships among people, things, feelings, and events—and to express these perceived connections to others.

In fact, storying seems to evolve as naturally as a child's language acquisition itself, long before the imposition of formal learning of rules. According to linguist Noam Chomsky, our predisposition for language is innate—that is, built into our brain. Because no one as yet knows exactly how language is learned, let's say children learn language simply by using it. No one, least of all the average mother, knows how to *teach* it to them. Children's innate capacity naturally shapes them to pay attention to it, and then—at a learning rate that is breathtaking—to tumble forth experiences and perceptions of the world in increasingly sophisticated ways.

Kornei Chukovsky calls every two-year-old a "linguistic genius":

> Beginning with the age of two, every child becomes for a short period of time a linguistic genius. . . . There is no trace left in the eight-year-old of this creativity with words, since the need for it has passed; by this age the child already has fully mastered the basic principles of his native language. If his former talent for word invention and construction had not abandoned him, he would, even by the age of ten, eclipse any of us with his suppleness and brilliance of speech.

As children, every time we told an experience or tried to express our feelings about something, we were storying, and through storying we built our sense of who we were and what was significant for our gradually expanding world view. Our mothers patiently reinforced our utterances, correcting us only when we called a pony, which we were seeing for the first time, a doggie—after all, both are four-legged, both have ears, tail, eyes, and so forth. Soon enough we learned to beg to ride that horsie, and when we were lucky enough to get permission, we uninhibitedly and excitedly told our father or sister what we had done, how we felt, and what the horsie looked like. Thus, through storying, an essential and natural expressive mode, our horizon and delight in words continually expanded, augmented by the wonder and joy in stories our parents read us out of books.

The same fascination these stories held for us as children played a significant role in our growing desire to get our own stories on paper: the wonder and surprise of holding the fleeting images of our mind fast on the page and the satisfaction in creating coherence out of the world at large.

The Magic of the Written Word

When at some point in our development—as early as age two and certainly by four—we realized that those black squiggly lines on pages in books made up the stories we loved to hear, it seemed so magical to us that many of us attempted to duplicate the feat by making our own squiggly lines and then "reading" the resulting "story" to our parents. Then, once we learned to identify letters, connect those letters with sounds, and combine letters to make words, a whole new world opened up to us. Gradually we gained the power to put stubby pencil to paper to hold fast our storying efforts—both real and imagined. Our story on the page became a silent testimonial of our mind's pictures.

In his autobiography, *The Words,* Jean-Paul Sartre recalled what drew his childhood self to writing—he felt the irresistible need to make the pictures in his head somehow real: "I'm playing moving-pictures" (I would answer). Indeed, I was trying to pluck the pictures from my head and *realize* them outside of me." Writing was so central to his life, he continues, that "when I began writing, I began my birth over again."

At the beginning, this desire to express the pictures in our heads through storying was as natural as our delight in making drawings or chanting jump-rope rhymes. There was no anxiety associated with it; we were compelled to communicate our thoughts. Rarely stumped or inhibited by what they don't know, children actually seem to thrive on novelty, which they appropriate to create their own meaning: elbow macaroni is transformed into a necklace; a box of plain wooden blocks becomes a thriving city; nonsense figures become a story. Given the nonsense markings of Figure 3–1, a first-grader detailed the following story.

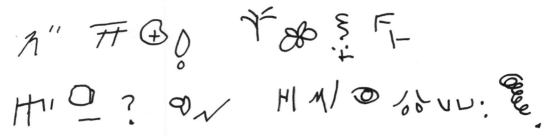

Figure 3–1

The Street Accident

A point is going into the street. Two cars crash in each other. Had to get to the hospital. Water came up. Saw a butterfly. They saw the terrible lights that they bumped into. Then they saw a full accident on the street. The whole world was bunked into the street of cars. Then they had to stay there in the one little box. Then they thought a little bit. Then a firefly came by the street. His name was Helper. He rescued them. Then they are free again on the street and could go anywhere. Then an eye appeared on the street. It was coming closer and closer until everyone rushed away. The End!

Tracy Owen, 6

No matter how crude their work appears to sometimes critical parents, it brings these small storytellers themselves profound feelings of satisfaction, just as their artful scribbles do.

The sense of wholeness and the sense of pleasure in storying are two important qualities you will learn to recapture in your own natural writing. They are the basis of aesthetic activity: consciousness of a unified whole and consciousness of intense pleasure. They are the result of having discovered or fashioned a form out of the chaos of one's experience. Aesthetic activity is not only a central feature of a child's development—for young children seem to be guided by aesthetic criteria rather than logical criteria much of the time—but a necessary ingredient of all creative activity.

Stages of Creative Development

In an article titled "Impression and Expression in Artistic Development," art educator Harry Broudy has classified three stages of aesthetic/creative development that are not only highly useful to an understanding of natural writing but correspond remarkably to the stages of brain development we will discuss in Chapter 4. He refers to them as the stage of the "innocent eye, ear, and hand," the stage of the "conventional eye, ear, and hand," and the stage of the "cultivated eye, ear, and hand."

The Innocent Eye, Ear, and Hand

This stage of innocent creative expression lasts from about age two to age seven. It is characterized by innocence of perception—that

is, children have few preconceived notions about what the world
ought to be like, about how they *should* feel, about what they *must*
do according to certain prescribed formulas. The world is sheer possibility and, as discussed, a child's characteristic stance toward it is
wonder. Each day is filled with the delight of new discoveries rather
than the dead weight of obligations; each minute, each activity is
experienced as "now" rather than as a worried look into the future.
Wondering is openness to the unknown; in fact, wondering makes it
quite acceptable *not* to know, precisely because it sets the stage for
spontaneous discoveries.

Writing in this stage is characterized, as we have already discussed, by wholeness at the expense of logic, by vivid images like
Volik's ladders, by accidental metaphors ("Can't you see I'm bare-
foot all over?"), by sensitivity to language rhythms, by frequent recurrence of key words, and by a juxtaposition of logically incom-
mensurate elements. This early stage clearly encompasses the most
salient features of natural writing. A poignant example is the recently
republished turn-of-the-century diary of a six-year-old girl, Opal
Whitely, entitled *Opal*. An orphan, she lived in a mining camp with
foster parents. Her original parents were well educated and had taught
her to read and write. To make sense of her existence, and also to
make it more bearable, Opal storied with ferocious intensity, using
whatever scraps of paper she could garner, often writing under the
bed where she was sent as punishment. Her writing attests to the
power of the imagination and reflects the wondering receptivity of a
child to all the world about her.

> Today the grandpa dug potatoes in the field
> I followed along after.
> I picked them up and piled them in piles.
> Some of them were very plump.
> And all the time I was picking up potatoes
> I did have conversations with them.
> To some potatoes I did tell about
> my hospital in the near woods
> and all the little folk in it
> and how much prayers and songs
> and mentholatum helps them to have well feels.

To other potatoes I did talk about my friends—
how the crow, Lars Porsena,
does have a fondness for collecting things,
how Aphrodite, the mother pig, has a fondness
for chocolate creams,
how my dear pig, Peter Paul Rubens, wears a
little bell coming to my cathedral service.

Potatoes are very interesting folks.
I think they must see a lot
of what is going on in the earth.
They have so many eyes.
Too, I did have thinks
of all their growing days
there in the ground,
and all the things they did hear.

And after, I did count the eyes
that every potatoe did have,
and their numbers were in blessings.

I have thinks these potatoes growing here
did have knowings of star songs.
I have kept watch in the field at night
and I have seen the stars
look kindness down upon them.
And I have walked between the rows of potatoes
and I have watched
the star gleams on their leaves.

There you have it: the intense openness to experience, the un-
clouded power of observation, the vivid images, the charming childish terminology—"well feels," "did have thinks." But what is most
striking in this excerpt of a child's writing is its sense of wholeness,
its completeness as a vignette. It is achieved through the unwavering
focus on potatoes, almost as if Opal had clustered. The opening line
explains that "the grandpa dug potatoes in the field," followed by
Opal's "conversations with them," followed by her near identifica-
tion with their "feelings," recognizing how much they "see and hear,"

followed by a profound (for a six-year-old) musing on the unity of the universe: "potatoes . . ./have knowings of star songs"; "the stars/look kindness down upon them"; "I have watched/the star gleams on their leaves." This, from a six-year-old, is an amazing example of natural writing.

Unfortunately, in the course of a child's writing development, wonder is eclipsed by the complacency inherent in valuing and writing about the conventional, the widely accepted, the correctness-dampened—hence the stage of the conventional eye, ear, and hand.

The Conventional Eye, Ear, and Hand

From about age eight through sixteen, our manual dexterity is considerably strengthened through continually improving eye-hand coordination. Consequently, there is considerable improvement in handwriting skills, and we gain mastery over the mechanics of language because of the heavy emphasis on these left-brain skills in school. We also gradually eliminate the logical gaps in our stories—characteristic of our earlier stage of perception—as intense preoccupation with the whole vision gives way to preoccupation with appropriateness of detail. As a result, our writing and oral storying become increasingly conventional and literal, with a concomitant loss of the spontaneity and originality of our earlier efforts.

The writing of my fourteen-year-old daughter Stephanie can be used to illustrate many of the characteristics of writing in the conventional stage. Rhyme tends to subtract instead of adding to the effect, and the content is unimaginative.

During these years of conventional perception and expression, we are well entrenched in a school curriculum that emphasizes logical/linear, rule-governed learnings taught piece by piece, and usually in the absence of a larger context that would allow us to hook these bits and pieces of learning to a larger picture. Education is compartmentalized as we begin to move from a class in English to a class in science to a class in mathematics, and so forth.

At this stage our vocabulary is firmly enough established so that we feel little need to invent metaphors in an effort to communicate meaning. By now we know that a star is, by definition, a "hot gaseous mass floating in space," in contrast to our innocent stage, when, looking out at the star-filled sky, we pointed to the largest one and excitedly exclaimed, "That star is a flower without a stem!"

Everyday Things
*My Birkenstocks
Are the neatest shoes
Without socks
I really groove
With those socks
My feet are warm
In my Birkenstocks—
They're such a charm!*
        Stephanie Rico

Yet, at this stage it is reassuring to "know" the same things our classmates know; it feels good to have familiar labels to classify the world around us; it feels good to be comfortably grounded in a consensual reality. (I know, for as an eleven-year-old German stranger in a land whose language was Greek to me, it was painful not to be part of the consensual reality my peers drew on as naturally as breath.) Children at this stage usually aspire to an exaggerated conformity.

Understandably, with such an imposition of rules and criticism about "the right way" and "the wrong way" to accomplish learning, our writing becomes more anxious, less spontaneous, far less daring and grandiose in conception. Imagine for a moment how young children would fare if they had to learn to speak by a process equivalent to the way they now are taught to write. We learn to speak largely in a yes-world, but learning to write tends to become a no-world of rules, corrections, and often artificial—and thus hard to follow—prescriptions that have little to do with natural expressiveness.

Yet the other side of the coin is that our increasing store of new words grounds us in the security of clear and unambiguous references. We happily begin to participate in certain uniformities of perception; for example, how we love to identify the different breeds of dogs or makes of automobiles at this stage. We also participate in uniformities of expression to a degree that adults often cringe at, slaves to the currently popular slang terms dictated by the generation that spawns them.

Our writing at this stage displays two distinct characteristics. First, it tends to be insistently literal, as this adolescent's typical note demonstrates:

Thursday

Stephers:

Hola! Heh! I am in a good mood. I am glad I went to third—otherwise Mr. P would have been ticked. I can't wait til Friday. It's gonna be so fun!

Stephie, now I am getting tired. This class is too boring (for me, at least). We are doing stupid grammar stuff. Hey, 17 days til my birthday EEEEE!!! Oh well,

Gotta go,
Love
Chris

Second, it tends to be highly clichéd—that is, riddled with overused and trite language or observations. My other daughter Simone's poem at age eleven will illustrate.

> *I Wish*
> I wish I could soar with the birds in the sky
> I wish I could run with a horse,
> I wish I could swim with the fish in the sea,
> I wish I could burrow with the ground squirrel on his underground
>   course.
> I wish everybody could forgive and forget,
> I wish everybody could love,
> I wish everybody could live in peace,
> Under the sign of the dove.

Most of us at this stage gradually slide into a negative attitude about writing, with the result that we write only when it is required of us: book reports, perfunctory thank-you notes, and tests, endless tests. Writing becomes synonymous in our minds with the hard labor of following impossible injunctions and, all too often, punishment. Thus, writing becomes tedious, anxiety-provoking, and pleasureless—thoroughly Sign mind. Perceived as a necessary evil, our once free-wheeling expressive powers that were grounded in an openness to wonder and an innate love of storying become mired in the ruts of convention.

And that's where most of us have stayed. Wonder was gradually replaced by the complacency of knowing what everyone else knew, of seeing what everyone else saw, and of writing what everyone else wrote. And our world began to narrow, our potential to constrict, and our erstwhile trust in ourselves to ebb away into the river of the commonplace.

Fortunately, the human brain is constituted to grow and learn and change as it comes across alternative ways of seeing and doing. When this happens, no matter what our age, we open ourselves to possibility and, consequently, to moving into a stage of creative expressive power, a childlike "innocence of eye" that Dorothea Brande calls the hallmark of the "author of genius." This is the stage of the cultivated eye, ear, and hand.

The author of genius does keep till his last breath the spontaneity, the ready sensitiveness, of a child, the "innocence of eye" that means so much to the painter, the ability to respond freshly and quickly to new scenes, and to old scenes as though they were new; to see traits and characteristics as though each were new-minted from the hand of God instead of sorting them quickly into dusty categories and pigeon-holing them without wonder or surprise; to feel situations so immediately and keenly that the word "trite" has hardly any meaning for him; and always to see "the correspondences between things" of which Aristotle spoke two thousand years ago.

> Dorothea Brande,
> Becoming a Writer

The child is father to the man.
                    Wordsworth

The Cultivated Eye, Ear, and Hand

In this stage, we recover the characteristics of the innocent eye, ear, and hand, beginning with wonder, and cultivating it for a mature expression of our innate storying impulses.

It is a paradox of creativity that the very way to move beyond the conventional stage is not to try harder, but to take a seeming step backward: to reawaken and cultivate in ourselves some of the ways we had of perceiving and expressing when we were children. Physician/writer Richard Moss, in *The I That Is We,* calls this step "a fundamental return to beginner's mind, to the child state, to Beingness prior to conditioned and memorized ideas about life."

In relearning to shift consciousness to the stage of cultivated freshness of perception and its accompanying wonder, we will not only begin to recognize, and then to overcome, the blocks to original and free expression built up in our conventional stage, but also to consciously redirect our energies toward developing the natural writing skills that constitute the forthcoming chapters of this book.

Directing Your Hand

Experience a return to the innocent eye, ear, and hand that characterized your interchange with the world when you were small.

1. Close your eyes and invite into your Design-mind consciousness a childhood memory of something that had an enormous impact on you, negative or positive. Stay receptive and quietly alert, letting images and their accompanying feeling-tones pass before your mind's eye until you come upon the experience that draws you to it most insistently.
2. Now cluster that experience by using as a nucleus the most dominant feeling and characterizing it, to which you give a name, for example:

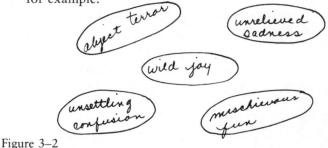

Figure 3–2

Cluster, for two to four minutes, for as many details as you can recall of that experience, letting the associations flow, knowing that one association will trigger the next; you'll be surprised by the richness of your cluster. Remember feelings, sights, sounds, smells, touches, tastes. Cluster until you have the sense that you have a focus and a sense of where and how to begin.

3. Now write your vignette in ten minutes or so, from the point of view of the adult looking back on this experience. Begin your vignette with "I remember . . ." and stay in the past tense while telling your story. As you write, occasionally refer to your cluster for direction or details.

4. When you have finished, read aloud what you have written, making any changes you feel would improve the whole.

5. Now do an about-face: retell your story in a second vignette from a radically different point of view: of you *as* that child having that particular experience. Write in the present tense, as though it were happening to you now. Eliminate "I remember . . ." Instead *become* that child in imagination as you write, recording your story, your feelings, your experience, as though you were there at that very moment, experiencing, feeling, doing, saying. Quote conversation if you wish. Refer to your cluster for direction and details; you may be surprised to discover that some of the details that did not get into the first vignette are finding their way into the second.

6. When you have come full circle, reread aloud what you have written and make whatever changes you think will improve the sound of the whole.

After Writing

Now read both versions aloud again and simply notice the differences. Your tellings probably differ considerably in intensity. The "I remember . . ." version often is more a ticking off of the events of the experience; sometimes it moves into an analysis of the experience. Very likely the quality of wholeness is missing. But most important, it is likely to be once removed from a feeling of direct emotional involvement.

*The child in man is his growing tip,
alive throughout our lifespan. . . .
One of the labors of adulthood is
to befriend in ourselves those
handicapped and underdeveloped
parts of our nature which we have
set aside.*

M. C. Richards
The Crossing Point

By contrast, the second version probably pleases you more because of its directness, its intensity, its immediacy. And the writing very likely exhibits a distinct full-circle wholeness. Re-entering childhood in imagination probably brought you much closer to a sense of receptivity and innocence than did the recall from the adult's point of view. Natural writing stems from this kind of immersion in whatever subject you are writing about.

A Last Word and Heading On

This chapter has shown that the natural process of creating meaning through wonder and storying and language is accessible to all of us as we learn to move beyond the conventional to the cultivated stage of the eye, ear, and hand. Many of us have become stuck in the conventional stage without ever experiencing the full force of our inner writer. The strategies of this book will involve your Design mind so fully that writing can once more become a natural expressive form of storying for you.

Chapter 4 tells its own story, as it clarifies the unique workings of your Design mind and its cooperation with your Sign mind in natural writing.

CHAPTER 4/ *Sign and Design: Words and the Brain*

To this point we have been alluding only to the different functions of the left and right hemispheres of the brain in the creative process. Now we'll look in a little more detail at just why the right hemisphere is the fertile repository of the powers we wish to develop for natural writing and how both hemispheres must be brought into play at appropriate times for the best results.

Perhaps the best way to start, before we investigate briefly how the hemispheres specialize to produce two separate ways of knowing, is to see two powerful examples showing hemispheric specialization at work. The first is a true story told by psychologist Richard M. Jones, in *Fantasy and Feeling in Education.* (Jones was writing before the recent advances in brain research.)

Billy was a sixth-grader. His teacher, reviewing the previous day's math lesson, called on him to define infinity. Billy squirmed in his seat and said nothing.

"Come on, Billy, what's infinity?" his teacher insisted. He looked at the floor.

Exasperated, she commanded him again to answer, whereupon he mumbled, "Well, infinity is kinda like a box of Cream of Wheat."

"Billy, don't be silly," she snapped, and called on Johnny, who was eager to share his learning.

"Infinity is immeasurable, unbounded space, time, or quantity," he said. The teacher was pleased, since this was the only appropriate answer she could imagine.

Yet here's the rub: Billy had verbalized a complex right-brain image and made a nonliteral statement. Literally, infinity is nothing like a box of Cream of Wheat, and the teacher, looking for a literal left-brain definition, understandably ignored his answer. But Billy knew something about infinity. Later, to a more sympathetic ear, he was able to explain his image: "You see, on a box of Cream of Wheat there's a picture of a man holding a box of Cream of Wheat, which shows a picture of a man holding a box of Cream of Wheat—and it goes on and on like that forever and ever, even if you can't see it anymore. Isn't that what infinity is?" Billy had a rich right-brain understanding of infinity. The left-brain definition fed back by his literal classmate meant so little to Billy that he could not reproduce it even though he had written it down the day before. This is an example of hemispheric dominance and two separate modes of processing the same information.

The second example is taken from *The Shattered Mind,* in which psychologist Howard Gardner of Harvard reports his exploration of the linguistic capabilities of Peter, a man with previously normal intelligence who had sustained severe right-brain damage. Left brain intact, Peter's use of language was nearly perfect despite the damage, with two qualifications: he could answer only questions that required the literal use of language and his literal responses were spoken in a monotonic voice akin to a computer print-out.

But when it came to evoking nonliteral responses, real difficulties became apparent. When Gardner asked Peter to interpret the proverb "Too many cooks spoil the broth," he was only able to answer, "Well, it means that if you have too many cooks cooking the soup, it'll spoil." Of normal intelligence and with our own right hemispheres intact, most of us will puzzle a bit and then suggest that the proverb could have something to do with raising a child, designing a building, training a dog, producing a work of art, or even writing a book! Proverbs are by nature nonliteral; they are meant to be interpreted, but Peter was unable to do this because understanding nonliteral language requires the participation of the right brain. Without it, we are left with only the denotative and literal. Interpretive meaning escapes us.

The Discovery of Cerebral Duality

From the rich, albeit often contradictory, world of brain research over the past twenty years, two irrefutable facts have emerged: (1) the brain is dual (Figure 4–1), and each hemisphere is capable of operating independently of the other; (2) each hemisphere interprets the world through a different lens—that is, each of the two minds processes the same information differently. Using the specialized

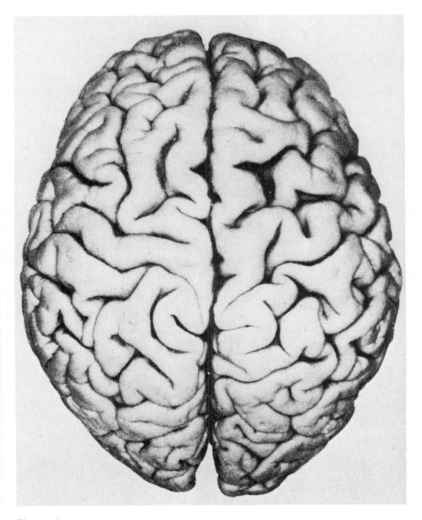

Figure 4–1

functions of both hemispheres in appropriate ways is crucial to the creative act and especially to cultivating your inner writer.

The discovery of brain duality really began with the observations of English physician A. L. Wigan in 1844. In performing an autopsy on a longtime friend and patient, Wigan discovered that his friend, whose behavior had been normal in every respect until his death, had only one cerebral hemisphere. This discovery led him to speculate that if only one hemisphere can constitute a mind—as clearly had been the case with his dead friend—then the fact that nature has given us two hemispheres means we may actually be in possession of two "minds."

Wigan's speculation was eclipsed for a hundred years by yet another medical discovery: damage to the left hemisphere usually resulted in *aphasia,* an impairment of the power to use and understand words. Left-brain aphasia can be contrasted to right-brain *visual agnosia* (inability to recognize faces and objects) as well as to right-brain *aprodosia* (inability to perceive and express emotions), subjects to be touched on later in this chapter because they are crucial to understanding the ways in which the right brain participates in natural writing. Since an impairment of language functions represented an obvious and dramatic loss of human faculties, the unexamined assumption took hold that the left hemisphere was the "smart" hemisphere while the right was much like a spare tire—good only in emergencies and only until the "real" one was operative once more.

Such assumptions were challenged by the first epileptic "split-brain" patient. He was operated on by neurosurgeons Phillip Vogel and Joseph Bogen in Nobel Prize-winner Roger Sperry's lab at the California Institute of Technology. Vogel and Bogen, believing that epileptic seizures originated in one hemisphere and spread to the other via the connecting bundle of nerve fibers called the corpus callosum, hypothesized that if the connecting nerve cables would be cut, the "electrical storm" of epilepsy, with its uncontrollable convul-

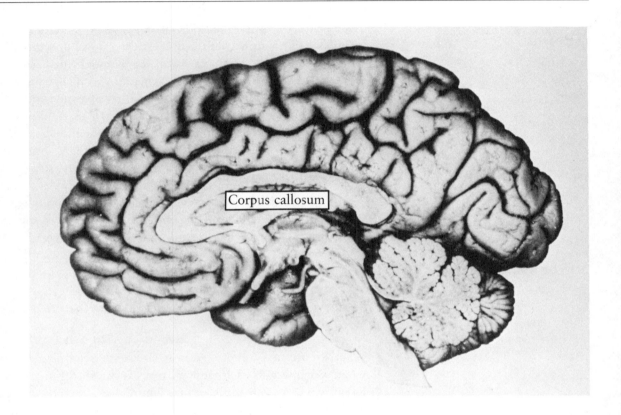

Corpus callosum

Figure 4–2

sions, could be contained. Accordingly, they performed a "commis-surotomy" by cutting through the 200 million nerve fibers of the corpus callosum (Figure 4–2). Their hypothesis proved correct: the electrical storm was contained, and the seizures, now confined to one hemisphere, could be treated and controlled.

The really fascinating findings began to appear as the patient was recovering from the surgery. Despite the cutting of some 200 million nerve fibers connecting one hemisphere to the other, at first glance the split-brain patient's behavior appeared to be quite normal. The disbelief and curiosity of the attending neurosurgeons led to the first of an extensive—and still ongoing—series of tests and experiments, which in turn confirmed Wigan's original speculation of almost a hundred and forty years ago: the human being has two minds in one head, and these two minds generate two independent streams of conscious awareness, each to some extent unaware of the other.

As experiments with these patients began to yield insight after insight, other researchers intensified the search with patients who had sustained damage in one or the other hemisphere. Still other researchers devised elaborate experiments with normal subjects, whose brain-wave patterns were measured during specially devised tasks to determine which hemisphere would show active brain waves and which would maintain an idling rhythm. Out of this enormous body of published experimentation, a profile of the workings of each hemisphere emerged.

Sign Versus Design Mind: A Complementary Division of Labor

What we are really interested in is how each hemisphere thinks, for we now know that each tends to process the world in radically different ways. As you can see from Figure 4–3, the most basic difference in how the two hemispheres see the world is that the left is specialized to process only one stimulus at a time, albeit at lightning speed, which leads to orderly sequences of thought and a focus on parts. The right brain, by contrast, can process a whole cluster of stimuli simultaneously, which leads to a grasp of complex wholes. This fundamentally different process largely accounts for the other differences delineated in Figure 4–3. The one-at-a-time processing of the left brain leads to the sequential, logical functions that produce linear thinking; they are also responsible for ordering language into syntactic units we can understand. Like a computer, the left brain's thought is rule-governed, drawing on pre-existing learned, fixed codes that were organized and stored very early in life. Like a computer, the left brain can recall complex motor sequences. In short, the left brain cultivates the repetitively predictable. And a good thing it does, because otherwise the world would forever appear to us to be in a state of unbearable unfamiliarity and chaos. In living, we could not

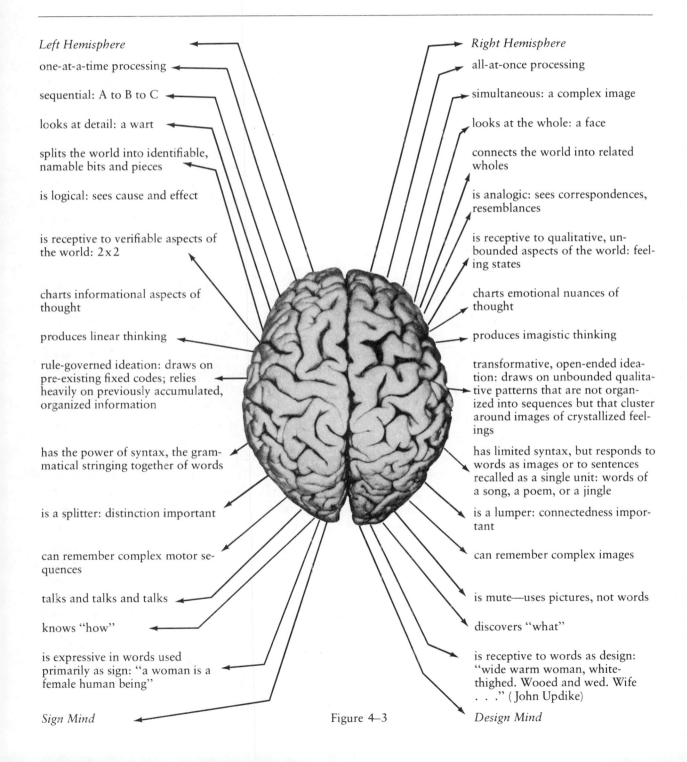

Left Hemisphere

one-at-a-time processing

sequential: A to B to C

looks at detail: a wart

splits the world into identifiable, namable bits and pieces

is logical: sees cause and effect

is receptive to verifiable aspects of the world: 2 x 2

charts informational aspects of thought

produces linear thinking

rule-governed ideation: draws on pre-existing fixed codes; relies heavily on previously accumulated, organized information

has the power of syntax, the grammatical stringing together of words

is a splitter: distinction important

can remember complex motor sequences

talks and talks and talks

knows "how"

is expressive in words used primarily as sign: "a woman is a female human being"

Sign Mind

Right Hemisphere

all-at-once processing

simultaneous: a complex image

looks at the whole: a face

connects the world into related wholes

is analogic: sees correspondences, resemblances

is receptive to qualitative, unbounded aspects of the world: feeling states

charts emotional nuances of thought

produces imagistic thinking

transformative, open-ended ideation: draws on unbounded qualitative patterns that are not organized into sequences but that cluster around images of crystallized feelings

has limited syntax, but responds to words as images or to sentences recalled as a single unit: words of a song, a poem, or a jingle

is a lumper: connectedness important

can remember complex images

is mute—uses pictures, not words

discovers "what"

is receptive to words as design: "wide warm woman, white-thighed. Wooed and wed. Wife . . ." (John Updike)

Design Mind

Figure 4–3

fall back on even the simplest of habitually used sequences like starting a car. In writing, we could not rely on knowing the alphabet and
our conventional ways of hooking letters together to make words, or
the grammatical forms we learned long before we could write, or
correct and consistent ways of spelling words, or that words are signs
having stable meanings, and so forth.

However, as Figure 4–3 indicates, we have evolved two thinking
apparatuses that not only dramatically increase our mental options
but make creative acts possible. As critical as is the contribution of
the left brain, we need not be dependent only on pre-existing learned
sequences that do not readily process novel information because the
right brain, with its simultaneous processing, can do this. It can take
in a whole face; it can connect parts of the world into fresh patterns
of meaning by perceiving correspondences or resemblances; it can
interpret the amoebic formlessness of intricate emotions and think in
complex images (dreaming might be called clustering in images). Instead of the repetitively predictable, the right brain is superior at
handling the unknown, the novel, the ambiguous, the paradoxical,
the unconventional, attempting to make sense out of it all by discovering workable patterns. And a good thing it does, because with only
the information-processing style of the left hemisphere our world
would be rigidly classified, our actions would have unvarying sequences and consequences—and human beings would have great difficulty formulating boundary-breaking ideas.

In terms of writing, the act would be highly mechanical instead
of organic. As Gertrude Stein said, "If we knew everything before-
hand, all would be dictation, not creation." Words would tend not
to move beyond their literal definitions, and thus we could not make
word designs, metaphors, images, nor could we respond to the subtle
shades of meaning and nuances that make language a living, dynamic, changing entity.

After reviewing an enormous body of research, two researchers—E. Goldberg of the State University of New York and Louis
Costa of the University of Victoria, British Columbia—have pro-
posed that these hemispheric differences exist because the two halves
of the brain are "wired" differently. They say that the right hemisphere has a greater neuronal "interregional connectivity" and so can
handle novel material better, whereas the left hemisphere, because of

its sequential neuronal organization, has superior compact storage of well-routinized pre-existing codes. They suggest that the right hemisphere has a greater neuronal capacity to deal with informational complexity for which no learned program is readily available. By contrast, the left hemisphere relies heavily on previously accumulated, sequentially organized information. Thus the right hemisphere is specialized for the initial orientation of a task for which no preexisting routine is available. Once an appropriate system has been discovered, they say, the left hemisphere holds a leading role in its utilization. If their conclusions are correct, it has much to tell us about the directionality of hemispheric involvement at different stages of the creative process or in any complex symbolic activity that moves from novel to known, such as natural writing.

Thus, in the human brain, the corpus callosum becomes a crucial channel of communication between two radically different thinking systems. When the specialized talents of each hemisphere are brought to bear on a given task, we can indeed make beautiful music.

Orchestrating Hemispheric Cooperation

The corpus callosum connects the two brain hemispheres primarily for two main purposes: it allows them to communicate with each other at the rate of thousands of impulses per second, but it can also inhibit this informational flow when it is more advantageous to focus the talents of one hemisphere alone on a given task. Such inhibition can be seen in an example from Einstein, who, from the age of fifteen on, engaged in what he called "thought experiments."

In one thought experiment, Einstein imagined what a light wave would look like if he were an observer riding along with it. In another, he imagined a man in a falling elevator and how that would "feel" and what would happen to his keys, and so forth. Einstein asserted that only when these images became so clear that they were voluntarily reproducible could he laboriously transform them into communicable language. Here we have a compelling example of callosal inhibition of logical "sign" information from the left brain so that the right brain can seek out, discover, and stabilize its images. (Clustering, as we saw in Chapter 2, creates a similar inhibition of logical left-brain thought while the nonlinear associations of the patterning right brain are spilling forth.)

The psychical entities which seem to serve as elements of thought are certain signals and more or less clear images which can be "voluntarily" reproduced and combined. . . . This combinatory play seems to be the essential feature of productive thought—before there is any connection with logical construction in words or other kinds of signs which can be communicated to others . . . . The above-mentioned elements are, in my case, of visual and some of muscular type. Conventional words . . . have to be sought for laboriously only in a secondary stage, when the mentioned associative play is sufficiently established and can be reproduced at will.

Albert Einstein,
Letter to Jacques Hadamard

However, once images are voluntarily reproducible (or, in our case, associations are held fast in clusters), the corpus callosum shifts from *stop* to *go,* making right-brain images and patterns accessible to the left brain, which in turn can give them sequential, communicable form. At this stage we benefit from the left brain's systematic application of learned strategies, of its ability to create "signs" which can be communicated to others.

Conversely, if a task is familiar, thus coded and stored as a repetitively predictable skill, the corpus callosum may inhibit nonproductive "help" from the right brain, which would only interfere. Imagine, for example, copying a poem, which requires left-brain skills almost exclusively. When one of his compositions was finished in his head, Mozart would have his wife read him stories to keep him entertained during the laborious, time-consuming, and sequential process of musical notation.

And here is the important point. The right brain plays a critical role in the initial stages of doing anything not already clearly laid out. Experimental evidence in the learning of novel tasks shows that, in the early stages of acquisition, the right brain shows superiority in performance. Then, as skills necessary for the execution of the task are acquired and routinized, the left brain attains superiority. Translated for our purposes, to achieve natural writing, we move from the wondering, exploring, inquisitive, receptive right brain in the productive, idea-generating stages to the sequential, syntactical, sequentially organizing capabilities of the left brain in the later stages of the writing process.

Precisely because the right brain is specialized for initial orientation of a task for which there is no pre-existing routine, it must be drawn into the writing process first, through clustering. You cannot routinize clustering. It is always a novel task, open to surprise, discovery, pattern. Once discovery has been accomplished, the left brain can enter the picture with its systematic application of learned strategies and sequencing abilities. In so doing, it draws on fixed linguistic codes and relies heavily on previously accumulated and organized information, such as syntax and vocabulary. Finally, the left brain imposes the limits of what it knows on the wide-ranging possibilities of the wondering right brain. Thus, natural writing is fully dependent on the cooperation and orchestration of both sides of the brain, but always *begins* with the right brain. Let's go back, for the moment, to an understanding of how, from a developmental standpoint, the two hemispheres came to be specialized.

The Development of Cerebral Lateralization

We have seen how, in the fully developed brain, the hemispheres function differently, sometimes independently of each other and sometimes in cooperation. Let's take a quick look at how lateralization develops, and the implications of this development for our use of language.

At birth, the corpus callosum—that bundle of nerve fibers connecting the brain's two hemispheres—exists and contains 200 million nerve fibers, but it is undeveloped. Our phenomenal ability to learn during infancy and early childhood may have something to do with the fact that the two brains do not as yet interfere with each other's mode of learning, although this is conjecture. Only gradually, over a period of approximately eleven years, do each of the corpus callosum's nerve fibers grow the fatty conductive myelin sheath that enables it to conduct electrical impulses from one hemisphere to the other, resulting in the constant communication that occurs between the hemispheres in the fully developed brain.

Neurologist Jason W. Brown and psychologist Joseph Jaffe have hypothesized that during infancy and before the acquisition of language the right brain is dominant. Thus we are able to shape the unfamiliar, uncatalogued world around us into meaningful image patterns. Then, as language begins to be lateralized to the left brain, we begin to master the shared sign and symbol world of our culture. Overall, however, our perceptions still seem to be heavily guided by aesthetic influences. We see wholeness rather than parts and sequences; we fashion stories as unified wholes despite gaps in logic; we imagine "wild things" and fantasize playmates that are as real to us as our neighbor's dog.

In this stage of the innocent eye, ear, and hand, the critical censor of the left brain still does not have much clout—that is, the left brain is not yet a strong contender for the chief position—and speaking and early efforts at writing are intensely natural aesthetic acts.

How to teach rigor while preserving imagination is an unsolved challenge to education.
R. W. Gerard,
The Biological Basis of
the Imagination

SIGN AND DESIGN: WORDS AND THE BRAIN

We tell stories, first verbally, then written, with easy strokes, impulsively following our immediate and most intense interests. And so we create patterns of words that are meaningful to us and give us pleasure. We enjoy language naturally—its sounds its rhythms, its picture qualities. This lasts for the first few years of life.

Young children are natural poets, until the left hemisphere takes over, between the ages of nine and twelve, correlating with the onset of puberty. By this time, the corpus callosum achieves full effectiveness as a conductor of information between hemispheres, and it has also begun to inhibit the transfer when the exclusive attention of one hemisphere is more appropriate to a given task. Language begins to be used largely informationally and thus becomes the specialty of the left brain. With our increased exposure to formal learning, the logical left brain is becoming dominant, with a continually expanding storehouse of words.

In school this left-brain bias is strengthened by the rewarding of left-brain skills and the general neglect of right brain-skills, as we saw in the story of Billy at the beginning of the chapter. The curriculum emphasizes parts-specific learning, and we are intensively exposed to and shaped by rule-governed left-brain thinking. This "conventional" stage of perception is both appropriate and necessary; our increasing vocabulary and command of language grounds us in the security of clear and unambiguous references, thus assuring us of a common framework for communication in the world.

Yet, given our left-brain education and the suppression of right-brain tendencies, many of us come to believe ourselves to be uncreative: we "can't" draw; we "hate" to write; we become inhibited in our body movements, in singing, and in other forms of creative expression. We begin to lose our spontaneity, our aesthetic sense, our trust in our abilities, our playfulness. And writing begins to be drummed into us as an unnatural, artificial act replete with contradictory rules, even requiring the formal breaking into parts of the language we had learned so effortlessly in our "innocent" stage. And so we stop writing.

A few of us come through this period with our ability to write, draw, and express ourselves naturally and creatively, intact. There may be two reasons for this: either such people have a very strong right-brain bias that continues to develop in spite of schooling (I believe Einstein was such a case), or they are recognized by teachers or

How does one bring the child to his full analytic powers in a discipline while at the same time preserving in him a robust sense of the uses of intuitive thinking, both in intellectual activities and in daily life?

Jerome Bruner,
The Relevance of Education

*My question is "when did other
people give up the idea of being a
poet?" You know, when we are
kids we make up things, we write,
and for me the puzzle is not that
some people are still writing, the
real question is why did the other
people stop?*

William Stafford,
Writing the Australian Crawl

parents and are encouraged in their creative endeavors. Most of us, however, feel stuck and creatively thwarted in this "conventional" stage of development.

From late adolescence on, the brain is fully lateralized and, in most cases, the left hemisphere has become completely dominant. The much neglected right side of our brain, with its aesthetic predilection for wholeness, images, metaphors, its ability to reconcile logical opposites, and its receptivity to creative play and wonder, has lost its primacy. Through regaining access to the natural functions of our right brain and developing a conscious collaboration between the essential abilities of both hemispheres, we can ultimately reach the cultivated stage of perception. The functions of the two hemispheres are complementary, and the basis of creative activity lies in the productive tension that connects the rule-abiding with receptive wondering and experimentation, literal language with metaphoric, imagistic expression, and the stasis of form with the dynamics of process.

Now let's focus specifically on language and the hemispheres.

Language and the Hemispheres

As we have already seen, achieving natural writing seems to depend entirely on hemispheric cooperation, each brain contributing its complementary capacities to the writing process at the appropriate times. Research shows that we are able to rely on the left hemisphere in writing while the right goes into an idling rhythm, although the result lacks the evocative dimensions characteristic of natural writing. Rather, the predominantly left-brain writing we are all too familiar with is usually dull, often uses inflated language, clichés, or jargon, and is lifeless and stiff. It is turgid precisely because it is once removed from its right-brain roots grounded in image, rhythm, wholeness, resonance, and the other nuances and subtleties of which language is capable.

Interestingly, until very recently researchers assumed that the right brain had relatively little to do with language because it thinks essentially in images rather than words and is predominantly "mute," leaving the left brain to do most of the verbalizing. However, researchers like Eran Zaidel of UCLA, whose main interest lies in exploring the linguistic capability of the right hemisphere, are demonstrating that just because the right brain is essentially mute does not mean it cannot process and comprehend language.

What the right brain cannot do well is string words together like the left brain does because it has a highly limited syntactical ability. For this reason, the right brain is not normally engaged in expressing itself in language, with a few exceptions first observed by the nineteenth-century neurosurgeon Hughlings Jackson in aphasic patients and experimentally demonstrated by Joseph Bogen, a pioneer in split-brain research. The exceptions proved to encompass emotionally charged units of language such as lines of a poem, songs, or proverbs—language that belongs to a rhythmic, imagined, semantic, or emotional whole where totality of meaning transcends grammatical components.

Zaidel calls his findings about the right brain's linguistic abilities "an unexpected and unusual form of natural language"—unexpected because brain researchers believed for so long that the right brain had at best only a token involvement in language; unusual because it is not governed by syntactic rules, as left-brain language is; natural because it is an inherent ability developed in infancy and early childhood in the right hemisphere, not one that is transferred and "learned" from the left. Herein lie many of the characteristics of natural writing, and here is our principal clue to the way the right brain helps to generate natural writing.

As we saw in Figure 4–3, the right brain, or Design mind, processes a face as a total unit, not just a small portion of it, such as hair on the chin, as the left brain does. Similarly, according to Zaidel, in the linguistic domain the right brain responds to verbal units as whole patterns without, however, having the ability to divide and analyze them into their component parts. A unit might be a whole poem, a stanza, a sentence, a phrase, or a word, depending on what the right brain perceives as a whole.

By contrast, division and analysis is the province of the left brain, or Sign mind, which can separate a word into its component letters or arrange a sentence into its correct grammatical form. The right brain's inability to analyze component parts while still expressing a

WRITING THE NATURAL WAY

The most enviable writers are those who, quite often unanalytically and unconsciously, have realized that there are different facets to their nature and are able to live and work with now one, now another, in the ascendant.

Dorothea Brande,
Becoming a Writer

Creativity, which is often considered the highest form of thinking, presumably involves an extraordinary degree of interplay of imaginal and verbal processes. Through its high memory capacity and freedom from sequential constraints, imagery contributes richness of content and flexibility in the processing of that content. . . . These imagistic attributes may underlie the intuitive leaps of imagination that often characterize creative thinking.

Alan Paivio,
Imagery and Verbal Processes

unified perception is illuminated by the response of a left-hemisphere-damaged woman to whom the French neurologist Lhermitte showed two paintings, asking her to describe what was in them. With her detail-oriented brain damaged, she was unable to identify any details—the church, the field, the clown, and so forth. But immediately upon seeing the paintings, she exclaimed, "Look! There are two Van Goghs!" Her right brain had a unified perception of the qualities of the painting that allowed her to recognize Van Gogh's work.

In sum, it appears that the left hemisphere (Sign mind) provides us with the solid stuff of language, including syntax, denotation, and correct spelling; it gives us language used as sign, which enables us to express ourselves literally, specifically, and verifiably. In turn, the right hemisphere (Design mind) has this solid base at its disposal, enabling it to transform these invariances toward different ends: it can create designs with images, recognize patterns of sound, reach out for metaphor, and play with recurrences, juxtapositions, and ambiguities, enabling us to make the rich and evocative patterns that give life to natural writing. So you see, even linguistically, the hemispheres cooperate to produce novelty and nuance, richness and expressiveness. In this cooperation lies our creativity.

Clearly, to great writers, philosophers, and psychologists, such two-sidedness in the creative process is nothing new. Over the centuries, they have made distinctions between artistic/critical, unconscious/conscious, imagination/analysis, inspiration/perspiration, intuition/reason, restraint/passion, to name but a few. All, sometimes obliquely, sometimes directly, tie in with the findings of hemispheric specialization: and suddenly these findings underscore what creative people have "intuited" all along.

Writing teacher Dorothea Brande would have been astounded at how accurately her 1934 positing of two metaphoric "selves," which she called "the artist" and "the critics," reflects what we are discovering about the two halves of the brain today.

In *Imagery and Verbal Processes*, creativity researcher Alan Paivio spoke of "interplay" between imaginal (Design mind) and verbal (Sign mind) processes.

Philosopher Susanne Langer foreshadowed hemispheric differences with extraordinary clarity when she spoke of a mind that is sensitive to forms, patterns, designs, wholes beyond mere (Sign-mind) "classification of things"—a reflection of right-brain processes.

A mind that is very sensitive to forms as such and is aware of them beyond the common sense requirements for . . . classification of things, is apt to use its images metaphorically, to exploit their possible significance for the conception of remote or intangible ideas.

Susanne Langer,
Problems of Art

Cognitive psychologist Jerome Bruner describes an alternate approach to knowing that approximates what we are learning about the modality of right-brain thoughts. Interestingly, he called his study *On Knowing: Essays for the Left Hand,* which implicates right-brain involvement, since we know with certainty that the right brain governs the motor functions of the left side of the body and vice versa.

And composition teacher Peter Elbow, in *Writing with Power,* speaks of different character traits that reflect a thirst for certainty on the one hand and an acceptance for uncertainty and ambiguity on the other. As we learn from studying hemisphericity, these traits reside in the same human being, as in the examples given in the following list:

Thirst for Certainty	*Acceptance of Uncertainty*
extrication, disengagement	involvement
rejecting or fending off what is new	willingness to explore what is new
closing, clenching	opening, loosening
literal	metaphorical
rigid	flexible
stubborn, hanging on	yielding
impulse for security	impulse for risk
unmoving self	floating self
learning to be sharper, finer, more piercing, harder, tougher	learning to be larger, more encompassing, softer, more absorbent

The Emotions and the Hemispheres

It is an approach whose medium of exchange seems to be the metaphor paid out by the left hand [right brain]. It is a way that grows happy hunches and "lucky" guesses, that is stirred into connective activity by the poet and the necromancer looking sideways rather than directly. Their hunches and intuitions generate a grammar of their own—searching out connections, suggesting similarities, weaving ideas loosely in a trial web.

Jerome Bruner,
On Knowing: Essays for the Left Hand

Three quite recent and related sets of findings regarding the right brain shed new light on the enormous difference between feeling emotion and *interpreting* or *expressing* those feelings. They also tell us something about the crucial role of the emotions in the creative process. In the first set of findings, neurologist Elliot Ross of the University of Texas discovered that just as damage to a particular region of the left hemisphere impairs speech, producing *aphasia,* so damage to a particular region of the right hemisphere impairs our ability to express or even interpret what we feel, producing what he has labeled *aprodosia. Feeling* an emotion, which originates in the midbrain's limbic system, is quite different from expressing or interpreting what we feel. The ability to interpret and express our emotional states is closely linked to the creative process and to natural writing.

Ross describes a thirty-nine-year-old schoolteacher who had a normal emotional profile before her right hemisphere was impaired by a stroke. After the stroke, he reports, she exhibited three striking characteristics: she was unable to laugh; she was unable to cry (even at her father's funeral, at which she said she experienced deep emotion); and her voice was so monotonous that she was unable to express anger or maintain discipline in her classroom. Ross notes that other right-brain-damaged patients who exhibited the physical symptoms of depression, such as loss of appetite and inability to sleep regularly, nevertheless insisted they were not unhappy.

These findings suggest that in the midbrain, in a region called the limbic system, these patients *"feel"* a certain way, but because of the interpretive right brain's impairment they are unable to do anything with these feelings. This aprodosic deficit refers to a loss of melody, pitch, rhythm, and intonation of the voice as well as to the nonverbal gestures accompanying speech that are necessary for the expression of feelings. One is immediately reminded of Peter, the right-hemisphere-damaged patient described at the beginning of this chapter, with his monotonic voice and his inability to go beyond literal— and, by implication, emotionally neutral—talk. What is most important for our purposes is that emotionally linked interpretive and expressive functions appear to reside in the right brain, the hemisphere we are learning to gain access to for natural writing.

In the second set of findings, William Gray, director of a psychiatric clinic in Massachusetts, has, after years of practice, recently developed a theory that we are feeling beings before we are thinking beings. Thus, he argues, emotional nuances play a primary and organizing role in cognition. (Think of the emotionally tinged associations that spill forth in clustering, which in turn involve us pleasurably—often intensely—in the writing that follows.)

Gray points out that in infancy we experience a basic set of global feelings such as contentment, anger, fear, rejection. These global wholes suggest right-hemisphere involvement and, as we grow up, continue to be refined and are interpreted and expressed as multifaceted nuances.

Gray asserts that in highly verbal cultures such as ours, "feeling-tones" are largely ignored, with a terrible loss to creative expression.

In the third set of findings regarding the hemispheres and emotion, researcher Shula Sommers of the University of Massachusetts demonstrates that the wider the range of our emotional expression, the more complex is our intellectual expression. Without the ability to be aware of what we feel, as Gray suggests, and without the ability to interpret what we feel, as Ross's study of the schoolteacher suggests, in effect we *have* no feelings, thus severely restricting our range of expression. Clustering, which often evokes the emotionally tinged associations interpreted by our right brain, activates our potential for greater intellectual and emotional breadth.

Let's look at the emotional intensity generated by a beginning writer's response to the nucleus word CLING (Figure 4–4). Many students wrote irritably about "clingy" girlfriends, "clingy" boyfriends, or "clingy" parents, but this writer, a mature re-entry student terrified of going back to school and having little confidence in her writing skills, generated highly sensitive emotional associations in her cluster. As they found their way into her vignette, she appeared to be a far more "natural" writer, in touch with her right-hemisphere knowings, than many in the class who had more writing confidence.

Clustering CLING evoked highly specific images of an infant's beauty, its fragility, its strength, and its scent coupled with intense feelings of maternal involvement. Paradoxically, in the end it is not the infant who does the clinging, as we might expect, but the mother herself because it makes her *feel* "rich and whole."

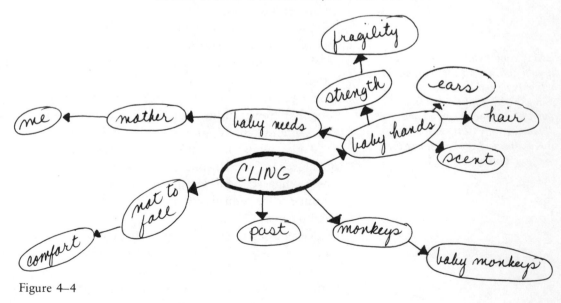

Figure 4–4

Baby hands are transparent, almost. So unbelievably delicate—
and mouth like a folded rose. How surprisingly powerful its suc-
tion. How urgent. The tiny, fuzzy head cradled in your hand,
how fragile, yet constant and indomitable is its effort to rise and
see the world around it. How it bobs and bounces against your
cheek and breast. The tiny ear is folded pink against soft brown
hair. And the new-born scent, a smell as filling as a meal, as full
of contentment. Blue eyes close beneath delicate lashes. And in
sleep, an angel smile. You cling tightly to the tiny body lying in
your arms, making you feel rich and whole.

Lavelle Leahey

There is an immediacy, a richness of detail, and an emotional
intensity reflected in this vignette that bespeak a rich feeling/image
response, evoked from the right brain's storehouse by the nucleus
word "cling."

All this suggests that the right brain, specialized for patterns,
emotions, and open-endedness, has much to do with our aesthetic
rendering of our world. To know something aesthetically means, as
already suggested: (1) consciousness of a unified whole in which our
usual preoccupation with particulars has been released; (2) consciousness of a sense of pleasure, the result of having discovered or
fashioned form and order out of the chaotic acts and facts of the
world.

Aesthetic mental activity, primarily a right-brain function, sows
the seeds of the creative act. But the creative act itself also demands
the specialized talents of the left brain. In fact, the creative act might
be characterized as the dynamic interplay between global and local
focus. A creator begins with global possibilities, which reveal new
details; the details in turn modify, strengthen, and clarify the initial
global design. The right brain envisions the whole structure or context . . . which, itself, is . . . still evolving through the left brain's
developing detail and sequencing skills. The creative act is a constant
back-and-forth movement between tentative vision and emerging
parts and sequences, to a more clearly delineated whole. Thus we begin to see that any language use of comparative richness and complexity demands active right-brain involvement. In natural writing,
each hemisphere plays an intensely cooperative role.

As long as we do not call on the specialized talents of both brains
to cooperate in writing, we will have to struggle to write naturally.

SIGN AND DESIGN: WORDS AND THE BRAIN

What is of overriding importance in the matter of the brain's hemispheres is not the division between them but the unity—a synergy. The corpus callosum is a busy two-way bridge, not a Berlin wall. There is interchange and there is wholeness. The information on either side is equally important to the whole—like stereo speakers. Balance is the key. Bring the percussion down so as not to drown out the strings.
Denise McCluggage,
The Centered Skier

A willingness to seek out what has real significance through clustering, a sensitivity to the nuances of language, an awareness of wholeness, an openness to feelings—all features of right-brain thought—create a maximum of creative freedom. Given those creative choices to work from, our left brain will gladly persevere in its task—with a minimum of anxiety—to write the words that pour out in endless succession, naturally.

Brain-research findings of recent years have done nothing more than crack open the "black box" to see what is actually inside and how it really works. Our understanding is still in its infancy. Yet the findings have not only confirmed, underscored, and refined our understanding of the creative process but have given us new ways of talking about it. For those of us who have always half yearned to write but believed we couldn't, this new understanding is altering the teaching and learning of writing forever by providing us with new tools.

Clustering and the Hemispheres

Since I specifically developed clustering as a way to gain access to the right brain, it becomes the first and most vital step in natural writing and serves as the basis for this book, leading to—and used in—the other techniques, which also tap the rich perceptions of the right brain. Accordingly, let me review clustering in view of what we have learned about our modes of thought.

1. Clustering forces the surrender of the left brain's step-by-step operation in favor of the right brain's seemingly random associations spilled nonlinearly onto paper.
2. In clustering, such left-brain characteristics of language as syntax, sequence, and cause/effect play little role. Thus words tend to move from their customary role of *sign* toward *design,* from literal meaning toward complex and evocative images.
3. Through clustering, the right brain has the opportunity to generate the fresh perceptions and meaningful patterns peculiar to its special cognitive style.
4. Clustering generates right-brain involvement through an unimpeded flow of images, ideas, memories—all emotionally tinged—which lead to the vision of a tentative whole, enabling us to begin writing easily and coherently.

5. Clustering taps the childlike, wondering, innocent, curious, playful, open-ended, flexible, pattern-seeking Design mind, allowing
us to play with language, ideas, rhythms, images, sounds, and
patterns creatively before committing ourselves to a fixed course.
In short, we avail ourselves of choices.

For the complex symbolic activity that writing surely is, the synthesis of our two modes of thinking seems to be the key. Our creative
acts bring us satisfaction, enrich and stabilize our lives, enable us to
express our own uniqueness, and clarify our flashes of insight into
our complex existence.

Writing Left, Writing Right, and Orchestrating

To enable my students to experience an approximation of predominantly left-brain versus right brain thought in writing, I asked them
to respond to the proverb "a rolling stone gathers no moss," first
from a pure Sign mind perspective, second from a pure Design mind
perspective through clustering, and finally through an integrated
perspective in a vignette. In order to prepare them, I charted examples of the two modes as a reminder of the distinctions as follows:

Left-Brain Response
Infinity is unbounded space, time,
  or quantity (pure abstraction)
Woman: a female human being
  (purely literal definition)

" 'Too many cooks spoil the broth'
  means that if you have too many
  cooks cooking the soup, it'll
  spoil." (literal/logical)

Right-Brain Response
Infinity is like a box of Cream of
  Wheat (pure image)
Woman: "The wide w. The receptive o. Womb . . . wide warm
  woman, white-thighed. Wooed
  and wed. Wife." (qualitative,
  patterning, imagistic, rhythmic)

" 'Too many cooks spoil the broth'
  . . . well, let's see [scanning
  possibilities], it could mean that
  a child subjected to too many
  conflicting disciplinary measures
  by too many well-meaning
  adults will probably become a
  confused adult. What do you see
  in it?" (metaphoric/interpretive)

What characterizes Sign-mind responses is that they are highly
literal; they can be looked up in the dictionary; they are logical and
explanatory; they do not go beyond what is given; they are precise.

What characterizes Design-mind responses is that they tend to be metaphoric (soup becomes a child), reflecting a complex image or a series of connected images in words; they are personal; they tend to be full-circle wholes; they go beyond the given and the literal.

The vignette is the result of the cooperative effort of both modes of thought, reminding us that writing at its best is a complex creative act, necessitating the orchestration of both sides of the brain.

Here is writer Art Carey's literal Sign-mind response:

A rolling stone is always mossless because it does not stay in one place long enough to allow the accumulation of living growth on its surface.

The cluster of Figure 4–5 is his pure Design-mind response in his search for something of significance to him.

And here is Art Carey's vignette.

Of Rootlessness

There are times when I envy the bristlecone pine. Nestled on the dry, windy, eastern slopes of the Sierra Nevada Mountains, the bristlecone pine is reputed to be the oldest living thing. Before Lincoln spoke at Gettysburg, before Washington crossed the Delaware, before Columbus sailed from Spain, the bristlecone seed sprouted, sent out tendrils, and grew roots.

It is the roots that I envy. Not the roots of a cultural heritage but the roots of permanence, of staying. My roots were first planted in Schenectady, N.Y., a no-nonsense, cold-as-sin-in-the-winter upstate city that boasted an Indian massacre before California had a white settlement. But the roots, shallow planted, didn't take. They tried the soil in diverse places: Kentucky, Missouri, and Michigan. Finally, itching for new ground to investigate, they settled in the peatdust of Central California, only to be transplanted to the concrete adobe hard pan of Los Angeles, the vanishing farmland of San Jose.

There is a loss in this. A loss of security, of identity, of attachment, both physical and emotional. Where I live is Nowhere city. Friendships are fleeting, attachments shallow, commitment negligible. Like an Arab following a desert star, I pitch my tent every five years and move on. The roots are weak and anywhere is everywhere.

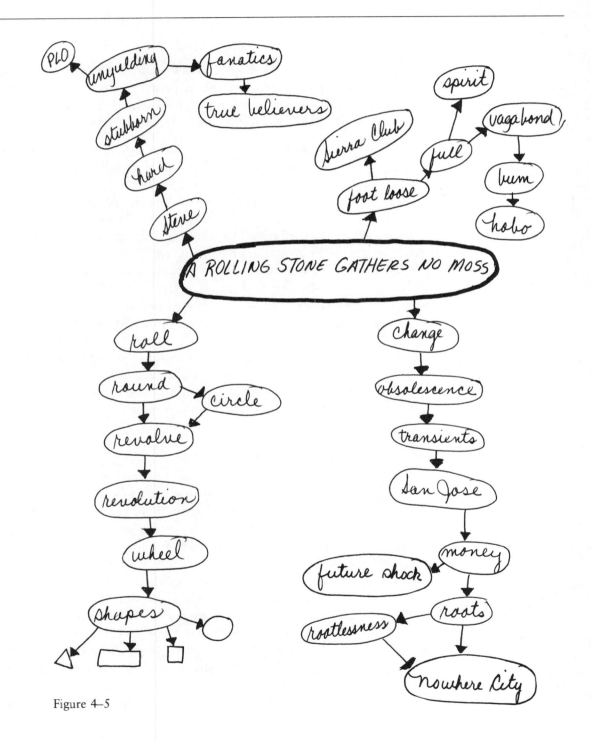

Figure 4–5

Directing Your Hand

Now it's your turn. Allow yourself to experience the two modes of knowing, and then the cooperative efforts of your combined Sign- and Design-mind talents. In your writer's notebook, write the proverb "Birds of a feather flock together." Draw a circle around it.

1. First, write as precise a literal definition as you are capable of. Use the dictionary if you think it will help. Keep track of how long it takes you.
2. Now cluster the proverb, generating Design-mind associations and patterns. Let go. Play. Be audacious. Be funny, if you wish. Cluster either the whole or single words, or both. Spend a couple of minutes doing this, until you experience a shift from randomness to a sense of purpose or direction, suddenly recognizing what you want to say.
3. Now begin writing immediately, drawing on your cluster. You may also incorporate part or all of the left-brain definition for juxtaposition, if it suits your sense of the whole. Otherwise, ignore it. Write for ten minutes or so until you feel you've come full circle with what you wanted to say.
4. Read your vignette aloud and make any changes that may bring you an even greater sense of satisfaction.

After Writing

What you probably noticed as you wrote the literal definition is the precision with which you searched for words to explain the proverb in a left-brain way. You may have experienced a struggle to avoid simply rephrasing the words of the proverb lest you give a totally circular explanation like that of the right-brain-damaged Peter with his cooks and broth.

Moving from left-brain explanation to right-brain clustering very likely released you into experimentation. You could wonder, entertain possibility, explore extraordinary notions, connect the widely divergent. Your entire response was probably very relaxed and fluid.

Now look at your vignette, which integrates the two ways of knowing. Chances are you focused on something that was not in your mind at all when you began clustering, so you may have experienced some surprise. You probably felt that your writing was out of character with what you normally produce; perhaps it came more easily, felt more coherent, more vivid, more detailed. As you compared your cluster and your subsequent writing you found that your cluster was somewhat of a self-organizing process—that is, you probably developed only one or two "arms" of the cluster rather than everything in it. Finally, you could not help but perceive the radical difference between your first literal effort and the vignette that grew out of gaining access to your Design mind.

As you write your way through this book, you will gain increasing confidence in the powers of your Design mind and the richness of the integrated creative experience. Learn once again to trust it, to be playful. The way to have one fresh idea is to have choices from among many.

A Last Word and Heading On

Brain-research findings richly substantiate many writers' intuitive recognition that the most creatively successful and productive writers are aware of two separate "selves," each of which makes its own unique contribution to natural writing. Framing this assertion in the brain terminology of today, the original vision of your Design mind—once it becomes accessible—is formed into something that can communicate beyond itself by the verbal sequencing capabilities of your Sign mind. In so doing, Roger Sperry noted, an actual physiological harmony occurs as the brain's diverse strengths work together. The reward of such cooperation is a psychological sense of wholeness. Herein lies our need and yearning for creative activity.

Clustering has been the first step in tapping your creative potential, and thus your expressive power. Now that we have explored the childhood origins of natural writing and the brain's role in creative activity, we come to the second major step in natural writing: the sudden shift of awareness, while clustering, from randomness to a sense of wholeness. I call this the trial-web shift, and it is the subject of Chapter 5.

CHAPTER 5/ *Discovering Design: the Trial Web*

Just as clustering represents the first critical step toward natural writing, so the trial-web shift represents the second. A trial web is your first awareness of a tentative vision, an idea of what you want to say. It happens when the seemingly random associations of your clustering suddenly take on coherence. In "The Making of a Poem," Stephen Spender compares this vision to a face, a telling comparison in view of our Design mind's predilection for faces: "A poem is like a face which one seems to be able to visualize clearly in the eye of memory. . . . [The poet's] job is to recreate his vision."

Trial web: the term itself tells you much. A web is something formed by weaving or interweaving. The word suggests complexity, unity, coherence, connectedness. The word trial (try-all) refers to a tentative experimental act. Thus, a trial web is exploratory, not definitive. It is your Design mind's way of expressing its awareness of a tentative pattern, a whole.

It is precisely this loosely floating vision of wholeness that gives focus, impetus, meaning, and direction to your writing. And your Design mind produces it because of its gift for seeing patterns and wholes rather than bits and pieces. With connectedness and pattern, meaning begins to emerge; we call this larger pattern *context*—literally, "that which is braided together." From it you get a sense of destination.

The trial-web shift is a tentative pattern only in the sense that it is a global Design-mind vision which gains solidity, form, and detail as you begin to write by calling on your Sign-mind sequencing skills. The trial web itself shows little concern with particular features. But when you begin to write, the broad vista of the trial web takes on substance as you work down into details and then back up toward a modified and richly expanded whole. Once you become aware of it, this primitive whole has the potential for generating a more complex structure.

For example, before I wrote the prospectus for this book, I sat down one day with a huge sheet of butcher-block paper and clustered around the nucleus (NATURAL WRITING) . It became an enormous cluster, for everything I had thought about for the past four years, in my teaching, reading, and research, spilled onto that page. I was so absorbed by the clustering that I lost all sense of time. As my momentum slowed, I experienced my first trial-web shift when I clearly saw in that welter the focus of at least four distinct chapters. In time, that first trial web spawned twelve separate clusters, which evolved into trial webs for each of the chapters of this book. Now that the book is written, I am delighted to see that, although the details have changed, the original vision is what directed the writing from its inception to its finish. My first "shock of recognition"—the trial-web shift into a sense of what I wanted to write—had guided the entire execution.

The clustered trial-web vision is a complex of memories, images, and emotional tones that have bunched together and demand attention precisely because there has been created a focus and feeling more powerful than each of them could offer separately.

The purpose of this chapter is to extend and deepen your understanding of clustering—the first nonlinear act of spilling and circling and connecting—through a feel for the trial-web shift, the second step toward becoming a natural writer. In fact, you probably already experienced it when you stopped clustering and started writing the vignette in Chapter 2. Now we're going to analyze in more detail what happens at that moment of transition.

The Trial-Web Shift: An Illuminated Landscape

The trial-web shift is movement from indeterminate form to focus. You are clustering, seemingly randomly, when suddenly you experience a sense of direction. The moment between randomness and sense

*DISCOVERING
DESIGN: THE TRIAL
WEB*

*Only an instant is needed for in-
sight to break through since it
comes always as a single unit, not
in some digital breakdown. Insight
is always complete and perfect in
its single instant's appearance, for
it is wholeness, or a power, that
can't be divided. It appears in all-
or-nothing form.*

Joseph C. Pearce,
The Bond of Power

*I sometimes begin a drawing with
no preconceived problem to solve,
with only the desire to use pencil
on paper and make lines, tones,
and shapes with no conscious aim;
but as my mind takes in what is so
produced, a point arrives where
some idea crystallizes, and then a
control and ordering begins to take
place.*

Henry Moore, sculptor

of direction is the moment of shift. It occurs during any creative act. Composer Paul Hindemith described it as a flash of lightning illuminating a landscape; writer Joseph C. Pearce, as a unified instant of insight; sculptor Henry Moore, as a crystallization that determines form; writing teacher Peter Elbow, as the moment when what was chaos is seen as having a center of gravity.

Psychiatrist Eugene Gendlin describes this sense of direction as a "felt shift." He applies what he describes as the physical sensation of this sudden shift therapeutically to get in touch with the true source of an emotional difficulty. His technique, called "focusing," involves sitting quietly relaxed, without expectations of any sort, waiting for the "feeling" of a problem to well up—anger or disappointment or shame, whatever emotion can be associated with it. Simultaneously, with the feeling of the problem, a word or phrase usually pops into mind, such as "I feel *hurt*." If this phrase is appropriate, according to Gendlin, the body responds with an unmistakable felt shift, invariably experienced as a feeling of relief. In his book *Focusing,* he compares this felt shift to remembering something you have forgotten.

Like Gendlin's "felt shift," the trial-web shift is unmistakable. It suddenly strikes you that you have *this* to write about. You suddenly perceive a direction to follow. Something stands out as significant for you here and now. A complex image coheres and connects the seeming randomness of your clustering. You have already experienced this sensation in doing your first cluster; now we are simply defining it and bringing it to awareness so you can recognize and cultivate it.

I tell my students it is like looking through the eye of a camera at a total blur only to discover, as you turn the focusing mechanism, a sudden broad vista or an expectant face or a grouping of clearly defined figures. Not only is this image focused, but it is *framed* to give you a sense that the objects you are focusing on somehow belong together. The trial-web shift is accompanied by sensations of pleasure/surprise/delight, as when you unexpectedly and gratefully recognize a familiar face in a crowd of strangers.

The trial-web shift is also inevitable, for your Design mind wants to make meaningful patterns out of whatever it encounters; thus you will, sooner or later, perceive a pattern in the seemingly random spilling of associations around a nucleus. That moment of recognition constitutes the shift to tentative trial web, and that awareness

The turning point in the whole cycle of growing is the emergence of a focus or a theme. It is also the most mysterious and difficult kind of cognitive event to analyze. It is the moment when what was chaos is now seen as having a center of gravity. There is a shape where a moment ago there was none.
                    Peter Elbow,
        Writing Without Teachers

You take off on a journey with that familiar, uneasy feeling that you have forgotten something. As you sit on the airplane you rummage through the possibilities. You may recall an item you did indeed forget, but there is no sense of relief; you know that isn't it. When the "real" item comes to mind, there is sharp recognition, a tangible shift, certainty that this was what was troubling you.
                Eugene Gendlin,
                        Focusing

triggers the impulse to write. And you do write, usually with surprising effortlessness, since so many of your previous experiences with writing were an excruciating stop-and-go affair. The most persuasive evidence is for you to experience it directly.

Directing Your Hand

Find a quiet place where you won't be interrupted. Use a new page in your writer's notebook and your favorite writing implement. Settle in comfortably. Natural writing is not chore but joy.

1. Cluster the word (WEB) for a minute or two. Be receptive to everything that comes, not only words, but phrases, lines of song, snatches of poems, proverbs, book and movie titles, pieces of conversation—anything within your experience. Do not let your Sign mind interfere by censoring.
2. As you cluster, allow yourself to move into a state of relaxed attention by simply letting come what will without judgment. Be alert for the trial-web shift without trying to force it. Just be open to it, expect it to happen, and it will.
3. The shift will happen in one of two ways. Most often, as already suggested, it will come as a sudden illumination of a connected complex of thoughts and feelings, but occasionally it is a gradual realization of a sense of a whole, accompanied by the urge to write. The trial-web shift is not a method; it is a phenomenon that cannot be standardized. A method can only be imposed from without; a trial-web shift always emerges from within—it is the response of your natural inner writer recognizing meaning.
4. Now simply follow the desire to write your vignette. It will become a process of discovering and recording what you have recognized in that trial-web shift. Your Sign mind now has full access to your Design mind's trial vision. It is time to crystallize that vision. Try to stay within the ten-minute limitation for both writing and clustering, but don't leave your writing hanging. Fulfill your Design mind's need to bring your thought process full circle.
5. Now read aloud what you have written. Spend a minute or two making any changes you feel will enhance your vignette.

After Writing

Let's focus for a moment on your feelings throughout the process you just went through. Now that you've done it a few times, quite likely you've begun to feel a sense of letting go as you cluster, trusting your Design mind to come up with something that holds meaning for you. The trial-web shift probably occurred as a mild shock of recognition, a sudden awareness of tentative design, the discovery of a focus. With this delicious sense of direction, your writing came as a flow instead of a trickle, accompanied by a sense of satisfaction, perhaps even exhilaration.

If you felt somewhat neutral or even disappointed, don't conclude that clustering won't work for you. It works for *all* of us because we are all equipped with patterning right brains. It is true that some Sign minds will put up greater resistance to novelty than others. This resistance will disappear as you continue to practice, and soon you will experience flow. If you experience really strong resistance, however, try drawing circles around a nucleus and connect them with lines and arrows, as suggested in Chapter 2. This doodling puts you into a state of relaxed awareness. When your resistance ebbs as you begin to relax, you will begin filling those circles.

The stricter your education in composition, the longer it may take you to get past your anxiety. Just know that no one but you is evaluating or judging your efforts. Remind yourself that clustering is playful; let go enough to enjoy it. All my students eventually cluster effortlessly, with great interest in what discoveries they will make. Let me share with you a few of their reactions.

Although clustering is a phenomenon unique to each individual Design-mind consciousness, it demonstrates certain characteristics no matter who is doing it. Students open themselves to clustering by relaxing their attention; this is like opening all the doors and windows on a summer night and then sitting in your favorite easy chair to let the night sounds pour in to your expectant ears. Relaxed attention leads to a receptive attitude, which permits the students to accept anything that comes their way—words and phrases, lines of songs, bits of poems, proverbs, book and movie titles, snatches of conversation, feelings—in short, anything within their experience. As they cluster, they experience a sense of randomness without distress because they know a shift will come.

And come it does. Students variously report it as a physically felt sense of unblocking often followed by a deep intake of breath, an opening up, a release of tension, "a burst inside of insight," a sense of exhilaration, a sudden sense of direction instead of scattered thoughts, an irresistible impulse to begin writing, a feeling that "writing is so easy it simply flows." Occasionally they have also reported a sense of physical lightness or of timelessness, or a "frozen moment" in which something of significance seemed to hover before them or in them. But most often they speak of a feeling amazed that, in letting go to allow *design* to happen, it actually happens! Poet Alastair Reid calls it "the moment when amazement ran through the senses like a flame," the moment of shift when the urge to write is overpowering. As Reid has written, "a word in that instant of realizing catches fire, ignites another, and soon, the page is ablaze with a wildfire of writing."

A Closer Look at an Elusive Process

The process of natural writing, then, occurs as follows: nucleus word leads to clustering, clustering to an internal pattern awareness, pattern awareness to the emotionally charged trial-web shift, trial-web shift to the impulse to write. Although the cluster itself is in the external world, accessible to the senses and visible on paper, the process of pattern awareness occurs in your right hemisphere, inaccessible to your logical Sign mind, and the trial web you recognize is the designation we give to your Design mind's sudden emotionally tinged perception of pattern and meaning.

From trial web to writing is like a camera zooming in for a close-up. As you write, using relevant words and phrases from your cluster, the encompassing shape of the trial web crystallizes into sharpness, detail, and a more complex structure than was initially apparent—that is, through the writing the trial vision continues to evolve. It evolves because the Sign mind has come into play, creating a dynamic interplay between global and local focus, the local detail shedding new light on the global possibility of the trial vision, the global vision generating new details. In this orchestration of talents lies the creative act.

Once you have experienced the trial-web shift, you have the answer to a paradox that has puzzled students of writing for centuries: how is it possible to structure the parts of a whole if the whole does not yet exist? The answer lies in the dual nature of the brain. The whole doesn't exist in the Sign mind, which can only process parts, nor does it actually exist in the Design-mind shorthand cluster on the page. However, from that relevant shorthand, the Design mind perceives the indefinite edges of a global vision, as one student expressed it:

To me, clustering is like blossoms on a branch. Each bud originates from its own main branch, sprouting and developing, yet always linked to its own source. The branch is constantly giving way to more and more blossoms, collecting them, linking them, and sending more stems out in new directions all the time. Individually, each bud can conjure up partial visual patterns in our mind, but when we see those buds clustered in bunches, we feel fulfilled, as if we had seen the whole picture.

That's what clustering does for me. It groups together many ideas that sprout from one main one and, when I stop to reflect upon what has been developed from clustering, I see the whole picture emerge. It enables me to understand more fully what I had trouble arriving at in the beginning, allowing the patterns and connections that are created to spur me into a more rounded grasp of meaning.

Once you begin writing, you initiate a natural collaboration between the two halves of the brain. Your Design mind has created a tentative whole and has made it accessible to your Sign mind through clustering. Now the very act of setting the emerging parts down in sequence stimulates an ongoing interaction between your Sign and Design minds.

So you see that writing naturally and effortlessly begins with generating a trial-web vision. This sense of purpose, of knowing what you want to say, not only minimizes the anxiety so commonly associated with writing but leads to a dynamic and absolutely essential collaboration between the two modes of thought.

Fear.
Afraid of self,
afraid of knowing,
running, hiding,
going nowhere, fading fast.
Then. Stop.
Turn and see,
turn about and face it.
It? Me.

Although it is difficult to discuss someone else's right-brain shorthand, let's look at the anatomy of a cluster to help us get the feel for one writer's associational response to CIRCLES (Figure 5–1). Doing so may help to show you that clustering is truly a receptive activity, and that a trial-web shift occurs sooner or later to anyone who clusters. It's built into our Design minds.

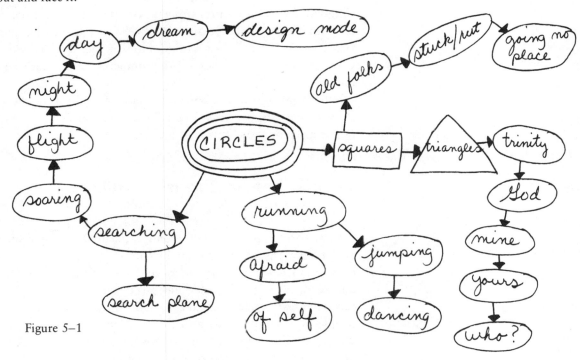

Figure 5–1

Even a cursory look at her cluster tells us that her associations naturally organized themselves into three main branches, one beginning with "squares," another beginning with "searching," and a third beginning with "running." Clustering "squares" brought no shift, so she remained in a receptive state and continued to cluster, taking off from "searching"; still nothing, but still receptive, alert for the shift, she clustered from "runnning" to "jumping" and "dancing." A look back at "running" triggered "afraid" followed by "of self."

Suddenly the shift illuminated a vision, a sense of direction, and she began to write immediately. Although she ignored the parts of the cluster that were not relevant to her trial-web vision, it is interesting that she took ideas from each of the three arms of the cluster:

Myself, my secrets, my soul
Growing, dreaming, dancing,
going, going someplace,
anywhere, searching for meanings
& motives & reasons why,
learning to fly, to soar again like
before, before fear made me run.
                              Donna Ducarme

"going no place" from one, the notion of flying and soaring from another, and, of course, from the third the idea of running away from one's self. In the effortless writing that followed, her clustered vision crystallized into a poem, all within a ten-minute time span.

The point of exploring this writer's cluster is that you may be too impatient to reach a trial-web shift. Trying harder or trying to force a creative idea is highly counterproductive. Do its opposite: simply *allow*. This natural process will take its own time, and your only obligation is to remain receptive and relaxed though alert as you continue to spill out Design-mind possibilities. It will come. It will come. Your right brain is programmed to see patterns and meaning.

Let's go on to experience one more dimension of the trial-web shift: being receptive to a dominant impression as you scan a painting or a sculpture or any work of art.

Trial Webs from Pictures: Dominant Impressions

All visual art forms, be they paintings, sculptures, or drawings, appeal to the Design mind's predilection for wholes. Recall that the right brain is superior at processing faces. When the right brain is damaged, patients often develop facial agnosia, and a patient with this condition cannot recognize familiar faces or discriminate among people in general. Recall also that the left brain is superior at processing detail. In looking at a friend's face, for example, your Sign mind will not be able to process the whole face whose totality signals "Suzanne"; rather, it will note her earring, her right eyebrow, or a mole on her cheek. Similarly, in looking at a painting, while your Sign mind focuses on specific details, the Design mind forms a dominant impression of the whole.

Accordingly, using a visual stimulus for clustering and the resulting trial-web shift gets directly at right-brain processing. It also allows you to discover your own nucleus by naming the dominant impression you get upon scanning a painting. The value of this exercise is that when you use these techniques for writing after you have completed this course, you will always be able to discover your own nucleus for a cluster before you begin writing. Knowing you can arrive at it naturally by being receptive to a dominant impression about any subject means you can discover it from within rather than being dependent on it from without; you gain a feeling of quiet self-assurance rarely experienced in most writing.

In looking at the visual arts, this nucleus or dominant impression is often a feeling evoked by the painting, such as sadness or joy, but it can also be simply a response to a dominant color, such as "grayness," or a shape, such as "angularity," or anything else that strikes you as you scan the painting. Whatever the dominant impression, it becomes the nucleus around which you can cluster your observations. The resultant writing will be much more meaningful than a simplistic "I like it" or "I don't like it." Nor will it be an art critic's Sign-mind analysis of style and technique, historial significance, or artistic merit. Instead, it will serve as a means of cultivating your aesthetic sense and expressing all the feelings that surface as a result of the associations triggered by the dominant impression. The trial-web shift and the resulting vignette become a way of unraveling what your Design mind sees and feels as it scrutinizes a work.

It works this way. You scan a given painting, sculpture, or photograph for a moment or two until a dominant feeling strikes you: restlessness, or chaos, or movement, or bitterness, for example. You capture that dominant impression in a word or phrase and circle it on the page. That word or phrase is your own discovered nucleus from which your cluster will grow as you continue to scan the painting.

Let's take a well-known painting, Grant Wood's *American Gothic*. Your Sign mind will tend to take charge with facts: Grant Wood is an American painter, *American Gothic* is his most famous painting, his sister posed as a model, it was painted in such and such a year, and so forth. By contrast, your Design mind is not interested in such detail. Instead, it scans the total painting and forms impressions, as you will see for yourself with the following exercise.

Directing Your Hand

Discover how fascinating and easy it is to generate a dominant impression by focusing on Grant Wood's *American Gothic* (Figure 5–2). Use a fresh page in your writer's notebook.

Figure 5–2   GRANT WOOD, *AMERICAN GOTHIC*, COURTESY OF THE ART INSTITUTE OF CHICAGO.

1. Contemplate the painting for a moment or two and let yourself become aware of the strongest feeling it evokes in you. If you are not relaxed, unfocus your eyes for a moment as you look at the painting and then refocus, which may help you slide into relaxed attention. Scan the painting, letting your eyes move wherever they wish.

2. When you become aware of a feeling or impression (a "felt shift"), give it a name. Should no dominant impression come immediately to mind, ask yourself "How does it make me feel?" "What is the main thing that hits me here?" Don't try for something profound or eloquent. Let what will come, come. Something will come; something always comes to us because our brains are rarely still. Just be patient and stay with it a minute or two longer.

3. The dominant impression you discover and name is your own experiential response to the painting and is the nucleus around which your cluster will grow. Write the word or phrase on your paper and circle it. Now, for a minute or two, continue to scan the painting and cluster whatever you see or feel.

4. In due time you will experience the shift from seemingly random association to a sense of pattern; that is the trial-web shift. It makes you aware of a sense of purpose and of something you want to say that allows you to begin writing.

5. Write immediately for eight minutes or so, using anything that seems appropriate from your cluster and ignoring whatever doesn't fit your sense of the whole. When you have filled the page, be sure to come full circle, referring back to the impression that triggered your writing.

6. Read your vignette aloud and then make any brief changes that will improve the whole.

After Writing

Now that you have had the opportunity to use a painting as a stimulus for experiencing the trial-web shift, let's explore the process.

What happens when you are confronted with a painting as stimulus for writing? Most significant, your Design-mind reaction is likely to be immediate and intense because you are confronting a complex whole. For example, your dominant impression of *American Gothic* may well have been triggered by something in those two faces. Then, as you clustered, the trial-web shift very likely occurred as an insight, illumination, or observation with respect to the expressions on those faces. The process worked as follows: your dominant impression triggered associations that you recorded in your cluster, and then the trial-web shift told you what you wanted to say about the expressions on those faces.

Let me illustrate by sharing with you four vignettes written in response to *American Gothic*. The vignettes were produced by first-year high school students with severe writing problems. Their experiences with writing had been so negative that they rarely even attempted assignments and, when they did, what they wrote was virtually indecipherable. Their teachers warned me that I should not be disappointed if they produced no writing. In this experiment, I asked this anxious, failure-oriented group of youngsters to focus on *American Gothic* projected onto a screen. "What is the main feeling you get?" I asked. "Give that feeling a word," I said, after showing them how to cluster and describing the trial-web shift.

All responded with a dominant impression; all began to cluster around their own generated nucleus until, one by one, each seemed to experience a trial-web shift, for they soon began writing, much to the surprise of their teachers, who were in the room. The results of their insights appear below (Figures 5–3 through 5–6). For readability, I have corrected spelling and added a few punctuation marks; otherwise they stand as written.

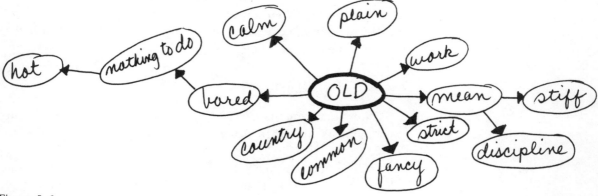

Figure 5–3

They are old. They have nothing to do but work. They look lifeless and stiff. They're trying to be fancy, but they look mean. They look bored. They're common country folks. They look like parents, strict and disciplined. And they look hot.

Peter Koleckar

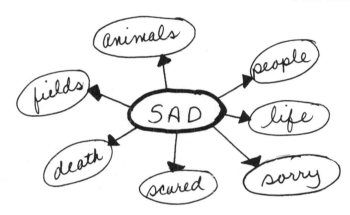

Figure 5–4

As sad as they look, they don't cry. Both figures stand side by side, one thinking of whatever has happened, and the other of who did it. Maybe someone died; maybe they're scared. I don't know. Maybe their fields were bad this season, or was it those little animals who ate their crops? Maybe that's the reason. Whether people made them angry or they're just sad, I wouldn't know, and I sure am glad.

Manuel Peña

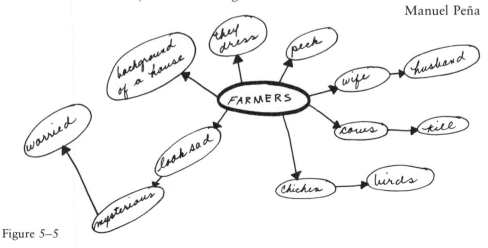

Figure 5–5

The farmers look worried as if the corn wasn't growing. The way they dress is as if they didn't have money. The cow's hungry, no milk; the chickens lay rotten eggs. The farmer's wife looks as if it's her fault about everything. The husband looks mysterious in a way that he is ready to kill for money.

Ricardo Rodriguez

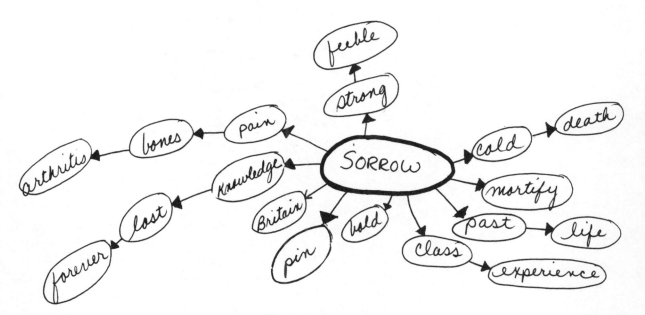

Figure 5–6

We are like a balloon, rising high and mighty in our youth. We bobble up and down, thinking, deciding, and growing. We sag, sink, go down, know all, and finally, land to die in sorrow, dust.

Andrew Naas

The last, cryptic vignette never specifically refers to the painting itself, but it potently reflects the mood of resignation this fourteen-year-old writer saw in those joyless faces.

As we have seen, responding to a work of art requires two shifts, in a sense: initially, the sudden recognition of a dominant impression, providing your own discovered nucleus to expand on, and, later, the trial-web shift from randomness to awareness of purpose and meaning. Experience these two shifts once more by responding to different subject matter in the form of a sculpture.

Directing Your Hand

The photograph of a sculpture (Figure 5–7) will provide the stimulus for your dominant impression and trial-web shift. It is an untitled work by Dutch sculptor Ole Langerhorst.

Figure 5–7   CLE LANGERHORST, *UNTITLED*, COURTESY OF THE SCULPTOR.

1. Quietly contemplate the sculpture for a few moments. Let a dominant impression come to you. Now give it a name. This dominant impression is your own discovered nucleus from which you will cluster. Write it on a sheet of paper in your writer's notebook and circle it.

2. Cluster any and all associations that want to come. Stay open and receptive. Continue to cluster until you experience the trial-web shift that signals your sense of direction.

3. Now crystallize your vision in writing. That means engaging your Sign mind sequencing powers—but don't forget, as you write, to rescan the Design-mind connections in your cluster. Your vignette is a cooperative venture between Sign- and Design-mind talents.

4. Take approximately ten minutes, as usual, being sure to come full circle.

5. Now read what you have written, preferably aloud. Make any changes that will make you feel better about the vignette. If you can get a friend to respond to this sculpture with you, you will be amazed at how the same sculpture can evoke such different responses.

As you develop your clustering skills, you can get Design-mind trial webs from any source you choose. Let me show you what my students did with poems as a stimulus for natural writing.

Trial Webs from Poems: Focusing Statements

Like a painting or sculpture, a poem is a whole, given form and content by another personality. Also like a painting, a poem can evoke in us a dominant impression, triggered by the emotions it elicits as we read it. But I wanted to challenge the Design mind with a slightly different approach, which promised to be effective with poetry because its medium is words. In so doing, we discovered yet another way to use clustering for evoking a trial-web shift. It yielded fascinating results.

I asked students to read the poem by the American poet Jon Stallworthy at least two or three times.

Lament
*Because I have no time
To set my ladder up and climb
Out of the dung and straw,
Green poems laid in a dark store
Wither and grow soft
Like unturned apples in a loft.*
                    Jon Stallworthy

Next I asked them to choose any three words or phrases that particularly struck them. They were to precluster these, not to achieve a trial-web shift but to identify a dominant impression. Unlike a painting, which can easily be scanned for a dominant impression, a poem must first be read linearly and only then approached as an aesthetic, nonlinear whole.

Scanning the three clusters will lead to a dominant impression. Given a name and circled on a sheet of paper, this impression became the nucleus to be clustered, triggering new associations along with any associations the students wanted to use from the preclusters. The students kept clustering until they experienced the trial-web shift.

Then, before writing, they were to put the trial-web vision into two or three "focusing statements," which represents a shift to Signmind processing and articulates the direction a writer will take. Normally, one of the focusing statements provides an even more specific direction than the others, whereupon students begin to write.

Let me share a strong example by a beginning writer whose clusters of (TIME), (DARK), and (SHRIVEL) comprise Figures 5–8, 5–9, and 5–10.

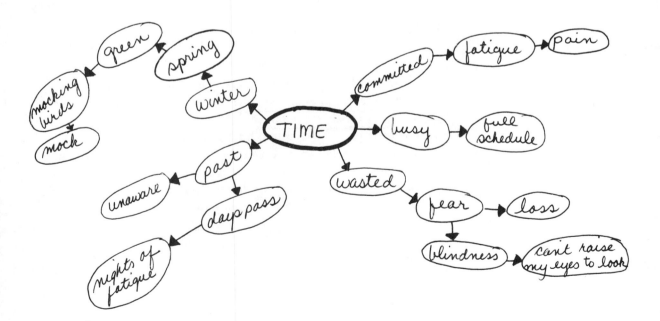

Figure 5–8

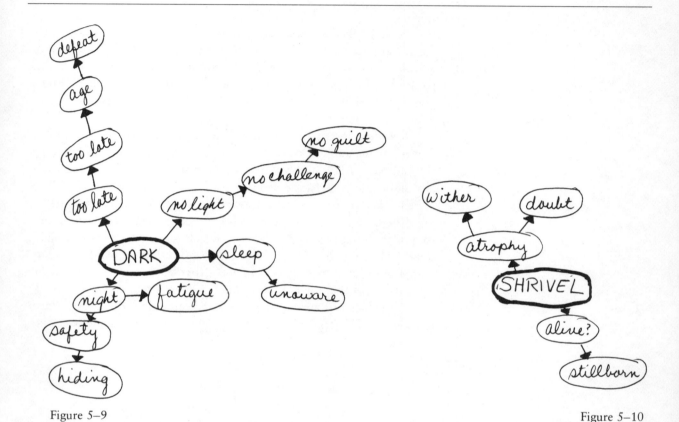

Figure 5–9   Figure 5–10

The precluster of "time," "dark," and "shrivel" already indicates considerable emotional involvement. The dominant impression, (LOSS OF CREATIVE CURRENT), was derived from scanning these preclusters; then she clustered for a tighter focus (Figure 5–11).

Next she held her trial-web vision fast with two focusing statements: "Loss of the creative current is death in the womb" and "In the dark, things do not grow." She selected the first one for writing, which flowed effortlessly to a close in a ten-minute period.

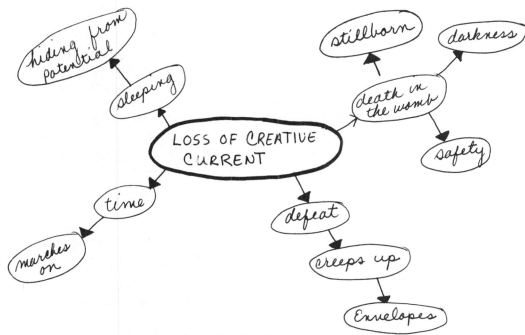

Figure 5–11

Death in the Womb
I have forgotten many poems
Because I slept when they were to be born,
For the dark hid me and made me safe.
And time, whose minutes became seasons—
As I wrapped defeat warmly on my shoulders—
Slid under the door behind the drapes.
And mocking birds mock me in the spring
As I carry my stillborn poems in my womb.

Lavelle Leahey

Although the vignette was ostensibly based on the focusing statement "Loss of the creative current is death in the womb," we can see that the vignette combines elements of both focusing statements. In fact, they seem to be restatements of the same idea that is expressed in the vignette. That's fine, for each attempt at focusing is a Sign-mind effort at clarifying the Design-mind trial-web vision. It is clear evidence of hemispheric cooperation in the complex symbolic activity that is writing; we are witnessing the move from Design-mind clustering to holistic vision to Sign-mind sharpening of that vision.

When you use a poem as a stimulus for clustering, you confront a fully shaped whole that exerts its own aesthetic influence on your Design mind. The words you choose to cluster, therefore, retain echoes of the context from which you took them. As you cluster, you may find that these words evoke particularly rich and potent images and feelings. The two focusing statements, which draw on the cluster, as well as on all three preclusters, clarify and articulate whatever trial-web shifts you may have experienced along the line. It's time to experience your own response to a poem using the process just demonstrated.

Directing Your Hand

Read the poem by William Butler Yeats several times.

Deep-Sworn Vow
*Others because you did not keep
That deep-sworn vow have been
    friends of mine;
Yet always when I look death in
    the face,
When I clamber to the heights of
    sleep,
Or when I grow excited with wine,
Suddenly I meet your face.*
            William Butler Yeats

1. Choose, without too much contemplation, three words or phrases from the poem and circle them on a page in your writer's notebook. Be sure to leave plenty of space for each cluster to unfold.
2. Cluster any and all associations that want to come. Finish with one nucleus before you go on to the next. Allow all connections to spill out; don't force; don't censor.
3. Now scan all three clusters receptively and allow a dominant impression to emerge. Give it a name, circle it on a page in your notebook, and cluster it until you experience a trial-web shift. Should nothing jell for the moment, reread the Yeats poem and rescan your preclusters, using whatever seems appropriate from them. Sooner or later a focus will swim to the surface.
4. When it does, shift gears to Sign-mind thought by crystallizing your trial-web vision into a focusing statement and record it in your notebook. For statement number two, shift gears back to a more diffuse Design-mind state, rescan your clusters, and crystallize a second focusing statement, writing it down too. These steps will take approximately five minutes.
5. Now choose the statement that strikes you as most meaningful, or combine them if they seem to overlap.
6. Begin writing and continue for ten minutes or so. When you finish your vignette, read it aloud and make any changes you feel will improve its wholeness, making sure to bring it full circle.

After Writing

This exercise helps you become aware of switching from Design- to Sign-mind thinking processes and back again. This shifting underscores an essential principle of natural writing—the oscillation from wholes to parts and sequences, then back to more clearly delineated wholes, from immersion in Design-mind processes to a Sign-mind perspective and back again to immersion in the whole. In thus learning to cooperate in the writing process, your two modes of thought join in the creative act to fashion something original and authentic, something you probably weren't even aware of as a possibility before you began.

A Last Word and Heading On

By now you have seen that clustering is the tool whereby we gain access to the rich and creative Design-mind processes essential for natural writing. In this chapter you have experienced the trial-web shift, the step that leads to discovery, unity, and meaning in the diversity of spilled associations. After you have clustered and before you start writing, the trial-web shift gives you a focus to use as a point of departure.

If you do not begin in the fluid Design mind—which can accept and work through that fullness of random images and feelings to discover patterns of meaning—you may get stuck in Sign-mind detail. You will worry about what to say and how to start, write fitfully and unconnectedly, sit in judgment on whether it sounds right instead of concentrating on the whole, and get bogged down in spelling, punctuation, topic sentences, supporting statements—any one of dozens of legitimate Sign-mind concerns that, when treated as a prime concern in the initial stages of writing, will block you from discovering a larger picture to give you focus and, ultimately, a loosely webbed structure to write from. A mind preoccupied with particulars cannot discover the larger picture; without it writing becomes a painful process of laboriously squeezing out sentence after sentence like too-stiff cookie dough out of a cookie press, producing a final product that is likely to be crumbly instead of cohesive. A trial web provides a controlling design, something to put into sequence. And focusing statements give you an even firmer sense of direction before you begin writing, in addition to making you intensely aware of the shift from Design- to Sign-mind processing and back again.

In Chapter 6 we will explore another important principle of natural writing: recurrence. Recurrence constitutes a natural unifying thread that you can develop consciously in your writing to give it increasingly sophisticated cohesiveness and pattern.

CHAPTER 6/ *Recurrences: the Unifying Thread*

Recurrence is a natural phenomenon. We have all had the experience of lying on a beach feeling pleasantly groggy in the heat, thoughts slipping in and out of our conscious awareness, when a sudden, inexplicable shift in attention makes us aware of nothing but the sound of waves: forward rush, momentary silence, backward sucking sound, coming again and again, not as isolated phenomena, which is how they reached our ears before, but as pattern. And we experience pleasure. Yet that pleasure comes not because the waves all sound alike, but because there is pattern, and within that pattern there is variation, irregularity.

Pattern recognition is the province of the Design mind. In writing naturally, recurring words, sounds, images, and feelings have the same powerful effect that a recurring melody has in music, recurring foliage in a landscape, recurring colors in a painting: we react to them emotionally and they intensify the unity of the whole. In language, we are more likely to remember recurring patterns—for example, "of the people, by the people, for the people" from the Gettysburg Address—because of their powerful effect on the right brain. For this reason, much persuasive writing, and especially speeches, contains recurrences, as do poetry and other writings with a strong emotional content. Learning to use recurrences—the *meaningful* repetition of words, images, ideas, phrases, sounds, objects, or actions throughout a piece of writing to unify and empower it—constitutes the third basic step in achieving natural writing. Beyond the cluster

111

*For constructing any work of art
you need some principle of repetition or recurrence; that's what
gives you rhythm in music and pattern in painting.*

Northrop Frye,
The Educated Imagination

*In all of us an ancient infant
Responds to the rhythm of the
   waves
As if to a lullabye.*

Lavelle Leahey,
student writer

and the trial web, recurrence is one of the simplest and most natural reflections of your Design mind's love of making patterns, of seeing wholes rather than discrete bits and pieces.

Childhood Origins

Recurrences are a natural characteristic of childhood language. Even before children can speak, they amuse themselves with a rhythmic jabbering of repeated syllables: "goo-goo," "ma-ma," "da-da." As they get older, they begin to delight in the rhythms and recurrences of such games as "Pat-a-cake, Pat-a-cake," "This little piggy," and countless others. Linguist Kornei Chukovsky suggests that the rhythmic recurrences of nursery rhymes actually grew out of children's intoxication with repetition, rhythm, and melodic lines. Children clap, chant, rhyme, and repeat words because such activity makes patterns, which produce intense pleasure.

As soon as children begin to write, recurrences find their way into their products. An example of recurrence came from a clustering experiment I was asked to do in my daughter Simone's second-grade class. We clustered the nucleus word ROUND on the board, all the children eagerly participating in filling the board with all sorts of "roundnesses" radiating outward from the center. Next I asked them to write about roundness—tell a story, describe something round, explain a "round" experience, anything they chose.

Simone's poem, written in twenty minutes, illustrates the extent to which the natural rhythms of language are used intuitively by a child. The repetition of "round" not only lends focus on "round things" but ties the poem into a coherent, self-contained whole.

What Is Round?
Round is a ball bouncing high in the air.
Round is a flea that crawls up in your hair.
Round is the earth that we're now standing on.
Round is the sun that goes up at dawn.
Round is an apple that blooms in the spring.
Round is a beautiful emerald ring.
Round is a planet up in space.
Round is a necklace made out of a shoelace.
Round is the super small moon.

Round is the head of a big baboon.
Round is a log floating down the stream.
Round is a pie topped with whipped cream.
Round is a little o.
Round is a tangerine that had a friend cow.
Round is a dime, a penny, a nickel.
Round is the end of a pickle.
Round is the doorknob that sits on a door.
Round is a table that stands on the floor.
Round is a tummy of a boy.
Round is the middle of a toy.
And that's all of this round tale
Goodbye, see ya after my bottle of ale!

As you recover the childhood "innocence of eye, ear, and hand" that took pleasure in the recurrences in language, you extend your Design mind's ability to become attuned to recurrences in life, in your experience in art, architecture, film, even in the speech of a friend—reaching the "cultivated eye, ear, and hand" of the natural writer. Accordingly, the purpose of this chapter is: (1) to sensitize your Design mind's natural affinity for recurrences, and (2) to enable you to use different types of recurrences to prod your Design mind into increasingly deliberate involvement in the writing process. Having mastered recurrence you can get past the conventional injunctions against using the same word twice because that is "wrong."

Read aloud this excerpt from the French diarist Anaïs Nin:

> I place my two hands on my stomach and very slowly, very softly, with the tips of my fingers I drum, drum, drum on my stomach, in circles. Round and round, softly, with eyes open in great serenity. The doctor comes near with amazement. The nurses are silent. Drum drum drum drum drum in soft circles, in soft quiet circles.

The most immediately apparent recurrence is the simple repetition of a single word, "drum." Its appearance seven times evokes feelings of intensity, tension, restlessness. But "drum" is counteracted by the variations on a key idea having to do with softness in the words "soft," "softly," "quiet," and "slowly." The drumming is not

Young children's concern with words is more like that of the poet, since they too are more than usually aware of their physical qualities, and show this by the way they play with sounds, making jingles and rhymes and puns and mixing in nonsense sounds.

James Britton,
Language and Learning

frantic; it moves in "soft, quiet circles." Thus the image of someone nervously drumming is altered by the softness of the act that supports the notion of "great serenity." Note that the passage begins with a circular movement of fingers and returns to it at the end, bringing it full circle.

Although we are not told exactly what is happening (it is Nin's description of her state of mind moments before her only child is stillborn), we get the feeling of a moment of great intensity which the drummer meets with ultimate calm. The passage is moving and powerful because of the sound of the language and the author's expert use of recurrence.

Recurrence Versus Repetition

My students have often asked me about the distinction between recurrence and repetition. The difference is subtle: repetition is rigid and orderly; repetition is the white picket fence you used to drag your stick along as a child in order to make that uniform clack-clack sound, interrupted only if there was a missing picket. Recurrence, by contrast, is much more fluid, often building on variations of the initial word or idea. To put it another way, repetition is heavy-handed while recurrence is much more graceful and filled with surprise.

One of the greatest writers of the twentieth century, James Joyce, experimented extensively with recurrences as a patterning technique to hold his narrative together since he used no punctuation or paragraphing to link or separate ideas. He invented the "stream-of-consciousness" style in an attempt to approximate the naturally erratic and associational flow of human thought.

In the final passage of *Ulysses,* the middle-aged Molly Bloom is thinking back on an event of her youth. As you read her welter of thoughts, one thing will strike you again and again: the strategic recurrence of the word "yes" until you develop a sense of what the insistently developing pattern is trying to tell you.

> . . . the sun shines for you he said the day we were lying among the rhododendrons on Howth head in the grey tweed suit and his straw hat the day I got him to propose to me yes first I gave him the bit of seedcake out of my mouth and it was leapyear like now yes 16 years ago my God after that long kiss I near

lost my breath yes he said I was a flower of the mountain yes so we are flowers all a woman's body yes that was one true thing he said in his life and the sun shines for you today yes that was why I liked him because I saw he understood or felt what a woman is and I knew I could always get round him and I gave him all the pleasure I could leading him on till he asked me to say yes and I wouldnt answer first only looked out over the sea and the sky . . . as a girl where I was a Flower of the mountain yes when I put the rose in my hair like the Andalusian girls used or shall I wear a red yes and how he kissed me under the Moorish wall and I thought well as well him as another and then I asked him with my yes to ask again yes and then he asked me would I yes to say yes my mountain flower and first I put my arms around him yes and drew him down to me so he could feel my breasts all perfume yes and his heart was going like mad and yes I said yes I will Yes.

The recurrence of "yes" juxtaposed against a whole series of sensual images, culminating in "yes I said yes I will Yes" evokes many impressions in the reader: Molly's knowing sensuality; her unqualified "yes" to life, which leaves us a little bit breathless; Molly as a driving elemental force; Molly as the image of a nurturing female; Molly whispering the most profound utterance of affirmation possible: yes! The recurrence builds momentum until it reaches the final dramatic climax.

Experience the power of recurrence for yourself. As in every exercise in natural writing, begin with a cluster.

Directing Your Hand

1. Cluster the nucleus word MAYBE in your writer's notebook. Spill your associations freely, letting them pour out until you experience the trial-web shift.
2. Hold that trial-web vision fast with one or two focusing statements, initiating participation of your Sign mind.
3. Use the focusing statement you like best to begin writing. Develop your vignette with an eye and ear toward recurrence of the word "maybe." You need not follow Joyce's stream-of-consciousness style, although, if you feel comfortable doing so, you may use it as a model.

4. Also keep in mind the recurrences in the Anaïs Nin exerpt; she repeats a number of words, sounds, and ideas. You might create several different recurrences, or you might want to play two recurrences off against each other. Writing can be playful as well as serious, or both. Play with your recurrences. Bring your writing full circle.

5. Now read your vignette aloud. Spend a minute or two making any changes you feel will improve the whole.

After Writing

In the context of what you wrote, consider what purpose the recurrence of "maybe" served. Did you find you also used related words, such as "perhaps," "someday," or "possibly"? You may have written, for example, about the eternal parental "maybes" that permeated some of the anxiety-filled hours and days of your childhood waiting for a parent to decide if you could go someplace. Would you say that "maybe" evoked positive or negative feelings in you? If "yes" is an affirmation and "no" negation, where does this leave "maybe" in what you have written? It's possible that you focused on the double bind of "maybe" in your writing.

The beginning writer in Figure 6–1, responding to the nucleus word (YES), produced an interesting, almost syncopated recurrent rhythm through the repetition of "if" and "I" and "will" and "wish" and the recurrent play on "twinkle, twinkle, little star."

> Yes! I will survive. I know I can. I will relate—if I try. I will love—if I may. I will strive—if I might. I will win—if I wish upon a star. Yes! I shall survive—if I get the wish I wish tonight.
>
> Susan Quinn

"Yes" evoked considerable intensity, bespeaking strong determination; the writer does not say "I will succeed" or "I will win" but "I will *survive*," as if at one time there may have been doubt about it. Yet at the same time there is an air of whimsicality about the vignette, brought about by the threading in of parts of a childhood rhyme. Here we see the influence of the childlike play with language brought about by clustering.

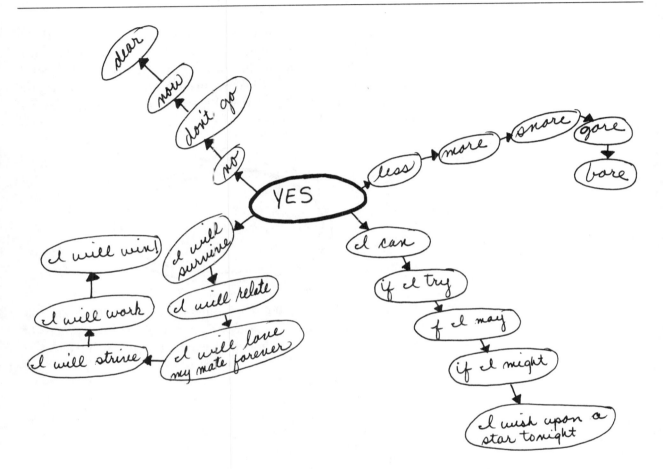

Figure 6–1

Recurrences can take many different forms beyond simple repetition of a single word: recurrence of full-circle wholeness, recurrence of sound, recurrence of key ideas, and recurrence of images. Let's explore their significance to natural writing.

Recurrence in Full-Circle Wholeness

When you expand your trial-web shift into a unified piece of writing, it "hangs together" much like a sculpture or a painting or the architecture of a striking building. When your writing coheres, all parts relate in such a way they form a continuous whole—and that includes the beginning and the end.

Recurrence is the easiest way to experience coming full circle; it is a repetition in your ending of some aspect of your beginning. I always remind my students that when I say "full-circle wholeness" they should think of the archetypal snake biting its own tail (Figure 6–2). It is a strong image that will help you remember the idea behind full-circle wholeness.

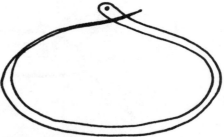

Figure 6–2

In his book *Telling Writing,* writing specialist Ken Macrorie calls this kind of recurrence the "fishhook," a metaphor for the process of referring back to the key thought, feeling, or image with which you began.

The fishhook is a recurrence that mentally hooks your reader back into your beginning, giving your writing the aesthetic quality of wholeness. Coming full circle doesn't mean merely repeating at the end of a vignette what has been said in the first sentence, but it does imply a link, something to tie the package together, the signal to a reader—and to yourself—that these words, these sentences, these paragraphs somehow belong together as a unified, meaningful design. As an example of recurrence to create full-circle wholeness, here is a vignette produced by a student writer (Figure 6–3). Triggering it was the nucleus word ⟨STILL⟩ .

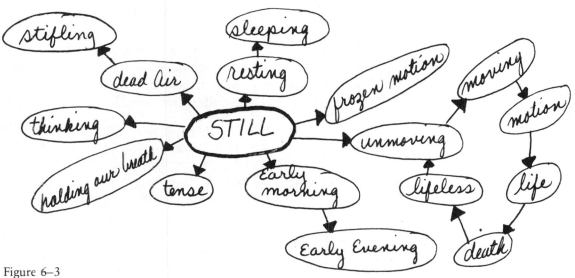

Figure 6–3

Runner
He is still,
Frozen by the photographer's lens
As he is about to break through the tape.
Look more closely;
Look at his expession,
His face contorted
In agony.
Look at his body,
His muscles tight
As steel bars,
His flesh soaked
in sweat,
His arms dangling with indifference.
Look at his stride,
The small stride of a tired runner.
He is almost at the end
Of his strength,
Almost,
But not quite.
He is still,
Frozen by the photographer's lens

Steve Sano

If you compare the cluster with the vignette, you will see that "frozen motion" became a pivotal idea by which the writer comes full circle: his vignette begins with "He is still/Frozen by the photographer's lens" and ends with the same statement, but not before we get a vivid image of what such stillness means.

You can reach toward full circle wholeness in one of three ways:

1. You may experience it as part of the trial-web shift—that is, you will intuitively use it to begin and end your vignette.

2. Your cluster itself may give you a clue as to what word, image, or idea would tie your vignette together. Rescan your cluster for words or ideas that crop up more than once.

3. If neither the trial-web shift nor the cluster produces the sense of full-circle wholeness, simply write and do not be concerned about it. As you draw to a close, glance back over your opening and find something in it to which you can return—either directly or obliquely—in your ending. Your vignette is a design in words, and full-circle wholeness is the finishing touch.

Now try it for yourself.

Directing Your Hand

1. Slowly scan the photograph of a sculpture by Ole Langerhorst (Figure 6–4) and be open to a dominant impression—a feeling, a memory, a cluster of images, the line of a song, poem, or saying that suddenly strikes you as being evoked by the work—just as you experienced in the trial-web chapter. In your writer's notebook, put this impression into words and cluster around it until you experience the trial-web shift. A minute or two should do it.

2. Before you begin your vignette, give your trial vision greater stability by writing two or three focusing statements, thus bringing your Sign mind into the act. Choose the statement that speaks to you most intensely and begin to write your vignette with an eye toward full-circle wholeness. Don't feel you must force it. If it didn't occur with the trial-web shift, you will discover a way, with the help of your cluster, to come full circle as you write.

Figure 6–4   OLE LANGERHORST, *UNTITLED*, COURTESY OF THE SCULPTOR.

3. If you still don't have a clear hook back to the beginning by the time you have finished writing, look specifically for an image, word, or phrase in your first two sentences that you can repeat meaningfully at the end to direct the reader back to the beginning.

4. Read your writing aloud. If your vignette does not feel complete, redesign words and ideas that seem out of place or ineffective. Then reread it. The sense of wholeness should give you satisfaction.

*As kingfishers catch fire, dragonflies
    draw flame*
*As tumbled over rim in roundy
    wells*
*Stones ring; like each tucked string
    tells, each hung bell's*
*Bow swung finds tongue to fling out
    broad its name . . .*
        Gerard Manley Hopkins

Sounding the Depths: Recurrence of Sounds

Developing awareness of sound recurrences in writing is another natural way to strengthen your patterning power. Sound recurrences
make you and your reader aware of the music in words; they act as
a unifying element in a vignette or across lines of poetry, as in the
manifold repetition of, say, the "s" sound to indicate harshness; they
contribute significantly to a vignette's meaning by creating a mood
appropriate to its content, such as a quiet, harmonious mood through
"m" sounds ("murmuring meadows meandering"). Hear the recurrence of "s" sounds, "f" sounds, "r" sounds, "fl" sounds, and so
forth in a poem by Gerard Manley Hopkins to the left.

Read the poetry aloud. There is much activity here: dragonflies,
stones, strings, draw and do, find and fling, and so forth. The sound
reinforces the idea that the things of the world are active and vitally
alive, for the next line is "Each thing does one thing and the
same/spells out that being indoors each one dwells." The tumbling
recurrences of sounds reinforce the sense of active participation in
life of "each thing."

Directing Your Hand

1. Without giving it much thought—in fact, as quickly as you can—
   get into the spirit of your childhood self by clustering the
   sound ⓜ for a minute or two, more if you wish. Let "m"
   words spill all over the page.
2. Be alert for a trial-web shift. It will come with an "m" word that
   carries particularly intense emotional associations.
3. Now write a brief vignette using as many "m" words as you can
   and still make sense.
4. Come full circle and then read your vignette aloud, changing anything that still doesn't sound right.

After Writing

If you felt a little foolish the first moment or so, that sense of
awkwardness probably soon gave way to a pleasant sense of release.

Your inner writer is playfully aware of language when you give it the chance to be so. It has merely been locked away behind the stultifying rules of convention for too long.

Your Design mind is aware of sound patterns. For instance, a Reno teacher in one of my workshops was astonished, in clustering around the word (AFRAID) (Figure 6–5), that his patterning Design mind had created a recurrence of "d" words that was totally outside the range of Sign-mind awareness. This was a first-time effort, and I had not discussed sound patterning at all.

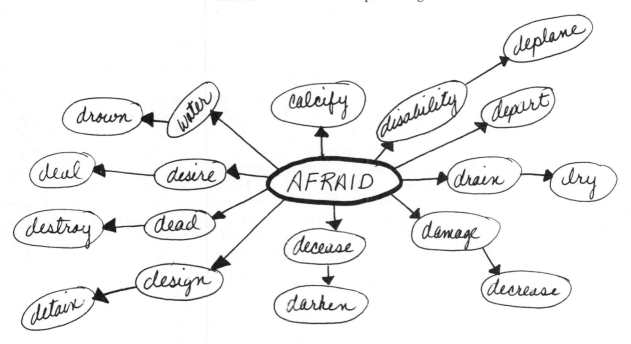

Figure 6–5

Afraid is the calcification of the will. It is the turning to stone of intention and the reduction of energy to zero. Destroy the sense of safety and the organism comes to a halt like a rabbit looking with glazed eyes at an oncoming car.

Interestingly, his vignette uses only one word starting with "d" since the assignment was only to cluster, experience the trial-web shift, and write. But his Design mind focused on the repeated sound of "d" and "t" throughout the pattern. "Destroy" is central to his description of fear.

Finally, there is repetition of sounds through rhyming. Rhyming, however, often interferes with the novice's natural writing, as it tends to become the primary focus. Beginning writers will force rhyme, often ending up with writing akin to "in the spring the birdies sing."

For this reason, I suggest you avoid conscious attempts to rhyme throughout this course. After you have experimented with all the techniques presented in this book, you will be prepared to tackle rhyming without producing doggerel, should you wish to try it.

Of all the types of sound recurrence, alliteration is by far the most natural, the easiest, and perhaps the most effective, as you saw in Anaïs Nin's selection, with its recurrence of "s" and "d" sounds.

Recurrence of a Key Idea

The repeated expression of a key idea for impact or illumination is a technique used in all kinds of writing—novels, short stories, essays, letters, and especially poetry. If a poetic line recurs, you can be sure it plays a key role in that poem. For example, poet Alastair Reid, in a poem entitled "A Lesson in Music," repeats the line "play the tune again" six times. For what purpose? To underscore the idea that only repeated *doing* will get you past the formal learning and into the *feel* of the music and the *pleasure* of it, which is its sole purpose. The recurring lines, juxtaposed against such sound recurrences as "lessons," "let flow," and "let's go," richly communicate his point about genuine learning. The poem is actually composed of a series of five vignettes, each a lesson in itself that comes full circle. All are unified by the recurrence of "play that tune again."

> *A Lesson in Music*
> Play the tune again: but this time
> with more regard for the movement at the source of it
> and less attention to time. Time falls
> curiously in the course of it.
>
> Play the tune again: not watching
> your fingering, but forgetting, letting flow
> the sound till it surrounds you. Do not count
> or even think. Let go.
>
> Play the tune again: but try to be
> nobody, nothing, as though the pace
> of the sound were your heart beating, as though
> the music were your face.

Play the tune again. It should be easier
to think less every time of the notes, of the measure.
It is all an arrangement of silence. Be silent, and then
play it for pleasure.

Play the tune again: and this time, when it ends,
do not ask me what I think. Feel what is happening
strangely in the room as the sound glooms over
you, me everything.

Now,
play the tune again.

When language is highly compressed, as it usually is in vignette writing, and particularly in poetry, your patterning Design mind is increasingly called into play to express or respond to those patterns, be they rhythmic, emotional, imaginal, or ideational. A recurring idea need not be as dependent on elaborate explanation as on the pattern it makes. The pattern-sensitive Design mind apprehends the recurrence, and thus it participates heavily in perceiving compressed meaning: "play the tune again," juxtaposed with gentle reminders of what it really means to play an instrument, unifies and clarifies the importance of subtlety and nuance in making music.

Before directing your hand at writing your own vignette using a recurring idea, let me give you a sense of what other beginning writers have produced. Read the "Lesson" poem, whose author appropriately enough clustered ⟨A LESSON IN WRITING⟩ from the other "lessons" she came up with in her precluster (Figure 6–6).

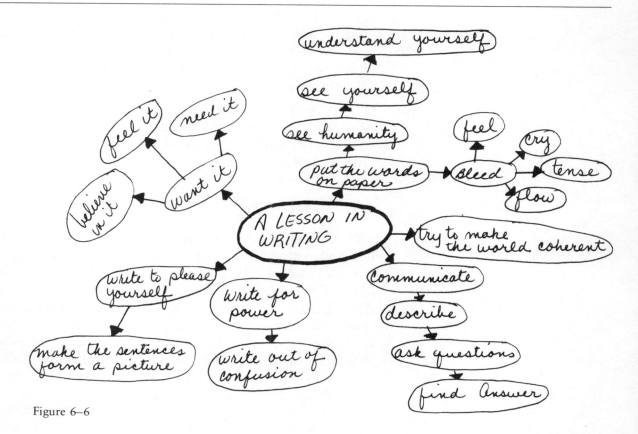

Figure 6–6

This writer, scanning her cluster, wrote three focusing statements: (1) write to please yourself; (2) try to make the world coherent; (3) put the words on paper. The last statement became the recurring idea around which she built her poem.

A Lesson in Writing
Put the words on paper; write because
you have questions, or answers, or just to remember.
Write because you feel and think
and cry and love.

Put the words on paper; try to make the world
coherent. Define yourself; define humanity.
What do you think? How does it feel?
Why does it matter?

Put the words on paper; see them,
believe in them, need them.
Bleed them from your soul and
let them spread before you.

Put the words on paper; make the sentences
form a picture; choose colored words.
Organize your thoughts and the universe.
Write out of understanding—
or confusion.

Now,
put the words on paper.

Lori Eickman

Now try your hand at letting an idea recur and reverberate in a vignette.

Directing Your Hand

1. In your writer's notebook, begin by preclustering (LESSONS) to give your Design mind options for finding a lesson of real significance to you. Preclustering should take only a minute or so.

2. Now cluster the lesson you would most like to "teach," perhaps *a lesson in love*. Continue to cluster until you experience the trial-web shift.

3. Glancing over your cluster, write two or three focusing statements with an eye to discovering the key recurring idea.

4. Choose the most effective as your recurring idea and plan to repeat it a minimum of four times in four self-contained vignettes. As you write, keep in mind the didactic nature of your subject: think in terms of really helping someone—or yourself—gain insight into something to be learned.

5. Complete your poem composed of four vignettes. Read it aloud and then rework it briefly until you feel satisfied that the recurring idea, coupled with what follows, progresses with each repetition to a clearer understanding of what or how that something is to be learned.

"—a conch; ever so expensive. I bet if you wanted to buy one, you'd have to pay pounds and pounds . . ."

Ralph took the shell from Piggy and a little water ran down his arm. In color the shell was deep cream, touched here and there with fading pink. Between the point, worn away into a little hole, and the pink lips of the mouth lay eighteen inches of shell with a slight spiral twist and covered with a delicate embossed pattern.

Ralph hit the shell with air from his diaphragm. Immediately the thing sounded. A deep, harsh note boomed under the palms, spread through intricacies of the forest and echoed back from the pink granite of the mountain.

"Gosh!"

His ordinary voice sounded like a whisper after the harsh note of the conch. He laid the conch against his lips, took a deep breath and blew once more. The note boomed again: and then at his firmer pressure, the note, fluking up an octave, became a strident blare more penetrating than before. . . . Ralph's breath failed; the note dropped the octave, became a low wubber, was a rush of air.

The conch was silent, a gleaming tusk; Ralph's face was dark with breathlessness and the air over the island was full of bird-clamor and echoes ringing.

"I bet you can hear that for miles."

William Golding,
Lord of the Flies

After Writing

If you have never tried to write poetry, or have always thought yourself incapable of doing so, this exercise will surprise you. In developing your four recurrences, you wrote four unified vignettes, which in effect are four stanzas of a poem, and they became unified precisely because of the recurrence of your key idea. Here is a discovery about the longer writing to come: the way of natural writing is to proceed in vignette fashion—little whole attached to little whole, which together encompass a total vision.

The Recurring Image

A fourth form of recurrence lies in the use of repeated images. We will discuss at length the power of images in Chapter 7, for images are an elemental Design-mind phenomenon. Here I simply want to make you aware that recurrences are not limited to sound or idea patterns but are found in images as well.

Images make possible the communication of what we see, hear, feel, smell, and taste; images are the expression of sense experiences in words. When images recur in a piece of writing, they serve to unify it by giving us dominant impressions: dark colors to convey a feeling of doom or danger, images of animals to say something about character, such as repeated references to birds of prey; the recurring image of an object. The conch in William Golding's *Lord of the Flies* points to something of real significance, telling the reader "Pay attention."

And that is the point of the image of the gleaming pink find. It holds the promise of calling together the scattered boys, who are abandoned on a deserted island, for the purpose of organizing and mobilizing a cooperative effort of survival.

To help make this point we find the repetition of the image and related words: "a conch," "shell," "in color the shell was deep cream, touched here and there with fading pink," "pink lips of the mouth," "slight spiral twist," "covered with a delicate embossed pattern," "the thing sounded," "a deep, harsh note boomed," "harsh note of the conch," "he laid the conch against his lips," "the note boomed again,"

Grandpa

As a youngster I visited my grandfather often; he would always make me feel so grown-up by giving me a firm handshake, except that my tiny little hand would get lost in grandpa's enormous paw. And so seemed the man to my childish eyes: absolutely huge.

As I grew up he gradually swam more into proportion—except for his hands, which remained larger than life. I remember how these huge hands would dig, dig deep into pockets and always find a quarter for me to buy ice cream with. When my little brothers were born, grandpa would cradle them in his hands, and they would virtually disappear. These same hands were always there to pick me up when I was learning how to ride a bike or to give me a hug when I was troubled.

Every so often I wish those big hands were still here to pick me up when I take a fall.

Mike Hughes

"fluking up an octave, became a strident blare," "the note dropped the octave, became a low wubber, was a rush of air," "the conch was silent, a gleaming tusk."

Image upon image reinforces for the reader the importance of this invaluable found tool.

A very simple student illustration of the power of recurring images is a "written portrait" for which this beginning writer chose his grandfather. As he clustered he was instructed to visualize the person of his choice as vividly as possible. The student was surprised to find that many of his associations referred to his grandfather's hands (Figure 6–7). Instead of fighting the pull of this recurring image, he allowed it to dominate his word portrait. His writing has strength because the recurring image of the hands shows us more about the grandfather's gentleness and caring than any lengthy description could have.

An image that is so prominent takes on the dimensions of *symbol,* which is one thing standing for something else. In the word portrait above, the grandfather's hands became a symbol of love and protection and gentleness. More than we generally realize, we associate people we know with certain objects or body parts. That is a Design-mind connection rooted in images. For example, your grandmother may be firmly associated with knitting needles, just as my grandmother is for me a set of lively jet-black gypsy eyes that flashed impishly as she told her grandchildren one terrifying ghost story after

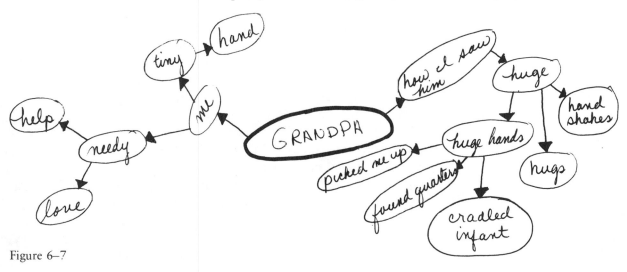

Figure 6–7

another. Were I writing a vignette about my grandmother, those eyes would be the recurring and unifying image. Someone else may be associated in your mind with a car, or dyed red hair, or an article of clothing, or tiny feet.

Whatever the image, let it surface by tapping your Design mind through clustering. Then develop that image through recurrence in your writing. In so doing you achieve power and unity, for recurrences always act as a unifying thread to the whole.

Directing Your Hand

In your writer's notebook, draw a word portrait of a person for whom you have strong feelings, either positive or negative.

1. Precluster the nucleus (PORTRAIT) to give yourself options. You may be surprised to find the most obvious name isn't the one you end up writing about.

2. Now cluster the name of your choice. Continue to cluster until an image (or more than one) presents itself as an apt representation of that person. Cluster associations around that image until you experience the trial-web shift. If your trial-web shift presented more than one image, make a choice. If that choice is difficult, quickly cluster each image in question. The richness of your associations will tell you which is the right one to develop in your vignette.

3. Once you have experienced the trial-web shift, write a focusing statement, initiating the shift from Design- to Sign-mind thinking. The focusing statement draws on the patterns spilled out by your Design mind and are thus made accessible. Now crystallize the trial web into a focusing statement, which usually functions as the main point (or thesis) in your vignette.

4. Now begin to draw your portrait in words, allowing your image to recur several times until it becomes a symbol for an aspect of the person drawn, as the grandfather's hands were a symbol of love and protection. The image surfaced because it has significance for your Design mind, and you can develop it intentionally now that it has become accessible to your Sign mind.

5. Come full circle; give your vignette wholeness and unity. Read it aloud. If something about it still doesn't seem right, experiment a little and make any changes that will improve the sound and feel of the whole.

Ringing the Bells
*And this is the way they ring
the bells in Bedlam
and this is the bell-lady
who comes each Tuesday morning
to give us a music lesson
and because the attendants make
     you go
and because we mind by instinct,
like bees caught in the wrong hive,
we are the circle of the crazy ladies
who sit in the lounge of the mental
     house
and smile at the smiling woman
who passes us each a bell,
who points at my hand
that holds my bell, E flat,
and this is the gray dress next to
     me
who grumbles as if it were special
to be old, to be old,
and this is the small hunched squir-
     rel girl
on the other side of me
who picks at the hairs over her lip,
who picks at the hairs over her lip
     all day,
and this is how the bells really
     sound,
as untroubled and clean
as a workable kitchen,
and this is always my bell respond-
     ing
to my hand that responds to the
     lady
who points at me, E flat;
and although we are no better for
     it,
they tell you to go. And you do.*
                              Anne Sexton

After Writing

As you focused on your image while writing, you probably experienced its richness and complexity as you tried to find words to express it. An image is never merely a single entity but a complex whole that resonates with feelings and other related images. You may have found yourself searching for different words, all of which were in some way related to the image you were trying to communicate. You may also have found yourself playing with coming full circle, using the image at the beginning and the end. Finally, you were probably pleased that your vignette really did become a portrait in words.

Looking to Other Writers: Modeling Recurrences

This final exercise will give you the opportunity to use the work of an established writer as a model for your own writing. Through modeling you will focus on the poet's recurrences, not to imitate them but to create your own. The poem "Ringing the Bells" by American poet Anne Sexton achieves its primary effect because of several recurrences. Read it aloud, noting that, except for the last two lines, it is all one long sentence held together by the word recurrence of ten "ands," several "E flats," "bell/bells," and "because." There are also sound recurrences of "b" and "s," an idea recurrence of the clearness of the bells juxtaposed against the "crazy" women, and image recurrences in "to be old, to be old" and "who picks at the hairs over her lip all day."

The many recurrences of "and" point, in their endless repetition, to the dull despair felt by the speaker through this bell-ringing "lesson." By contrast, the two unexpected image repetitions—"who picks at the hairs over her lip" and "to be old, to be old"—evoke the irrationality of human behavior gone awry in "Bedlam." These recurrences are in turn juxtaposed against the fivefold recurrence of "bell"—sounding "as untroubled and clean/as a workable kitchen." This image of a clear-sounding bell so ludicrously placed among these troubled people forces us into awareness of the pathos of muddied mental states.

Using this poem as a model will give you a form within which to discover your own idea, sound, and image recurrences.

Directing Your Hand

1. In your writer's notebook, precluster the phrase (AND THIS IS THE WAY) . . . for possibilities to give you choices, such as . . .*you write a poem* or . . . *you plant an orchid* or . . . *you meditate.*

2. Glance over the precluster, choose the focus that intrigues you the most, and cluster that choice until you experience the trial-web shift, the "aha!" that lets you know you have something to write about.

3. Write a focusing statement recording your trial-web shift. This is the bridge from Design- to Sign-mind thinking. Some writers prefer to write two or three focusing statements in order to have additional choices.

4. Now begin writing, opening with "And this is the way . . ." and letting the word "and" be your basic recurrence. Also let a recurring image (like Sexton's bells) tie the whole together. Be aware of shifting continually back and forth between Design-mind whole to Sign-mind parts and sequences, and back again to a more clearly delineated whole.

5. Make a point in this vignette. Ask yourself, "What do I want to say with this whole?"

6. Be conscious of full-circle wholeness. Achieve it by pulling something from the beginning into your final lines.

7. Read your poem aloud. Briefly make any changes you feel will improve it.

After Writing

By way of comparison with your associations to the Sexton poem, read the writing of a beginning student who had considerable writing difficulties before she tried natural writing (Figure 6–8). The recurrence of "ands" cataloging the unending effects of poverty thread the whole together. She also gives us several images of poverty, and she makes a point: That life is worth living "just as long as you're beautiful and clean." The vignette exhibits a simplicity that belies its strength.

Focusing statements: (1) poverty can kill; (2) poverty doesn't mean life can't be beautiful, too.

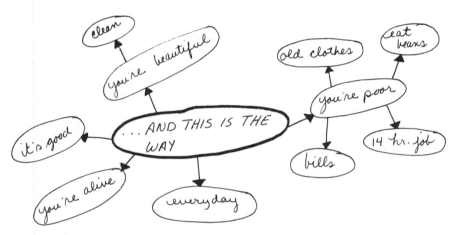

Figure 6–8

An Everyday Life
And this is the way you're poor and your dreams are big enough only to survive the next day: and this is the way you see the mailman coming with the bills, and your parents are out working for the next month's rent; and this is the way the beans sound which become the main course: breakfast, lunch and dinner; and this is the way you see your father in pain at night from a fourteen-hour job, and at dawn he's up ready for the next work day; and this is the way your old blue jeans and white T-shirt become your Sunday clothes, and your mother tells you, "just as long as you're beautiful and clean"; and this is the way you realize it's nice to stay alive to see another beautiful day.

Georgia Palmer

A Last Word and Heading On

Recurrence, one of the simplest and most readily apparent of strategies leading to power in writing, has allowed you to play with a new element in your writing. Carry it into the writing you do in subsequent chapters: practice it, play with it, experiment with it. Its effects are inexhaustible. You can now cultivate all kinds of recurrences to reflect your Design-mind awareness of patterns. As a result, your writing will become more fluid, more aesthetically pleasing, more rhythmic, more unified. The sound and rhythm of the *whole* will suddenly strike you more forcefully than ever before.

Now that your inner ear has become attuned to recurrences, you are ready for the more subtle recurrences of language rhythms, described in the next chapter.

CHAPTER 7/ *Language Rhythms: the Music in Words*

Robert Louis Stevenson once referred to the rhythms of sentences as "the pattern of sound in time." Before we were born, we were attuned to the rhythms of our mother's voice, an influence that continued after birth. As infants we were rocked, sung to, talked to. As babblers we were enchanted with the sounds we made in early attempts at approximating language. As toddlers we became absorbed with the strong, regular rhythms of chants, nursery rhymes such as "Peter, Peter, Pumpkin Eater," tongue twisters such as "Peter Piper picked a peck of pickled peppers," counting rhymes such as "One, two, buckle your shoe," and jump-rope rhymes such as "Lady bird, lady bird, turn around."

Dylan Thomas seemed to know that we are born with a hunger for the harmony, melody, and rhythms of language.

The music in words is Design-mind territory. In this chapter we focus on *cadence*, the rhythmic flow of language that provides the sense of continuity and wholeness in writing. Through the exercises you will learn to recognize and use language rhythms as expressive patterns. Such practice will continue to attune the inner ear of your Design mind to the music in the language patterns you began to recognize with recurrences in the last chapter, and it will prepare the way for sharpening your Design mind's inner eye for images, to be discussed in the next chapter.

LANGUAGE RHYTHMS: THE MUSIC IN WORDS

The first poems I knew were nursery rhymes, and before I could read them for myself I had come to love just the words of them; the words alone. What the words stood for, symbolised, or meant, was of very secondary importance. What mattered was the sound of them as I heard them for the first time on the lips of the remote and incomprehensible grownups who seemed, for some reason, to be living in my world. And these words were, to me, as the notes of bells, the sounds of musical instruments, the noises of wind, sea, and rain, the rattle of milk-carts, the clopping of hooves on cobbles, the fingering of branches on a window pane, might be to someone, deaf from birth, who has miraculously found his hearing. I did not care what the words said, overmuch, nor what happened to Jack and Jill and the Mother Goose rest of them; I cared for the shapes of sound that their names, and the words describing their actions, made in my ears; I cared for the colours the words cast on my eyes.

Dylan Thomas,
"Notes on the Art of Poetry"

Natural writing depends heavily on the multisensory nature of language; we are all too little accustomed to hearing, seeing, and feeling as we write, because we are generally taught writing as though it were a business apart from our five senses. We lose the innocent pleasure of language rhythms as we become grounded in the conventions of writing. So in this chapter we will attempt to cultivate the Design mind's natural attunement to the fundamental rhythms of language and the connectedness of words to make aesthetic rhythmic patterns. We will focus on retraining your sense of hearing to attend to the cadences of language and, in the process, to discover the essence of your writing: your *voice*.

Voice is the authentic sound, rhythm, texture of a unique consciousness on the page. It is the written expression of the endless oscillation between, and cooperation of, your Sign and Design minds in such a way that the resulting unique personality is powerfully expressed on the page. Voice is an expression of the natural you unfettered by the stultifying injunctions about writing you have labored under. Any first-rate writer is almost by definition one whose voice is distinctive. Milton, for example, had a rich and resonant voice; Frost, a relaxed, conversational voice; Hemingway, a masculine, direct voice; Emily Dickenson, a spare, cryptic voice; Faulkner, a flowing, elaborately meandering voice.

Jim Crosswhite of the Writing Program at the University of California, San Diego, claims that, contrary to popular belief, students are actually doing more than mastering the basics of English and are quite sophisticated in grasping the technical aspects of writing. He complains, however, that they rarely write authoritatively, honestly, or in their own voice. In the framework of this book, "voiceless" writing might be called Sign-mind writing in the extreme. The active participation of your Design mind in the writing process adds authenticity as you listen with your inner ear and see with your inner eye. When our Sign and Design minds learn to cooperate, our words take on the rhythm and resonance that Peter Elbow insists are essential to voice: "Real voice is whatever yields resonance, whatever makes the words bore through."

Finding your own distinctive voice is the actual goal of learning natural writing. Great writers like Ernest Hemingway and William Faulkner are great precisely because they have distinctive voices. Begin to foster the "cultivated ear" by reading aloud three excerpts by

*This is the feeling for syllable and
rhythm, penetrating far below the
conscious levels of thought and
feeling, invigorating every word.*
                                T. S. Eliot

*Apart from a few simple principles,
the sound and rhythm of English
prose seem to me matters where
both writers and readers should
trust not so much to rules as to
their ears.*

                                *F. L. Lucas,
                                Style*

writers with distinctive voices. The first is a passage from Hemingway's *For Whom the Bell Tolls*.

> He would not think about that. That was not his business. That was Golz's business. He had only one thing to do and that was what he should think about and he must think it out clearly and take everything as it came along, and not worry. To worry was as bad as to be afraid. It simply made things more difficult. . . . Think about them being away, he said. Think about them going through the timber. Think about them crossing a creek. Think about them riding through the heather. Think about them going up the slope. Think about them O.K. tonight. Think about them traveling, all night. Think about them hiding up tomorrow. Think about them. God damn it, think about them. *That's just as far as I can think about them,* he said.

What characterizes the cadences of the famous Hemingway voice is, first, recurrence used almost to excess: "think about" is repeated fourteen times. Thinking, under the circumstances, is what the protagonist has a hard time doing; in his staccato language rhythms we sense a thinly controlled panic. Second, as you read aloud you noticed that the sentences were very short, the whole piece in the hard-driving, punctuated rhythm of a man's thought, a trapped man in danger of his life. Third, the passage feels "masculine"—that is, it contains no unnecessary description, no long flowing lines. Fourth, the language is so simple as to be elementary. All these effects are achieved through sensitivity to cadence, the natural rhythm of language.

You probably became aware of most of these characteristics as you listened with your inner ear. If you truly listen to yourself read, your Design mind cannot stay oblivious to the nuances and flavors of language rhythms.

Next we have a passage from William Faulkner's *The Hamlet*, from a short story entitled "The Long Summer." Read it aloud, pausing when you encounter commas and periods.

LANGUAGE RHYTHMS: THE MUSIC IN WORDS

He was a man past middle age, who with nothing to start with but sound health and a certain grim and puritanical affinity for abstinence and endurance had made a fair farm out of the barren scrap of hill land which he had bought at less than a dollar an acre and married and raised a family on it and fed and clothed them all and even educated them after a fashion, taught them at least hard work, so that as soon as they became big enough to resist him, boys and girls too, they left home (one was a professional nurse, one a ward-heeler to a minor country politician, one a city barber, one a prostitute; the oldest had simply vanished completely) so that there now remained the small neat farm which likewise had been worked to the point of mute and unflagging mutual hatred and resistance but which could not leave him and so far had not been able to eject him but which possibly knew that it could and would outlast him, and his wife who possibly had the same, perhaps not hope for resisting, but maybe staff and prop for bearing and enduring.

As you read, you may have noticed that none of the qualities of Hemingway's voice is found in Faulkner's. Instead of the staccato cadences of short, choppy sentences, we hear the flowing cadences of Faulkner's inordinately long sentences; in fact, the entire paragraph is one long sentence, with the ebb and flow of a minister intoning dire predictions about the wages of a life of sin. Next, Faulkner almost miraculously compresses one man's history from youth to "past middle age"—including what happened to his five children and an observation on his wife's personality—into one brief vignette. Finally, the language is far more demanding than Hemingway's; observe such words as "affinity," "eject," "puritannical," and "abstinence."

The passages have two things in common, however. First, each is absolutely distinctive; it is nearly impossible to confuse a passage of Hemingway's with one of Faulkner's—and the reason is largely a matter of language rhythms creating distinctive resonances. Second, each uses recurrences: the unifying thread of recurrence in the Hemingway is "think about" and in the Faulkner "resist," "resistance," and "resisting," echoed by such emotionally related words as "bearing," "grim," "enduring," "mutual hatred," and "eject." Just as the

Writing without voice *is wooden or dead because it lacks sound, rhythm, energy, and individuality. . . . Writing* with voice *is writing into which someone has breathed. It has fluency, rhythm, and liveliness that exist naturally in the speech of most people when they are enjoying a conversation.*
                              Peter Elbow,
                    Writing with Power

recurrence in Hemingway dramatizes and unifies the feeling of a man trying to induce coolness and concentration amidst mortal danger, so the recurrence in Faulkner makes a unified resistant whole of his passage. In fact, there is so much resistance, resisting, bearing, and enduring in his description of a man in harmony with nothing and no one that the reader can hardly bear the negative emotional impact.

Here you see and hear the effects of the cadence and resonance of two writers following the inclinations of their own natural rhythms, thus achieving expressive power. As you increasingly allow your Design mind to participate in writing through the techniques in these chapters, your inner and authentic voice will come to the fore and begin to reflect cadences and resonances unique to it.

Finally we have a distinctive passage from Gertrude Stein's *The World Is Round*. Listen to it by reading it aloud.

> But mountains yes Rose did think about mountains and about blue when it was on the mountains and feathers when clouds like feathers were on the mountains and birds when one little bird and two little birds and three and four and six and seven and ten and seventeen and thirty or forty little birds all came flying and a big bird came flying and they flew higher than the big bird and they came down and one and then two and then five and then fifty of them came picking down on the head of the big bird and slowly the big bird came falling down between the mountain and the little birds all went home again.

If you listened carefully with your inner ear, you probably recalled the James Joyce passage from *Ulysses* quoted in an earlier chapter, as both Joyce and Stein are stream-of-consciousness writers. In the Stein passage, as in the Faulkner passage, you saw the cadences of one long sentence. But the two are nothing alike. Faulkner's is carefully punctuated, guiding the sweep of the language, giving it a serious, sonorous ebb and flow. Stein's passage, by contrast, rushes headlong without pause, connected only by a myriad of "ands" and a pattern of interlocking recurrences: "birds," "mountains," "down," "flying/flew," "feathers," all of which set up their own punctuated rhythm. Stein once compared her writing technique to the frames in a motion picture that present a moving series of instantaneous visions in a rhythmic pattern.

LANGUAGE RHYTHMS: THE MUSIC IN WORDS

In this chapter you are learning that the fourth major step to becoming a natural writer is to learn to listen beyond literal content to the patterns the language makes and how these patterns give the content further meaning. Closely attending the rhythms of distinctive voices such as Stein's attunes your ear to the subtleties and nuances of cadence and helps you learn to distinguish between resonance and flatness of voice. By the chapter's end you will be ready to write richer, more meaningful vignettes, modeling the language rhythms of Faulkner, Hemingway, or Stein.

Most of us can muster considerable expressiveness in speech and yet, mired in the stage of conventional writing, we seem unable to transfer the subtle nuances of rhythm to the written word. Begin to break this barrier by listening with your inner ear: listen as you read, listen to news commentators' voices—not just to what they have to say, but to the ebb and flow of language—and really listen to the rhythms of the upcoming model sentences and their student imitations.

Within a few days of birth, babies will flex their limbs and move their heads in rhythm with the human speech they hear around them.
Paul Bohannon,
Science, *October 1980*

Sentences as Rhythmic Mini-Wholes

Just as recurrences make the Design mind aware of patterns that unify meaning, certain repeated and repeating rhythms in sentences, through their aesthetic qualities, please the Design mind's ear and give writing wholeness. Some years ago I realized that, if students couldn't *hear* these rhythms in language, no amount of grammatical analysis would enable them to re-create them in their own writing. Accordingly, I had students experience some of these rhythms through modeling very short passages, thereby attuning their inner ear at sentence level.

We began with the simplest and most powerful rhythmic form: parallel rhythm. The Sign-mind principle behind parallel forms is simple: let words and phrases seek their own kind—noun to noun, verb to verb, and so forth. And so we get:

· A *jug* of wine, a *loaf* of bread, and *thou* . . . (nouns)
· I'll *beg, borrow,* and *steal* . . . (verbs)
· He spoke of tyranny, of poverty, of disease, and of war itself. (phrases)

The appeal of parallel form for the patterning Design mind runs much deeper, to an emotional and aesthetic satisfaction; the structure of parallel forms is not only explainable in terms of grammar but is also highly audible and memorable. My students learned to trust their inner ears rather than rules, and in a moment you will see how successful they were by the sentences they produced.

Let's begin with a very simple model of parallel form by writer Sam Keen; the model is followed by several student modelings of the original. Read all the models aloud to attune your ear to the similarities between model and student writing.

Original Inspiration

> I am tired of being hard, tight, controlled,
> tensed against the invasion of novelty.
>
> Sam Keen, *To a Dancing God*

This simple sentence gains power from the explosive rhythm derived from piling up four parallel feelings, one after the other, in a tightly controlled space, only to be followed by the surprising explanation, "against the invasion of novelty."

Before the students began to model, they took fifteen to thirty seconds to create brief clusters, like the one in Figure 7–1.

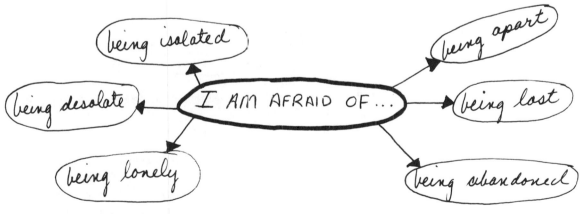

Figure 7–1

Once they had their focus and a number of choices, students could arrange their emerging content according to the rhythm of the model. Since they were working at the level of the sentence rather than of a vignette, trial-web shift and focusing statement were not necessary. Here are several student samples re-creating Keen's parallel rhythm.

Parallel Student Outpourings

I am tired of being used, mistreated, unappreciated, trampled on by freeloaders.

I am tired of being checked, inspected, hounded, forced into conformity by my friends.

I am sick of being controlled by, forced by, pushed by, shoved into, the traditions of the past.

I am afraid of being lost, desolated, abandoned, pitted against the devastation of loneliness.

Directing Your Hand

In your writer's notebook experience for yourself the power of parallel form. Use the Keen model to produce your own sentence, or two or three.

1. Read the model aloud once more.
2. Quick-cluster for the content that will make up your parallel sentence. Use I AM TIRED OF . . . or a similar phrase that has meaning for you as the nucleus of your cluster.
3. Write your parallel sentences, using whatever is appropriate from your cluster.
4. Read your writing aloud, listening to its rhythms.

The second model comes from the first lines of a poem entitled "There is a sadness to this world" by contemporary poet/novelist Al Young. He achieves intense compression—saying much in a small space—and aesthetic unity by piling up parallel nouns that turn into metaphoric equivalents of sadness: "grimness," "nastiness," "foulness," "slackening," and "chill."

Original Inspiration

> There is a sadness to this world, a grimness, a nastiness in the throat, a foulness of breath, a slackening of the penis into sorrow, a chill in the bloodstream that hurts.
>
> Al Young, "There is a Sadness"

Parallel Student Outpourings

> There is a quietness to this room, a noiselessness, a soundlessness in the ear, a speechlessness of the mouth, a soothing of the eyes into sleep, a warmth in the body that relaxes.

> There is an emptiness to this relationship, a hollowness, a nothingness to the taste, a vagueness of consciousness, a withdrawing of the self into glumness, an icicle in the heart that aches.

> There is an electricity to the touch, an intensity, a shivering through the arm, a feeling of the unknown, a surge of power that is erotic.

Directing Your Hand

In your writer's notebook imitate the rhythms of Young's model.

1. Quick-cluster THERE IS A(N) . . . for focus and images.
2. Now, using from your cluster whatever fits, write a minimum of one sentence, but preferably two or three, after Young's model.
3. Read them aloud, really listening with your inner ear, and change anything that would improve or intensify the cadence.

The third model sentence is more complex because it has both parallel and balanced elements. Balanced sentence rhythms evoke the image of an old-fashioned scale: a chunk of meaning laid on the left side of the scale is counterweighted on the right. Another way of saying this is that each part of the sentence has a similar design and its echo fuses into wholeness. Balanced rhythm, like parallel rhythm, brings texture and cohesion to writing. When the thoughts of a balanced sentence are in agreement, there is a sense of mutual reinforcement; when in contrast, a sense of tension. For example:

> Speech is silver; silence is golden
> Love not pleasure; love God

> Thomas Carlyle,
> *Sartor Resartus*

Let us never negotiate out of fear, but let us never fear to negotiate

> J. F. Kennedy,
> Inaugural Address

And so, my fellow Americans, ask not what your country can do for you; ask what you can do for your country.

> J. F. Kennedy,
> Inaugural Address

He who enters the sphere of faith enters the sanctuary of life.

> Paul Tillich,
> *The Dynamics of Faith Original Inspiration*

The three parallel rhythms of the model below are "profession but," "knowledge but," and "ideas but." Within each one of these is a balanced phrase, pitting "this" against "that."

I had a profession, but nothing to profess, knowledge but no wisdom, ideas but few feelings.

> Sam Keen,
> *To a Dancing God*

Parallel Student Outpourings

I had feelings but no one to convey them to, ideas but no way to express them, beliefs but no way to free them from my soul.

I had secrets but no one to tell them to, dreams but no reality, foresight but no destiny.

I had an education but nothing to teach, answers but no questions, religion but few convictions.

I had a destination but no road to follow, sight but no vision, a plan but no guide.

I had a dream but nothing to aspire to, potential but no determination, strength but little courage.

Directing Your Hand

In your writer's notebook write your own combination of parallel and balanced rhythms following Keen's model.

1. Reread Keen aloud to let your inner ear hear the rhythm.
2. Cluster (I HAD (A)) . . . (or I have (A)) . . . to discover your own focus and to give you choices.
3. Now follow the model rhythm and create your own rhythmic sentence, or two or three.
4. Read your own version aloud and quickly make any changes that will enhance rhythms and/or meaning.

Before we leave this section to go on to somewhat more complex exercises on rhythmic patterning, I remind you that in writing these exercises, your Design and Sign minds have been cooperating in a complex symbolic activity; your Design mind holds the totality of a given sentence's rhythmic pattern in mind—hears it with its inner ear, so to speak—and it quick-clusters for a focus such as newspaper printing or army haircuts; then, your sequencing Sign mind writes the sentence, all the while governed by the pattern's echo in your Design mind. When we allow our Design mind, with its sensitivity to the rhythms and patterns of language, to participate, there is no limit to the powerful sentences we can create.

Thus I urge you to hone your new awareness of parallel and balanced rhythms by looking for them in everything you read. You'll be surprised at the frequency with which they appear in good writing. If you find a particularly good rhythmic sentence, copy it in your writer's notebook and practice following it as a model. A student writer who had done extensive parallel patterning in my class richly applied his new understanding of parallel rhythms to an assignment to write an autobiographical sketch:

> In some of my worst nightmares, I am Mr. Smith, a supervisor or business executive who has an ordinary nine-to-five job, wears a typical business suit and tie, performs mundane assignments for a faceless bureaucracy, fights rush-hour traffic, watches prime-time television for entertainment, attends parties and social gatherings for recognition, and retires to a life of golf and bingo games.

In some of my best dreams . . .

The piling up of the "bad" images creates a rich picture of what this writer abhors. But how this writer sees himself in his worst nightmares is balanced against how he sees himself in some of his best dreams.

Here is your opportunity to discover your own worst and best "dreams" through clustering and writing your own brief autobiographical vignette.

Directing Your Hand

1. In your writer's notebook cluster both

   Cluster at least five minutes or more to give yourself plenty of choices and to get beyond the obvious.
2. Now take about fifteen minutes to write your vignette, modeling the parallel patterns of the student writing you have just read. Both nightmare and dream segments use parallel patterns throughout.
3. Read your vignette aloud. The compression you achieved by piling parallel element upon parallel element in quick succession allows you to reveal much about yourself in a small space—and elegantly make any refinements you wish.

The following model sentences, each with a single student sample, may spur you on to additional practice for your cultivated inner ear.

Model

And I have learned how to live with it, learned when to expect it, how to outwit it, even how to regard it when it does come as more friend than lodger. We have reached a certain understanding, my migraine and I.

Joan Didion, "In Bed"

Student Outpouring

And I have learned to understand them, to remember them, to look forward to them, to bask in their imagery, how to accept them as more friend than foe. We have marveled at each other, my dreams and I.

Model

Society's teaching time begins the process of informing the child of its smallness in relation to the far larger, its ignorance measured against great intelligences, its ineptitudes contrasted to vast skills, its lack opposed to fullness, its basic inconsequentiality within the context of things that matter.

Jean Houston,
Dromenon

Student Outpouring

Reflection begins the process of clustering a word to identify its hidden associations, its relations to a larger pattern of meaning, its rich possibilities contrasted to unimaginative usage, its creative potential contrasted, or opposed, to artistic sterility, its basic importance as the pivot upon which all communication is based.

Should you want additional practice for internalizing language rhythms, here are six beautiful examples to model:

My lack of excitement, of curiosity, of surprise, of any sort of pronounced interest, began to arouse his distrust.

Joseph Conrad,
The Secret Sharer

The whale is massive, brutal, monolithic, but at the same time protean, erotically beautiful, infinitely variable.

Richard Chase,
The American Novel and Its Tradition

Where the throng is thickest, where the lights are brightest, where all the senses are ministered to with the greatest delicacy and refinement, Lady Dedlock is.

Charles Dickens,
Bleak House

They were drinking ginger ale on her front porch and she kept rattling the ice in her glass, rattling her beads, rattling her bracelet like an impatient pony jingling its harness.

Flannery O'Connor,
"The Displaced Person"

It was one of his own cousins, rigid as iron, clean as the atmosphere, hardy as all virtue, tenacious as leaves, leaves that did not shrivel but kept their wintry life, firm shields, painted in fast colors.

Van Wyck Brooks,
"Thoreau at Walden"

It is a face seen once and lost forever in a crowd, an eye that looked, a face that smiled and vanished on a passing train, it is a prescience of snow upon a certain night, the laughter of a woman in a summer street long years ago, it is the memory of a single moon seen at the pines' dark edge in old October—and all of our lives are written in the twisting of a leaf upon a bough, a door that opened, and a stone.

Thomas Wolfe,
Of Time and the River

Poems as Rhythmic Wholes

As I have noted repeatedly, the right brain is more attuned to rhythmic wholes than it is to parts, just as it is more attuned to visual wholes than bits and pieces. The form that poetry takes on the page appeals to the Design mind for its rhythmic and its visual aspects. In fact, some poems have such a distinctive rhythm that all the parts are molded into an indivisible rhythmic unit. e.e. cummings' "Portrait VIII" is such an example. The poet carefully controls his rhythms by the way he places the poem on the page; not even punctuation is necessary to guide the reader. Read the poem aloud, noting cummings's placement of words; he intended the end of each line to constitute a pause.

Portrait VIII
Buffalo Bill's
defunct
            who used to
            ride a watersmooth-silver
                            stallion
and break onetwothreefourfive pigeonsjustlikethat
                            Jesus
he was a handsome man
                        and what i want to know is
how do you like your blueeyed boy
Mr. Death

In the student modeling, entitled "Portrait VIII½," the writer not only sustained cummings's rhythm but showed a keen ear for cummings's eccentric word use as well. He had read much of the author's poetry and his Design mind had internalized cummings's characteristic cadences and word ways; for example, "busy ones" and "by dong and by ding" are two of several expressions drawn from cummings's other work. The total student poem is clearly and delightfully evocative of cummings's style.

Portrait VIII½
e. e. someone
buried by busy ones
                used to
                wish yes aprils with a you
                                and a me
and write onetwothreefourfive poems justlikethat
                        by dong and by ding
he was a perceptive man
                        and what i want to know is
where is he now when we need him
Mister Death

                                                    Bill Irwin

A second example of distinctive rhythm creating an indivisible whole is D. H. Lawrence's "Bavarian Gentians," a poem about his own impending death written only days before he died. Read the poem aloud slowly, emphasizing the sonorous and solemn cadences by almost chanting it as though it were a prayer. The rhythm has a funereal grandeur and stateliness of cadence, a proud acceptance of the terrible beauty of death, intensified by references to Pluto, the Greek god of the underworld, and to Pluto's ravished bride, Persephone. In this poem, through its rhythms as well as its words, Lawrence transforms the normal terror of death into a solemn marriage "of the living dark."

Bavarian Gentians
Not every man has gentians in his house
in soft September, at slow, sad Michaelmas.

Bavarian gentians, tall and dark, but dark
Darkening the day-time torch-like with the smoking blueness of
                      Pluto's gloom,
Ribbed hellish flowers erect, with their blaze of darkness spread
                      blue
Blown into points, by the heavy white draught of the day.

Torch-flowers of the blue-smoking darkness, Pluto's dark blue
                      blaze
Black lamps from the halls of Dis, smoking dark blue
Giving off darkness, blue darkness, upon Demeter's yellowpale
                      day.
Reach me a gentian, give me a torch!
Let me guide myself with the blue, forked torch of a flower
Down the darker and darker stairs, where blue is darkened on
                      blueness
Down the way Persephone goes, just now, in first-frosted Sep-
                      tember
To the sightless realm where darkness is married to dark
And Persephone herself is but a voice, as a bride
A gloom invisible enfolded in the deeper dark
Of the arms of Pluto as he ravishes her once again
And pierces her once more with is passion of the utter dark,
Among the splendour of black-blue torches, shedding fathomless
                      darkness on the nuptials.
Give me a flower on a tall stem, and three dark flames,
For I will go to the wedding, and be wedding-guest
At the marriage of the living dark.

Lawrence achieves this solemn rhythm through a piling on of parallel constructions, such as "Torch-flowers of the blue-smoking darkness, Pluto's dark blue blaze,/Black lamps from the halls of Dis, smoking dark blue/Giving off darkness"; through manifold recurrences of such solemn words as "dark/darkness/darkening" and "torch" and "dark blue/blue-black"; and through the many recurrences of "d" sounds and "o" and "ah" vowel sounds, which slow down the cadence to a crawl. That this poem is very serious is inescapable as we read it aloud.

I asked students to model this poem. To my surprise, instead of the serious poem I expected, one student turned in "My Filter Long Gentians," keeping the serious and sonorous cadence but applying it to a trivial subject. She had written a delightful parody: by applying the organlike cadences of the Lawrence poem to something as trivial as cigarette advertisements, she made fun of every absurd claim ever made by a cigarette company.

My Filter Long Gentians
Not every man has gentians in his house
in Sparkling Spring, at saffron-scented Lawrencemas.

Virginian gentians, long and fresh, only fresh
freshening the heavy air with the taste of extra coolness,
Menthol and filter longs, stretching out
along the stair, a millimeter longer,
Salems ushering in a salubrious spring, a lush and flavorable
                                        freshness,
as lower tar and nicotine are loosed upon the scene,
I seek flavor, down home country taste,
flowing, smoking gentians leave a linger of taste in the air,
lead me, lead me to the flavor.

Reach me a gentian, give me a cigarette!
I'd walk a mile for a Camel,
let this flavorable flower guide me
down, past Surgeon General's warnings,
through Cancer's craggy cavern, and
into Marlboro's realm where freshness feeds upon freshness
and gentians taste good like a good gentian should,
I stand in a smoke-filled heaven,
                    L.S./M.F.T.

                                        Susan Jones

Parody is different from modeling in that parody makes us smile precisely because the sonorous cadence of the original is in all fidelity applied to something trivial. This writer had a fine inner ear for the rhythms of language—and a wonderful sense of humor.

It's your turn to exercise your intensified Design-mind awareness of the music in words through modeling the e.e. cummings poem yourself. You may choose to model it, but if parody appeals to you, you may juxtapose cummings' rhythms against a trivial subject.

Directing Your Hand

Begin by rereading the cummings poem several times, aloud.

1. In your writer's notebook, precluster around the nucleus PORTRAIT OF. . . for names of possible persons, since the model is a character portrait. Preclustering gives you choices, often of persons your Sign mind would never have thought of otherwise: perhaps Henry Ford, Thomas Edison, John F. Kennedy, Picasso, Michelangelo—you name it. Each has tremendous possibilities for straight modeling or parody. But the choice must be yours because only you know who piques your vital interest or emotional involvement.
2. Having discovered your subject, cluster around this nucleus all associations that come to you for about two minutes, until you experience the trial-web shift and, with it, a focus.
3. Now call your Sign mind into the act by writing a clear focusing statement drawing on your Design-mind-generated trial-web vision.
4. Now *play* with your content by adapting it to the rhyhms of the cummings poem. Take as long as you wish. For some, the writing takes fifteen minutes; for others the writing is much more leisurely. Enjoy the process. Humorous or serious, you will gradually mesh rhythms and subject into a harmonious whole. Frequently glance back at the original for its cadences, its recurrences, its ebb and flow of words that will give your own poem its unity.
5. Read your creation aloud, making any changes you wish.

After Writing

You probably experienced this as a playful exercise, surprising yourself with your own final product. That is the usual experience of my students. Should you have had some difficulty, it may have been caused by a couple of reasons. Possibly you tried parody and felt your vignette turned out to be less than adequate. If that was your problem, don't worry about it; not everyone's temperament is suited to writing parody, although all of us are equipped to become high sensitized to the cadences of language if we become receptive enough. Simply go back, recluster, and play with a straight modeling of the cummings poem.

In addition, you may have tried too hard, forcing your ideas into a rhythmic mold and finding they didn't fit. In effect, you have shut off the rhythm-and-pattern-sensitive Design mind, which does not function well under brow-furrowed mental strain. Ease up, go back, *allow* the cummings cadences to sink in by rereading the poem several times. Then play. Don't take the writing too seriously. Invite, allow, be receptive to the rhythms, and your poem will fall into place without a gnashing of teeth. Think of yourself as a child playing once again with language that holds infinite surprises.

Now that you have attuned your inner ear to the rhythms of language, you are ready to model your writing after one of the distinctively rhythmic voices whose passages we read aloud at the beginning of this chapter.

Directing Your Hand

Let's come full circle in this chapter by ending where we began: with Hemingway, Faulkner, or Stein. Choose your favorite passage of the three to model and read it aloud once again so your Design mind can internalize its distinctive rhythm.

1. In your writer's notebook, cluster around an interesting word or phrase taken from the selected passage, for example THINK ABOUT . . . or RESISTING or ROUND Or choose something opposed to one of the words or phrases, for example DREAM ABOUT or SQUARE or FLOW WITH. Cluster for associations for two to five minutes, until you experience the trial-web shift signaling that you have discovered a focus.

2. Shift to Sign-mind thinking by writing two or three clear focusing statements from the Design-mind cluster. Choose one to develop.

3. Begin writing your vignette, with conscious attention to the particular rhythm of the writer of your choice. Students usually write a vignette consisting of a half to a full page, although some get carried away and write more. That's fine. Use the momentum to carry you as far as you wish to go, as long as you come full circle.

4. Read aloud what you have written and make changes until you are satisfied when you compare your rhythms with the cadences of your chosen passage.

A Last Word and Heading On

The exercises in this chapter have first, reacquainted you with the child's way of listening to language for its rhythmic qualities and, second, applied such listening to showing you how to cultivate your natural writer. By modeling the quality of rhythmic wholeness, you have exercised the playful dimension of your Design mind and reawakened your inner ear.

The rhythm of language is emotionally satisfying from infancy on. As adults, we take pleasure from a beautifully rhythmic parallel sentence. When we consciously engage in such emotionally satisfying rhythmic activity, we enlist the Sign mind in a Design-mind activity, bringing about cooperation between our two asymmetrical brains. Since natural writing can only come about through orchestration of Sign and Design minds, that is exactly what we are after.

In the next chapter you will recapture the power of the inner eye—the fresh and authentic perception of the world you had in childhood. Just as, at the beginning of this chapter, Dylan Thomas told us he "cared for the colours the words cast on my eyes," so poet Peter Meinke writes, "The mind can't sing a poem without the eye," affirming that natural writing cannot occur without access to the Design mind's rich storehouse of images.

CHAPTER 8/ *Images: Inner Eye directing Writing Hand*

Virginia Woolf once said that her novel *The Waves* unfolded like a poem from a germinal image—the image of a "fin turning in a waste of water." In a famous passage from Marcel Proust's *Remembrance of Things Past,* the images evoked by dipping a teacake in a cup of tea trigger childhood memories in a middle-aged man that give shape and color to the experiences of his past. Images play a central role in art and in our lives. Much of what we remember is carried as images, especially memory charged with emotion. Picture for a moment the circumstances surrounding the instant you learned that President Kennedy had been shot. There will likely be an immediate flashback to a scene as sharp and vivid as though nearly twenty years had not passed, and you re-experience it as a visual, auditory, tactile whole, a spontaneous total picture of a moment in time.

You have the same ability to conjure up pleasurable images of the past: a picnic in the country, an afternoon on a sailboat, a sunset walk with someone you love. Ask a child what he or she remembers of a particular event and chances are it will be a vivid image that encapsulates the experience. Remember an emotionally powerful moment in your life and you will probably see it as vividly as if it had happened yesterday. That is the Design mind's special province—the ability to bring forth complex internal wholes in the absence of sensory stimuli.

IMAGES:
INNER EYE DIRECTING
WRITING HAND

She went to the fence and sat there, watching the gold clouds fall to pieces, and go in immense, rose-colored ruin towards the darkness. Gold flamed to scarlet, like pain in its intense brightness. Then the scarlet ran to rose, and rose to crimson, and quickly the passion went out of the sky. All the world was dark grey.

D. H. Lawrence,
Sons and Lovers

So with the lamps all put out, the moon sunk, and a thin rain drumming on the roof, a downpouring of immense darkness began. Nothing, it seemed, could survive the flood, the profusion of darkness which, creeping in at keyholes and crevices, stole round window blinds, came into bedrooms, swallowed up here a jug and basin, there a bowl of red and yellow dahlias, there the sharp edges and firm bulk of a chest of drawers.

Virginia Woolf,
To the Lighthouse

An image is an internal whole in the mind's eye, complete with all the sensations surrounding it, full of meaning for the writer. Images have strong visual significance, but they also evoke the feel or sound or smell or taste of things. Images are the constant in all natural writing, for they heighten or intensify the implicit, often becoming interlocking patterns of related images resonant with meaning.

In natural writing, an image is a word picture charged with feeling, which has freshness of vision, intensity, evocative power—freshness to reveal what we had forgotten to see; intensity to concentrate the most significance into a small space; evocative power to elicit emotional response. D. H. Lawrence pulls us into the moving image of a sunset. Virginia Woolf steeps us in images of darkness. And contemporary novelist John Hawkes entangles us in extraordinary images of wind.

Like language rhythms and recurrences, images in writing make a passage memorable. They add facets to meaning, stimulating our minds to see, understand, play with ideas, wonder, interpret emotional nuances—in short, to come alive. An image tells us more than pure fact: "the sun went down," "night came," "the wind blew." It makes us *experience* the crumbling of a multicolored sunset, the gobbling darkness, the all-enveloping island wind through carefully chosen words that strike the tuning fork of our senses and resonate through intellect, emotions, and body—if we can come to it with a childlike "innocence of eye."

Language scholar James Britton tells of reading a group of eight-year-olds some poems, one of which was about a night watchman in winter, another one about cold wind. When he finished, a small boy in the back row sat hugging himself like a street vendor in winter, pleading, "Please, sir, would you read us a *warm* one?"

In Chapter 7 we reawakened the inner ear's sense of language rhythms that empowers the cultivated hand to write naturally. In this chapter we will reawaken your inner eye to make you receptive to the imaging ability that resides naturally in your Design mind. Images are nonverbal. The purpose of this chapter is to put you in touch with ways of tapping these reservoirs of remembered or perceived experience and then making them accessible to your Sign mind for verbal expression.

The Childhood Origins of Imaging

Before there are words, there are images. We perceive and respond to images from the moment we are born. Our mother is our most primary image, which comes to represent security and nourishment. Certain objects come to mean pleasure or discomfort. "To the infant," remarked the Swiss psychologist Jean Piaget, "the world is a thing to be sucked." Our earliest images were all-encompassing. Only gradually did they take on the aspect of separate, discrete experiences.

In the stage of the innocent eye, ear, and hand, images began to evolve new dimensions through the child's observations of the external world as well as through imaginary creatures such as monsters and witches and fairy godmothers. Psychologist Bruno Bettelheim has written extensively on the power of fairy-tale images in the child's psychic development. As he wrote in *The Uses of Enchantment*, "Fairy tales describe inner states of the mind by means of images and actions."

Emotional states attached to fear, joy, courage, or isolation are translated into the visual images that people the world of fairy tales. These images and the feelings they characterize are unforgettable precisely because they reflect the child's inner states of mind. In addition, for both children and adults, images manifest themselves powerfully in nightmares. The popularity with children of such books as Mercer Mayer's *There's a Nightmare in My Closet* and Maurice Sendak's *Where the Wild Things Are* attests to the fact that children seem to find comfort in objectifying and externalizing these dream images.

A fundamental characteristic of early-childhood images is their interrelated multisensory nature. Psychologist Howard Gardner calls this phenomenon crucial to a child's aesthetic development:

Reawakened in the stage of the cultivated eye, ear, and hand, we can interchange sensory modalities in perceptive new ways, as Peter Meinke does in his line "the mind can't sing a poem without the eye." Stuck in the conventional stage, we might ask what singing poems have to do with the eye. But in the cultivated stage we realize that powerful images are the source of the poems we sing—that is, recast into aesthetically pleasing rhythms.

But the wind, this bundle of invisible snakes, roars across our wandering island—it is a wandering island, off course, unlocated in space and quite out of time—and seems to heap the shoulders with an arm-like weight, to coil about my naked legs and pulse and caress the flesh with an unpredictable weight and consistency, tension of its own. It drives, drives, and even when it drops down, fades, dies, it continues its gentle rubbing on the skin.

John Hawkes,
Second Skin

We enter an age of synesthesis: a time when, more than at any other, the child effects easy translations across sensory systems—when colors can readily evoke sounds and sounds can readily evoke colors, when motions of the hand suggest lines of poetry or lines of poetry or lines of verse stimulate a dance or a song.

Howard Gardner,
Artful Scribbles

IMAGES:
INNER EYE DIRECTING
WRITING HAND

There are other similarities bet-
ween poetry and young children's
speech. Poets tend to look for
significant evocative detail—
something straight out of life—to
carry their meaning, and to avoid
the vaguely general or abstract
terms. . . . With young children it
is not a matter of choice. Their
ideas must take a concrete form of
expression because they have not
yet mastered the art of making and
handling [Sign-mind] abstraction.
A five-year-old boy in an infants'
class once said, "Oh, yes, I know
Geography. It's polar bears at the
top and penguins at the bottom!"

James Britton,
Language and Learning

Impressive testimony of children's imaging powers comes from an experiment in a New York elementary school by a visiting poet, Philip Lopate, who wrote about the experience in his book, *Being with Children.* Lopate had been hired to encourage children to write. One day he was approached by eight-year-old Tommy, an "average" student who on this day could think of absolutely nothing to write about. Several suggestions failed. At the end of his rope of ideas, Lopate handed Tommy a poem by Guillaume Apollinaire: "Translate this." Puzzled, Tommy looked at the poem, then at Lopate: "But I don't know French." Lopate reassured him, "Just say the words over and over to yourself and write what you *think* it means." Reluctantly, Tommy went to work, responding to the images the sound of these totally foreign words produced in his Design mind.

The original Apollinaire poem and Tommy's inspired "translation" follow. Read Tommy's translation aloud, watching for the images.

Photographie
>Ton sourire m'attire comme
>Pourrait m'attirer une fleur
>
>Photographie tu es le champignon brun
>>De la forêt
>>Qu'est sa beauté
>>Les blancs y sont
>>Un clair de lune
>>Dans un jardin pacifique
>>Plein d'eaux vives et de jardiniers enviables
>>Photographie tu es la fumée de l'ardeur
>>Ou'est sa beauté
>>Et il y a en toi
>>Photographie
>>Des ton alanguis
>>On y entend
>>Une melopée
>>Photographie tu es l'ombre
>>Du soleil
>>Qu'est sa beauté

Guillaume Apollinaire

Photograph
The town squire's mattress came back to town.
Poor mattress fell on the floor.
She photographed the champion broom.
She found herself in the forest
In quest of her Beauty.
The blankets shone.
Her chair was held up by balloons.
She found people dancing in jars.
As they were dancing, they were making
some dough as flat as a plain.
She photographed some fumes from the
dust that rose in quest of her beauty.
She photographed tons of languages,
They entered a melody.
She photographed two lumps of soil
in quest of her beauty.

Out of words totally meaningless to him, Tommy had created a coherent whole because the strange words suggested images to him that he tried to fit into a meaningful configuration. How wonderful that our brains are so constituted that one side of it is not put off by the unknown and unfamiliar and simply creates its own sense of what the left brain must perceive as arrant nonsense.

In our early years, images are omnipresent and powerful. Later, by age ten or eleven, we lose much of our imaging power because reality replaces myth and fantasy. The stage of the conventional eye, ear, and hand sets in. Not only does schooling not cultivate our image-making, but our peers help reinforce the commonplace, as we begin to feel secure in our new fund of commonly shared knowledge that is readily communicated and clearly defined. Sign-mind definitions take the place of images. We learn that "a star is a celestial body which is a self-luminous mass of gas visible at night as twinkling points of light." This is a far cry from a four-year-old's observation that a star is a flower without a stem. And fairy tales, any ten-year-old will tell you, "are only for kids!"

According to psychologist Robert Sommer, television further reduces the child's natural need to conjure up personal images.

We can reach the stage of the cultivated eye, ear, and hand only if we relearn to tap the imaging powers of our Design minds: only

The image cannot be dispossessed of a primordial freshness, which idea can never claim. An idea is derivative and tamed. The image is in the natural or wild state, and it has to be discovered there, not put there, obeying its own law and none of ours.

John Crowe Ransom,
Poems and Essays

Why go to the trouble of con-
structing fantasies when a flick of
the dial will produce them ready-
made? There was a time when a
child expected a bedtime story be-
fore yielding the house to the
adults. Today television is the
baby-sitter and soporific. Most
adults have lost the capacity to tell
a good story. A good storyteller
follows internal sights, sounds, and
movements. A nonimager knows
what is important and can recite
general principles but has difficul-
ties describing the particulars,
which are the basis of a good story.
> Robert Sommer,
> The Mind's Eye

then can we recapture this childlike way of seeing and express our fresh perceptions authentically. Poets and creative writers, as William Stafford and Dorothea Brande have told us in another chapter, are people who never lost this authentic vision. Without Design-mind images we do not have natural writing.

Clustering for Images

A powerful way to experience the multisensory nature of images is to cluster a color and then shape the images that spill out into a coherent whole, as this student writer did in Figure 8–1. She preclustered (COLOR) to avail herself of choices, choosing "purple" as the color of greatest intensity for her, which she then clustered in turn. As you read her vignette aloud, see which senses this writer appeals to with her images of purple.

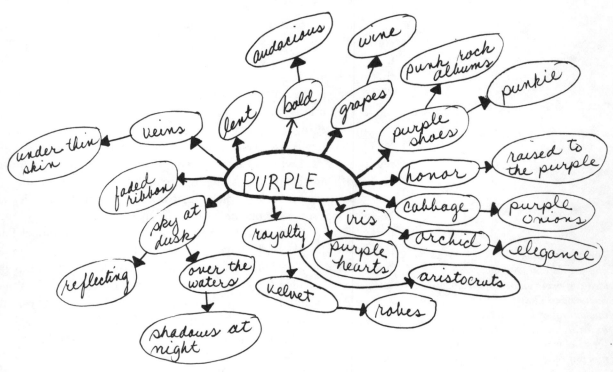

Figure 8–1

Purple Wine
As you sit and sip a dark wine,
remember the Latin masses
with statues draped in Lenten purple;
or Grandma's veined skin and bruised
arms; Uncle Harry's purple heart
under glass; how Daddy reminded
us about purple onion
and cabbage salads of
depression years and gangsters
driving purple Lincolns.
Or ponder purple shoes,
lavender stockings with purple
butterflies dancing under blacklights
of a purple punk band.
Or dream of a batik-draped
body, printed with iris and
orchids strolling through
purple-shadowed palm leaves
in a Hawaiian sunset.
Or just sit and sip a dark wine
and smell its ripeness.

Nancy Drummond

Purple, this writer tells us, can be tasted: "sip a dark wine," "purple onion/and cabbage salads"; it can be touched: "veined skin and bruised/arms"; it can be heard: "purple punk band"; it can be smelled: "smell its ripeness"; and, of course, it can be seen: purple heart, purple Lincolns, purple shoes, orchids, purple-shadowed palm leaves, to name a few.

But notice that this seeming cataloguing of purples has a subtle structure delineating three distinct experiences: "remember," "ponder," and "dream of" framed by "sit and sip" at the beginning and the end, bringing it full circle. This structure patterns the writer's experiences of images of purple and integrates them into a feeling, thought, and image whole.

Directing Your Hand

In your writer's notebook extend your awareness of the multi-sensory nature of images by focusing on a color.

1. Quick-cluster the nucleus ⟨COLOR⟩ to give you choices; my students are often surprised that their "favorite" color, which first comes to mind, is not the one they write about.

2. Scan your quick-cluster and choose a color that resonates for you, strikes an emotional chord, or simply interests you more than the others. Cluster it for the images you associate with it. Cluster a lot in order to get beyond the most obvious, most immediate associations (red—Valentine), allowing yourself to be open to more subtle images from your personal experience (purple—"how Daddy reminded/us about purple onion and cabbage salads of/depression years"). Cluster until you experience a trial-web shift that gives you a sense of direction.

3. Write a focusing statement, bringing your Sign mind into the act.

4. Now write your vignette, focusing on images of color, allowing them to reflect the full range of your senses. Be sensitive to the possibilities for recurrences, parallel forms, language rhythms, and any other qualities that will enrich the vignette and make it unique to you.

5. Be sure to come full circle, and revise as you feel necessary.

6. Read it aloud, perhaps to a friend, and see how far your writing has come, even using fewer than half of the elements of natural writing.

Where Do Images Come from?

Most fundamentally, images have three basic interrelated sources: (1) images from external reality directly presented to the senses reflecting the world we move in; (2) images from internal sources derived from daydreams and fantasy, internalized experiences of sight, sound, touch, smell, and taste as well as even more powerful images from sleeping dreams and nightmares; and (3) images simultaneously external and internal, derived from myth, religion, and the arts, sometimes called archetypes, meaning that they are common to all humanity, including such images as birth, love, nature, death. Let's begin with the waking experience of our everyday world as a source of images for natural writing.

The Real World As a Source of Images

Our world is full of images, but our senses are often dulled to them. Seen with new eyes, heard with new ears, the commonplace can be elevated through fresh perception. Focusing on a particular element of a commonplace experience can bring forth new meaning. A new look at the broad leaf of a banana palm, seen year after year as merely "background noise," triggered this momentary musing from a free-lance writer:

> I focus on the broad leaf of the banana palm outside my window and it represents for me Southern California, the isolation of my career as a free-lance, feeling closed-in and stagnant amidst the luxuriant life and growth that takes no notice of my frame of mind.

The banana-palm image evoked some profound feelings of withering in the midst of nature's abundance. The most commonplace objects are at the heart of sharpening the eye of the natural writer.

Witness poet Robert Hass, whose rich images of an empty house nevertheless bespeak love and caring.

IMAGES:
INNER EYE DIRECTING
WRITING HAND

Song
Afternoon cooking in the fall sun—
who is more naked
                              than the man
yelling, "Hey, I'm home!"
                    to an empty house?
thinking because the bay is clear,
the hills in yellow heat,
& scrub oak red in gullies
                    that great crowds of family
should tumble from the rooms
                    to throw their bodies on the Papa-body
                              I-am-loved.

Cat sleeps in the windowgleam,
                    dust motes.
  On the oak table
 filets of sole
stewing in the juice of tangerines,
  slices of green pepper
  on a bone-white dish.

                                        Robert Hass

    We are surrounded by images of everyday experience. Only when
we *really* open the mind's eye to see what is unusual about one of
these—seeing it "as if for the first time"—can we write about it in
such a way that we and the reader perceive it as an illumination, a
small epiphany, a new awareness of what life is all about. Remember
when the discovery of the first furry black spring caterpillar sent you
into horror or ecstasy? Remember when the crunchy, brittle sound
of the orange-red leaves as you marched through them on the way
home from school gave you the "good feels," to use Opal Whiteley's
phrase? Explore your "now": look gently at the dandelions on your
lawn; watch the face in the car next to you in a freeway traffic jam;
observe a child playing with blocks in total absorption—really see it
and create an image, a sensual picture in words with emotional un-
dertones. An image, suffused with feeling, conveys more than an accurate reflection of external reality ever can.

Directing Your Hand

1. To intensify your awareness of the images around you, in your writer's notebook precluster (IMAGES) and jot down all images that impinge on your consciousness right now, images seen, heard, tasted, touched, smelled. The precluster will open your Design mind and give you many options from which to choose.

2. Choose the image that has the greatest emotional texture for you and cluster it. Cluster for as many specifics as you can gather. Be receptive, open, flexible. Don't censor. Continue to cluster until you experience a trial-web shift, which is likely to occur when you suddenly see particular significance or some truth in a specific image or cluster of images.

3. Write a focusing statement in which you articulate that significance, thus inviting the participation of your Sign mind in the creative act.

4. Now re-create your significant image colored by certain emotional nuances in words. As you write, continually shift from the sequencing Sign mind to the guiding Design-mind vision until the vision and the words on the page are in alignment with each other. Use all the senses that seem relevant, as well as any memories or experiences that will enrich the texture of your writing.

5. Read your vignette aloud. Reshape anything that still does not please you—remember recurrences, full-circle wholeness, and language rhythms, but above all bring this commonplace event to life in words by re-creating what you see, hear, smell, taste, touch.

After Writing

This writing exercise should make you highly conscious of one thing: that the sources for natural writing are everywhere; we need only become receptive and *see,* thereby investing that seeing with our own meaning, expressing it in our natural voice.

Figure 8–2 is a student "commonplace" vignette about waking.

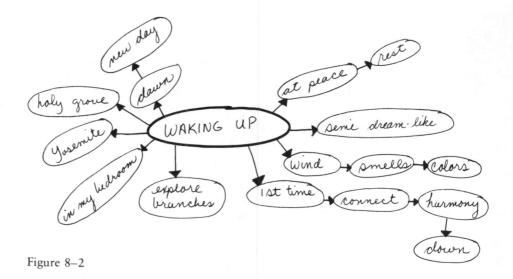

Figure 8–2

Arousal
Dawn dappled ceiling
Yosemite in my bedroom
holy grove where I
awake for the first time.
I watch life's kaleidoscope
branching, and in my reverie
I see a sun being born

Karen Nelson

Dreams As a Source of Images

A rich and often untapped source of images comes from a nightly event in our lives: dreaming. Dreams are the Design mind's way of expressing itself in pictures sometimes so overpoweringly vivid that we are not sure if we are experiencing dream or reality. After working with dreams as a rich source of images for some weeks, a student remarked, "A dream is clustering in images." And so it might well be.

As early as 1844, A. L. Wigan suggested that our two brains are relatively independent during sleep, with a suspension of the power of the Sign mind over the Design mind. His hypothesis has been confirmed by studies showing greater electrical activity in the right brain during dreaming. Recently, David Galin of the Langley-Porter Neuro-Psychiatric Institute further supported Wigan's hypothesis by suggesting that most dreaming is done with the right brain, hence the nonsequential, nontemporal nature of dreams, with their overlapping images drawn from time past as well as time present, from familiar and unfamiliar, from geographically near and far. And Canadian brain surgeon Wilder Penfield found that mild electrical stimulation of a patient's right temporal lobe usually produced visual illusions of vividly recalled memories—images—while probes of the left hemisphere did not. If we produce images with our right hemisphere, clustering can help bring them to consciousness.

For some it may be difficult to unplug the logical Sign mind, which dismisses dreams as puzzling at best, meaningless nonsense at worst. Yet great writers have always recognized the potency of dream images, using them as inspiration for poetry and prose, among them Poe, Coleridge, John Hawkes, John Cheever, Hermann Hesse, Doris Lessing, and D. M. Thomas—just a handful of examples from the past century. Doris Lessing's *The Golden Notebook* is filled with dream images:

> I dreamed marvelously. I dreamed there was an enormous web of beautiful fabric stretched out. It was incredibly beautiful, covered all over with embroidered pictures. The pictures were illustrations of the myths of mankind but they were not just pictures, they were the myths themselves, so that the soft glittering web was alive. In my dreams I handled and felt this material and wept with joy.

And since the advent of psychoanalysis, all therapies have focused on the interpretation of dream images as keys to our mental states. For Freud, all dream images were at root sexual symbols. For Jung, all dream images reflected the archetypal concerns of the collective unconscious (which we will deal with later in the chapter). And for Gestalt therapists, dream images represent parts of ourselves often in conflict.

When we dream, it is in the language of our imaging Design mind, which uses a logic quite different from that of our Sign mind. In the Design mind there is no logical cause and effect: time is telescoped in such a way that past blends with future, and present images appear on our dream stage with past images, often coalescing.

IMAGES:
INNER EYE DIRECTING
WRITING HAND

The Far Field
I dream of journeys repeatedly:
Of flying like a bat deep into a nar-
rowing tunnel,
Of driving alone, without luggage,
out a long peninsula,
The road lined with snow-laden
second growth,
A fine dry snow ticking the wind-
shield,
Alternate snow and sleet, no on-
coming traffic,
And no lights behind, in the
blurred side-mirror,
The road changing from glazed
tarface to a rubble of stone,
Ending at last in a hopeless sand-
rut,
Where the car stalls,
Churning in a snowdrift
Until the headlights darken.
                    Theodore Roethke

Every night we spontaneously create vivid images, complex and compelling stories. Learn to attend to dream images and you will come into contact with the mystery of your life, for dreams are important communications from ourselves to ourselves.

Theodore Roethke, for example, plagued by recurring bouts of manic-depression, recorded a dream journey shortly before his death in a poem in which the images indicate increasing bleakness, isolation, terror, and, finally, total blockage—clearly a description of the poet's mental state.

For the next week—in fact, for the rest of the time you spend developing your natural writing skills—record your dreams by clustering them in your writer's notebook as soon as you awake. Some of you will argue that you don't dream. Not so—all of us dream. "Well, then," you may say, "I can't remember my dreams." Resolve this difficulty by telling yourself, just before you fall asleep, "I will recall my dream on awakening." Within a few days your autosuggestion will bear fruit; when you do wake up recalling a dream, you will find it enormously satisfying to experience a part of yourself that has been tucked away.

In recording the dream when you awake, treat it as you would a painting. That is, begin with the dominant impression of the dream and capture it with a word or phrase as the nucleus of the cluster, such as (ECSTASY) or (TERROR.) A dominant impression is a De-sign-mind phenomenon, an overall feeling characterizing the totality of the dream. For example, I often have "house" dreams. I will be in a house that is at once strange and familiar, walking through it with great curiosity. (CURIOSITY) might be my nucleus. At other times I will be living in a Victorian mansion, apprehensively opening doors to rooms I didn't know existed. My dominant impression then might be (APPREHENSION.) Recently I dreamed I was in a lovely new house overlooking the ocean; it was totally devoid of furnishings and I somehow knew I was responsible for choosing the furniture. (MAKING CHOICES) might have been my nucleus. Find your dominant impression and, in your writer's notebook, cluster it in as much detail as you can recall.

Directing Your Hand

1. After a week of collecting clusters of dreams, select the dream impression that seems most compelling to you, or perhaps most puzzling.
2. Glance over your cluster, letting the words re-create the dream for you. If you recall any more details, add them to your cluster before beginning to write. You might even wish to recluster the same dream for new associations.
3. Rescan your cluster until you experience the trial-web shift, giving you your focus. Record a focusing statement to help clarify your impression. Now write about your dream in the first person and in the present tense as though it were happening right at this moment. Even if you can only recall fragmentary images of the dream, re-create these images in words. A dream is rarely logical and sequential. As you write, keep in mind recurrences (phrases or words that are especially significant to underscore the mood of the dream), language rhythms to suit the often conflicting feelings, parallel structures to pile on image after image to achieve the compressed quality of a dream.
4. Come full circle. Read your vignette aloud and make any changes that will improve the quality of natural writing.

After Writing

The experience of expressing a dream in words almost always intrigues my students. One beginning writer described the state in which she wrote the dream as "a kind of floating," so absorbed did she become in her attempt to re-create the images. Another student noticed that although there was no logical sequence to her retelling, the repetition of certain key images unified her vignette and allowed her to retain the dream quality of the original vision. Both these experiences signify a creative immersion in Design-mind processes and strong emotional connection to the material.

The cluster of Figure 8–3 was produced in the second week of one of my writing courses after the students had actively kept track of their dreaming through clustering. At first this student had insisted she could not remember her dreams, but bedtime autosuggestion and the tool of clustering to tap the Design mind's dream images soon made them accessible. Observe the rich detail that emerges, coupled with the absence of a logical cause/effect sequence. As this writer's dominant impression indicates, the dream was soothing rather than threatening.

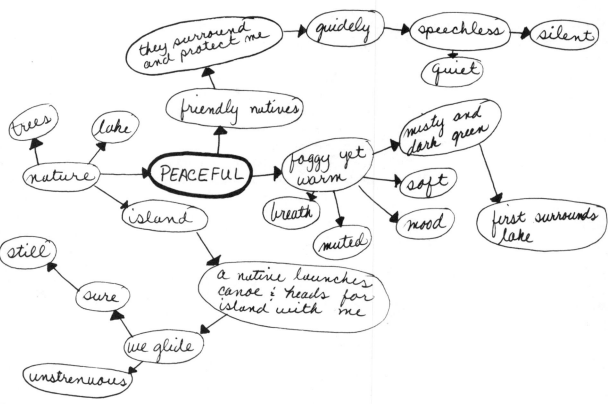

Figure 8–3

Dream Image
I don't care where we are going.
Friendly natives surround me
as we journey down a narrow mulch path
winding in a misty green forest, quickly, quietly.
The air is a soft breath.
We stop at the edge of the lake, yet
I don't recall stopping,
for I am in a delicately carved, ivory canoe, gliding,
gliding on a smooth mirror of water.
A speechless native makes sure, steady
strokes on the oars, pulling, pulling, easily
pulling toward the island
in the very center of the lake.
Swiftly, silently we glide,
cutting through unmarred water.
We never land.
Our haven is the peaceful water.

Laura Gesso

The first image is that of a journey and the dreamer's full acceptance of it: "I don't care where we are going"; it is an expression of
the desire for discovery and change. The second image is of "friendly
natives" who are "speechless" as well as highly competent, making
"sure, steady/strokes on the oars"; one sees them as guides or guard-
ians. A third image is the "narrow mulch path," related to the journey—of life? Into the self? A fourth is the "green forest," which,
according to Jung, is an archetypal symbol of the unconscious. A
fifth is the lake, often associated with the watery deep, the abyss,
hence with death. This vignette, however, focuses on the lake's
smooth, mirrored, "unmarred" water—that is, on its surface, which
suggests a mirror, presenting an image of self-contemplation.

A central image is the canoe, a vehicle facilitating the journey.
Another is the island, a complex symbol. Jung sees it as a refuge
from the menacing assault of the "seas of the unconscious," but at
the same time the island is a symbol of isolation and solitude. "The
center" is also an archetypal image, suggesting movement from outer
to inner, to the mystic middle that reveals the primordial meditative
state, the state in which the meditator experiences a profound sense
of unity with all the universe. But the dreamer of this poem is at
home in the waters: "We never land."

IMAGES:
INNER EYE DIRECTING
WRITING HAND

The images create an atmosphere of support, beauty, and cooperation in this venture of self-discovery. The language rhythms underscore the feeling of trust and joy in their smoothness: "I don't care where we are going" and "Our haven is the peaceful water." The recurrences, too, add to the calm but efficient movement: "quickly, quietly"; "gliding, gliding"; "sure, steady strokes"; "pulling, pulling, easily pulling"; "swiftly, silently."

The writing of dream images leads to more intense compression of language than in normal prose, or even fiction. Although there are also more gaps between images, they do not seem to disturb us but rather sustain the dreamlike quality of the whole.

Archetypes As Images

Closely related to dream images, as you can see from the dream poem we just discussed, are archetypes. Your dream images are your own unique creations; archetypes, however, are certain images in dreams and literature that have been reported to recur again and again in many different individuals at many different times and in many different cultures. According to Jung, these are images preserved in the memory of the race because of innumerable repetitions of certain modes of experience: images of birth, love, and death, and images from nature—seas, mountains, deserts, tunnels, valleys. We respond powerfully to them because they hold a universal truth for all of us.

Archetypal images bring us into touch with communal experience, general truths which have eternally bound mankind together.
C. Day Lewis,
The Poetic Image

These images are so powerful that they cross all cultural boundaries. For example, water is an archetypal image that all cultures associate with life and birth; the desert is an archetypal image associated with sterility and lifelessness; spilled blood is associated with death; and so forth. Other archetypal images are the journey (we are all on a journey), the Earth Mother (nurturing, protective, fertile); the hero, the monster (the monster, in all cultures, encompasses what we fear most, possibly something in ourselves), the shadow (our dark side, our repressed self), towers, stairs—the list goes on and on. Such images that occur spontaneously in our dreams and in imaginative writing, says Jung, lie deep in our "collective unconscious" and stir our feelings because they touch the very core of our psychic being and our deepest concerns: death, sexuality, abandonment, freedom, and so forth. Thus these images act as powerful motivators for natural writing.

*I dreamt of falling trees in a wild
    storm
I was between them as a desolate
    shore
came to meet me and I ran, scared
    stiff,
there was a trapdoor but I would
    not lift
it, I have started an affair
with your son, on a train some-
    where
in a dark tunnel, his hand was un-
    derneath
my dress between my thighs I
    could not breathe
he took me to a white lakeside ho-
    tel
somewhere high up, the lake was
    emerald
I could not stop myself I was in
    flames
from the first spreading of my
    thighs, no shame
could make me push my dress
    down, thrust his hand
    away. . . .*

D. M. Thomas,
The White Hotel

D. M. Thomas's *The White Hotel* begins in the Freudian "land-scape of hysteria," but it also contains Jungian archetypal images, all of which describe the speaker's state of mind.

Here, too, archetypal images abound, underscoring the heavy sensuality of the passage as it unfolds: "tree" archetypally suggests life, thus a falling tree—destruction; a dark tunnel calls to mind femaleness; a storm suggests archetypal creative intercourse among elements; a trap door is also a female image because it gives access to tunnels; a lake suggests the unconscious and also life-giving water. So, in these first few lines of the opening passage, Thomas sets the stage for this unabashedly Freudian novel of a journey into the unconscious.

Archetypal images arise naturally in our dreams and in writing that has been allowed to draw on Design-mind images. Becoming aware of these ancient images and tapping them for their psychic power will give your writing more richness and depth. When you explore an archetypal image of your own through clustering, processing it with your Design mind and filtering it through your own unique experiential sieve, you will discover the meaning it has for you.

Let us focus on the archetypal image of flying, for example. Many of us experience flying dreams, which often elicit pleasurable sensations. Flying signifies transcending the body's limitations, being unencumbered by gravity. But beyond that we also associate flying images with raising ourselves morally or spiritually. Flying, as in the myth of Icarus, is also a symbol of separation from a parent, of disobedience and its consequences—growing independence always tinged with sadness because it can result in a fall. Flight has also been associated with the flight of the imagination. As noted earlier, symbols are images elevated to the level where they come to stand for something else.

Directing Your Hand

Let the archetypal image of flying stimulate your Design mind so that you can discover which accumulated associations spill out and what patterns they will generate in your own writing. They are fertile stimuli with which to reawaken and develop your own image-making powers.

1. In your writer's notebook focus on the archetypal image of flight. Begin by clustering the nucleus word (FLYING) . Let go. Be receptive by widening your attention as though you were squinting your eyes to get a fuller, richer picture. Let all the associations you have ever experienced about flying spill out.

2. Continue to cluster for a minute or two until you experience the trial-web shift from randomness to a sense of focus, of direction, of a tentative whole.

3. Clarify that sense of direction by writing a focusing statement, initiating the shift from Design- to Sign-mind thinking.

4. Now spend eight minutes or so—more if you have come in touch with emotionally laden associations—writing a vignette inspired by the image of flying. Let your focus dictate the shape your writing wishes to take. It may be prose, but it may also evolve into a free-verse poem. Whatever it turns into, it will be a self-contained whole. Think of the qualities that give expression, richness, and authenticity as you write—rhythm, recurrence, freshness of vision.

5. Now read aloud what you have written. How did you come full circle? What recurrences help to unify the whole? When you read aloud, do you hear some parallel constructions? Reshape anything that still jars your sense of wholeness, cut whatever doesn't really fit, until you have a configuration that pleases you.

After Writing

The cluster (Figure 8–4) has no immediately discernible pattern but the archetype of flight is explored from many different angles, from its many and varied sensations to a variety of images of flight found in nature: birds, dust particles in sunlight, wind, insects, flower seeds, petals, leaves, volcanic ash, and so forth. As we explore this writer's Design-mind shorthand further, we discover the genesis for the vignette that evolved: adjacent to "advanced flying," listing spaceships and planes, we see "primitive flying" from which emerges "swing." Swinging is a more fettered variant of the archetypal image of flying, and poets have used it to symbolize parent-child relationships centering on pushing the child away, but only momentarily, for the arc of the swing brings the child back to the waiting hands of the parent who pushes again, harder, longer, only to have the child return stronger. On another level, every child knows the exhilaration of flight—tethered or not—through swinging, and this is the focus developed by the writer of "The Swing," albeit with a surprising and highly archetypal twist.

As you read this beginning writer's vignette, note how much of her cluster finds its way into her work. See also how the vignette unfolds quite realistically, then gradually, almost imperceptibly, takes on the surrealistic dimensions of a dream sequence. Finally, the restricted flight of the swinging motion is transformed into the archetypal flight away to freedom, unfettered by parental restraints and strictures: "Her arms reach for me./I smile/because it is too late. . . . I am free from my cage."

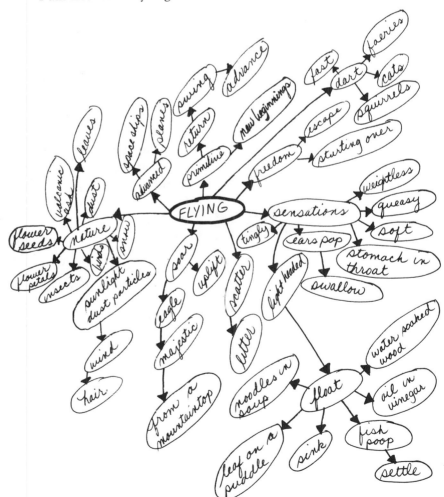

Figure 8–4

The Swing
The swing haunts me.
I am drawn to it.
I sit in the hard rubber seat; it conforms to my body.
The chains are bright and cold. I wrap my hands around them.
I close my eyes, push off with my legs.
The swing is in motion, a slow easy motion.
My muscles contract; I feel stiff and tense.
My stomach is churning.
I feel sick.
My hands begin to sweat.
My brain screams, get off the swing, get off now!
I try,
but I can't.
My chance is gone; I hear my brothers.
"Mom says she's not supposed to swing."
"It's OK this once. I'll push her."
My brother puts his hands on my back and pushes.
The swing surges forward.
Harder and harder he pushes.
Higher and higher I soar.
The wind blows my hair, whips it over face and arms.
He pushes harder.
I soar higher.
My muscles relax.
My stomach calms.
I begin to tingle all over.
My hands feel weak; so hard to hold on.
I feel like a bird in a cage. I know I can fly if I can just
free myself from this restraint.
My head feels light.
My body feels light.
I open my eyes.
I see my mother. She is running towards me. Her eyes are wide.
She is screaming. Her arms reach for me.
I smile
because it is too late.
My hands fall from the chains.
I am free from my cage.

I begin to fly.
I glide on the air with ease.
I am joined by the flying things of the world: flower petals,
leaves, seeds, sea spray, raindrops, and snowflakes. All
birds and insects, too.
We all float slowly and softly on the wind like dust particles
caught in beams of sunlight.
The motion of the swing has stopped,
but
my flight
      will
         last
           forever.

Jennifer Hubenthal

As you can see, archetypal images hold great power of inspiration for the inner writer, becoming accessible to us through plumbing the depths of our Design mind, thereby retrieving and reinterpreting those images which are significant for us in very profound ways.

Art As a Source of Images

In Chapter 5 we used a work of art to generate a dominant impression that, when put into words, served as your nucleus, which in turn was clustered to trigger a trial-web shift to your own discovered meaning. In this chapter we will focus on the visual images of a painting or sculpture to stimulate our Design mind to re-create our own personal images in words.

The complex wholeness of a work of art, like a face, strongly appeals to the Design mind. As we gain experience in responding to art images, we increase the Design mind's sensitivity to the expressiveness and emotional qualities of another human being's creation. According to poet/critic C. Day Lewis, the images of natural writing, like the inspiration for a painting or a sculpture, arise out of a demand of the Design mind to give form to an idea or feeling it wishes to convey. The writer "wishes to get something off his mind . . . a complex of memories which have clustered together unconsciously" and which demand expression.

IMAGES:
INNER EYE DIRECTING
WRITING HAND

Because all forms of artistic expression may be said to arise from this same impulse to give form to a Design-mind vision, art images serve as a strong stimulus to natural writing. In the process we become active participants in the creation of new meanings from those images.

The practice of using the images of art for one's own expressive purposes is an old one; many writers have transformed their own vision of a painting into a poem, short story, or novel. The poem by contemporary poet Donald Finkel was inspired by Katsushika Hokusai's early-nineteenth-century painting, *The Great Wave* (Figure 8-5).

Figure 8–5

KATSUSHIKA HOKUSAI (1760–1849), *THE GREAT WAVE AT KANAGAWA,* COURTESY OF THE METROPOLITAN MUSEUM OF ART, THE HOWARD MANSFIELD COLLECTION, ROGERS FUND.

The Great Wave: Hokusai
It is because the sea is blue,
Because Fuji is blue, because the
bent blue
Men have white faces, like the
snow
On Fuji, like the crest of the wave
in the sky the color of their
Boats. It is because the air
Is full of writing, because the wave
is still: that nothing
Will harm these frail strangers,
That high over Fuji in an earthcol-
ored sky the fingers
Will not fall; and the blue men
Lean on the sea like snow, and the
wave like a mountain leans
Against the sky.

In the painter's sea
All fishermen are safe. All anger
bends under his unity.
But the innocent bystander, he
merely
'Walks round a corner, thinking of
nothing': hidden
Behind a screen we hear his cry.
He stands half in and half out of
the world; he is the men,
But he cannot see below Fuji
The shore the color of sky; he is
the wave, he stretches
His claws against strangers. He is
Not safe, not even from himself.
His world is flat.
He fishes a sea full of serpents, he
rides his boat
Blindly from wave to wave toward
Ararat.

Donald Finkel

Now that you have read the poem, look at the painting again. In the first stanza we are bombarded with the poet's detailed observations: "the sea is blue," "Fuji is blue," "the bent blue/men have white faces," Fuji has snow, the crest of the wave is white. Then the poet shifts our consciousness to the fact that the painting is illusion: "the wave is still" and so, because it cannot fall, "in the painter's sea/all fishermen are safe."

The second stanza shifts our attention to the "observer," who comes upon the painting unexpectedly; the illusion of mortal danger overwhelms him as he identifies with the men one moment, the threatening wave the next. The painting fills him with existential terror, for it depicts a world in which "he is/not safe, not even from himself." We are left with the sense that our imagination creates the illusions we come to fear—and so we fish a "sea full of serpents" that in reality do not exist.

The quality of your response to a work of art depends on your ability to shift to Design-mind knowing. The Design mind, as we saw in the chapter on the brain, is better at scanning the painting for an overall impression than is the Sign mind, which wants to look at detail. Shift to your Design mind by scanning the whole painting and allowing a dominant impression to surface. Acknowledge this strong feeling by giving it a name.

Once you have your nucleus, explore the painting leisurely, clustering what you see, clustering what and how you feel, what you imagine—in short, any and all associations the artwork evokes. In so doing, your Design mind responds to the richness and resonance of the images, exploring patterns, relationships, context. As you begin writing, you become an active participant in creating meaning for yourself and your reader, transforming the visual image into patterns of your own.

Here is how a student writer responded to Hokusai's *The Great Wave.* As you can see in Figure 8–6, his dominant impression was (DREAMLIKE) .

His cluster—as clustering often does—exhibits a self-organizing thrust, as if the Design mind were already creating patterns of its own. As you read the subsequent vignette, you will also see that, as this student began to write, new connections came to the fore that were not in the original cluster.

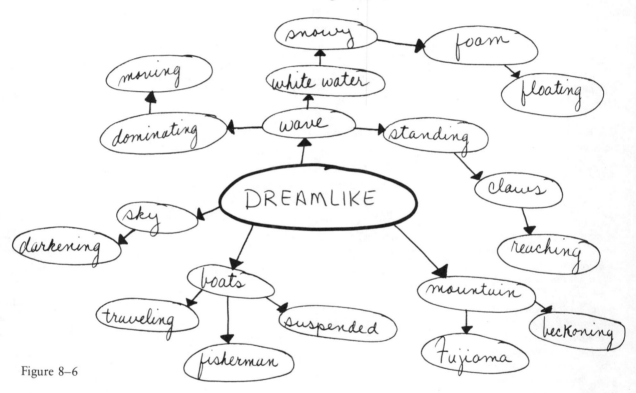

Figure 8–6

To suspend yourself in Hokusai's *The Great Wave* is to put yourself in a dreamlike state, for it contains many of the paradoxical qualities found in a dream.

The whole painting is unreal, yet more real than reality itself. The wave, boats, and men seem to be moving, yet simultaneously standing still. The sky gets darker as it gets closer to the horizon, with Mt. Fuji way in the distance, as if to beckon the dreamer.

The waves and ocean are topped by a whitewater which seems to float, detached from the body of water. The crest of the wave seems to be a collection of many claws, reaching to grab the fishermen, yet never quite reaching them.

Everything happening: the wave reaching, the fishermen rowing, Mount Fuji beckoning, seem to work cooperatively in the unfolding of a great destiny; the destiny is itself a paradox: The fishermen following their own will, yet blindly following fate and the forces of nature; the ocean and wave a spontaneous force yet all within the ordered will of God; the mountain a sign of steadiness amidst turmoil, yet too passing away.

Dreams are our own code of life symbols. When we awaken, we find those same symbols. Do we really know dreams from reality?

"Dreamlike" was this writer's dominant impression, and he developed this focus carefully by choosing simple, clear images from the painting, which reflect his impression of unreality:

- wave/boats/men move, yet simultaneously stand still
- Fuji is in the distance as if to beckon the dreamer
- The crest is a collection of many claws grabbing but not reaching
- waves reach
- fishermen row

His language rhythms naturally achieve richness and compression through parallel and balanced sentences:

Parallel

- "wave, boats, and men"
- Everything happening: the wave reaching, the fishermen rowing, Mt. Fuji beckoning

Balanced

- "The whole painting is unreal, yet more real than reality itself."
- "The fishermen following their own will, yet blindly following fate . . ."
- ". . . the ocean and wave a spontaneous force yet all within the ordered . . ."
- ". . . the mountain a sign of steadiness amidst turmoil, yet too passing away."

Recurrences thread their way to unify the whole:

·   dream/dreamlike/dreams
·   wave, boats, men (several times)
·   unreal/real/reality/really
·   yet . . . (underscores the paradoxical qualities of the dreamlike state of the painting)

Full-circle wholeness is achieved by reference to dreams at beginning and end.

Let's see what happens when you experience your own Design-mind involvement with a sculpture.

Directing Your Hand

Using photographs of the bronze and rock sculpture *Homo-chronos* by Greg Hill (Figures 8–7 A and B), create your own images in words.

1. Begin by relaxing and letting your eyes sweep over the entire sculpture, encompassing all angles, as if you could move around it and see it in three dimensions. A sculpture can be scanned by your Design mind in microseconds. Be alert for a dominant impression. Usually your first response will be most authentic and most telling. Trust it.
2. Put that impression into words, which constitute your nucleus.
3. Now explore the painting further by clustering what you see, feel, interpret, associate—in short, anything that comes to your Design mind. Recall that the very nonlinearity of clustering tends to shut down your Sign mind's logical, sequential, "scholarly" processes, allowing your Design mind free play, at least for the moment. Enjoy this play.
4. Watch for the trial-web shift, which always comes, signaling your sense of direction.
5. When you experience it, shift to Sign-mind process by writing a clear focusing statement.

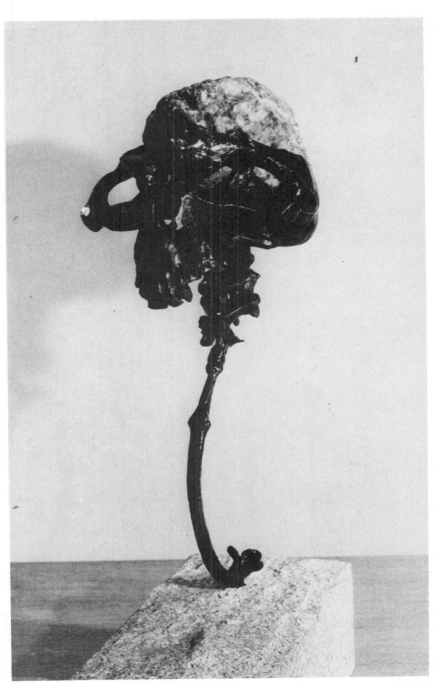

Figure 8–7(A)

GREG HILL, *HOMOCHRONOS*, COURTESY OF THE SCULPTOR.

IMAGES:
INNER EYE DIRECTING
WRITING HAND

Figure 8–7(B) GREG HILL, *HOMOCHRONOS*, COURTESY OF THE SCULPTOR.

6. Now begin writing, oscillating between global whole and emerging detail, thus eliciting both Sign- and Design-mind participation in this natural writing process. Allow your vignette to take any shape, be it prose or a free-verse poem.

7. Once you have finished, read your work aloud and look and listen for full-circle wholeness, recurrences, language rhythms, images. Quickly make any changes that contribute to the power of the whole.

After Writing

Very likely the strongest experience you had in doing this exercise was the sensation of intense involvement with an image, almost a sense of being pulled into it, participating in the feeling generated by the image. A second and perhaps unexpected experience may have been the way your writing took a certain shape, almost as if the sculpture, itself an image of someone else's making, were dictating the shape your words were taking.

A third discovery my students often report is the strong negative or positive pull an art image exerts. The ambivalence of *Homochronos* as an image may have caused you to perceive it as either negative, associating it with skulls and skeletons, or positive, associating it with brains and our visionary capability. The term *homochronos*, coined by philosopher Tobias Grether, actually means "time-conscious man." Time-consciousness fills us with uncertainty, uneasiness, restlessness, and we know the sculptor wished to render some of these qualities because he gave the work this title. A fourth discovery often has to do with the strange combination of bronze and rock, bronze suggesting skull-like hardness, and rock paradoxically suggesting the malleability and softness of the expanding human brain. In your own writing you rendered the qualities you perceived in the sculpture. The creative process is often a reinterpretive process, a variation on a theme of potentially infinite variations.

A Last Word and Heading On

*So the point of my keeping a note-
book has never been, nor is it now,
to have an accurate factual record
of what I have been doing or
thinking. . . . Perhaps it never did
snow that August in Vermont; perhaps there never were flurries in
the night wind, and maybe no one
else felt the ground hardening and
summer already dead even as we
pretended to bask in it, but that
was how it felt to me, and it might
as well have snowed, could have
snowed, did snow.*

How it felt to me: *that is getting
closer to the truth about a notebook.*

Joan Didion,
"On Keeping a Notebook"

As plentiful as images are, many of them are fragile, fleeting, insub-
stantial, for they are Design-mind associations, flashes of insight often
connected to emotional nuances we but half understand. To cultivate
your natural writer, you must not only be receptive to the images of
both your waking and dreaming worlds but also record them in clusters in your writer's notebook lest they fade and disappear. Transformed into vignettes, they may constitute some of your most meaningful writing.

Capturing these elusive images is precisely Joan Didion's reason
for keeping a notebook, as explained in her essay "On Keeping a
Notebook" (in *Slouching Towards Bethlehem*):

An accurate factual record is a sequential Sign-mind effort, and
is appropriate in certain instances; but to render "flurries in the night
wind," "the ground hardening," pretending to bask in a summer already signaling the winter to come, is a patterning Design-mind
awareness in which the writer goes beyond the given, the actual, the
factual. And so, for Joan Didion, "it might as well have snowed,
could have snowed, did snow."

When such images of snow and hardening of the ground and
snow flurries are connected to and equated with something radically
dissimilar, we get metaphor, which depends on the Design mind's
ability to process these complex and nonlogical connections. Thus
this chapter on images leads naturally to the next chapter on metaphor, for metaphor can come into being only through the mediation
of images and can be understood only by connecting Design-mind
image to Sign-mind idea.

CHAPTER 9/ *Wedding Word to Image: Metaphor*

In F. Scott Fitzgerald's *The Great Gatsby,* Gatsby, referring to the wealthy Daisy, tells the narrator:

> "Her voice is full of money."
>
> That was it. I'd never understood before. It was full of money—that was the inexhaustible charm that rose and fell in it, the jingle of it, the cymbals' song of it. . . .

Fitzgerald could have written "Daisy gives the impression of being very rich," but the author's metaphor goes far beyond the givens of literal language to resonate and suggest, creating shock waves of deeper meaning.

Metaphor consists of images connected to something they literally cannot be. Literally speaking, a voice cannot be full of money, yet the fusing of these dissimilar entities into one new image tells us something about Daisy's personality that is inexpressible in denotative language. Metaphors create tension and excitement by producing new connections, and in so doing reveal a truth about the world we had not previously recognized.

Images, as we have seen, are word pictures that give language power and richness by involving our senses in the experience. When an image is wedded to something totally unexpected, we produce a new pattern—metaphor—that creates a powerful picture for us. For example, if an instructor told a skier, "The mountain is a dish of vanilla ice cream and you are hot fudge—flow down the slope" (as Denise McCluggage did in her book, *The Centered Skier*), the skier would have an image of gliding and connectedness that would convey something important about a skier's proper relationship to a hill. Consider the Sign-mind alternative, which might go something like this:

> Now plant the pole on your right, then swing your body and skis around it, keeping your skis parallel and shifting your weight to the downhill ski as you go into the turn. Ski downhill a few yards to gain momentum, skis parallel, and then plant your pole on the left; swing around your pole, paying attention to the parallel of your skis, and then shift your weight to your right, the downhill ski.

Of course, the mountain is *not* ice cream and a person is *not* hot fudge, yet that advice communicates the proper feel of skiing, the sense of a whole fluid movement, more directly than a sequence of technically correct instructions can.

This chapter offers yet another aspect of natural writing: the Design mind's ability to make fresh connections, to see, hear, and feel metaphorically. This will bring additional dimension to your evolving writing capabilities and help in training your thinking in Design-mind ways. Metaphor generates new means of expression when the conventional or denotative will not suffice, thus extending your power over language and expanding your inherent creative potential. Since each of us has the natural potential for making connections and seeing relationships in our own unique way, metaphor-making is a highly personal, richly creative phenomenon.

An experiment with split-brain patients described by Robert Nebes (in *The Human Brain*, edited by Merle Wittrock) underscores the Design mind's metaphoric view of the world, contrasting it with the Sign mind's stolidly logical view. A picture of a round cake on a plate is flashed on a screen to a split-brain patient's right visual field, which feeds into the logical left brain. The patient is then instructed to choose an object from a large array that is pictured with the cake. The left brain invariably makes a logical choice, such as a knife or fork, for naturally you need the one to cut the cake with, the other to eat it with. But when the same round cake on a plate is flashed to the patient's left visual field, which feeds into the right brain, the patient invariably chooses—a round straw hat with a brim! Perceiving similarity of shape in dissimilar things is certainly not logical, but it strikes us as ingenious—and that is the power of metaphor: to surprise us, make us catch our breath, illuminate an aspect of the world that is totally at odds with the conventional way of seeing it.

In Chapter 4 I described Sign-mind thinking as computerlike. In a government-funded automatic-language-translation project, experimenters discovered that even the most elaborate computer is utterly baffled by fairy tales and metaphors. In asking a computer to translate "The spirit is willing, but the flesh is weak" from English to Russian and then back to English, it came up with "The wine is agreeable, but the meat has spoiled." When given the proverb "Out of sight, out of mind," the computer decided it meant "Blind and crazy." We can get beyond the literal and conventional only through Design-mind participation.

Let me use another visual illustration. In Figure 9–1 you see a pair of bicycle handlebars; in Figure 9–2 you see a bicycle seat. When you logically process these two objects with Sign-mind expectations, you see the parts and think "bicycle." But if, like Picasso, you see from a Design-mind perspective, bicycle handlebars and bicycle seat do not add up to bicycle, but rather to the head of a bull (Figure 9–3). For Picasso, the literal bicycle parts coalesced and were transformed into something each was literally not: the seat was not a head, nor the handlebars horns. Yet, combined, the two elements created a strong new image that cast each element in a new light.

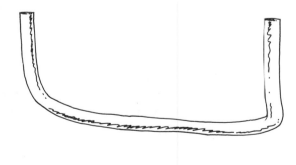

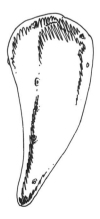

Figure 9–1

Figure 9–2

*WEDDING
WORD TO IMAGE:
METAPHOR*

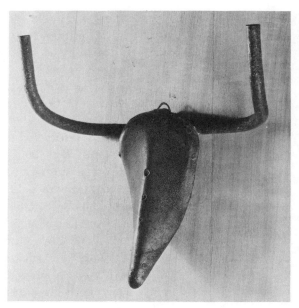

Figure 9–3

PABLO PICASSO, *TÊTE DE TAUREAU*,
© SPADEM, PARIS/VAGA, NEW YORK, 1982.

Picasso's bicycle bull is a visual metaphor. Let us turn now to linguistic metaphor, which is equally grounded in image and which graces all potent writing.

Metaphor: A Bilinguist for the Brain

Linguistic metaphor is simultaneously sign and design, and, as a consequence, it has the power to connect our two modes of knowing. Denise McCluggage, in *The Centered Skier,* suggests that metaphor is a "bilinguist" for the brain, drawing on the power of both hemispheres: verbal for the left and image for the right. When we use a metaphor, she says, a spark arcs from Design to Sign mind, making a connection. The metaphor as image resonates in the right brain with pictures, or complex wholes, which the left hemisphere expresses in words that imply a similarity in dissimilarity; in joining word and image, a sudden illumination takes place, a perception or insight that sheds new light on a familiar feeling/idea/event. For example, in *Second Skin* novelist John Hawkes describes a scream as a black bat, telling us something new about the character and quality of a scream by joining unexpected image to idea.

The scream . . . that was clamped between my teeth was a strenuous black bat struggling, wrestling in my bloated mouth and . . . I, with my eyes squeezed tight, my lips squeezed tight, felt that at any moment it must thrust the slimy black tip of its archaic skeletal wing into view.

John Hawkes,
Second Skin

*There are techniques that can help
us name our dreams and dragons.
They are designed to reopen the
bridge between right and left to
through traffic, to increase the left
brain's awareness of its counterpart. Metaphor builds a bridge between the hemispheres, symboli-
cally carrying knowledge from the
mute right brain so that it may be
recognized by the left as being like
something already known.*
Marilyn Ferguson,
The Aquarian Conspiracy

Metaphor does not substitute for Sign-mind meanings, but adds to those meanings by articulating Design-mind perceptions. In so doing, metaphor enormously expands our ordinary resources for both perception and expression. We have to *perceive* a similarity in dissimilar entities before we can articulate it, a talent we have possessed since childhood. In natural writing, we need only reawaken these perceptions.

Childhood Origins of Metaphor

Children learning language create meaning by grasping a relationship between a new experience and past experiences already coded and stored in the brain. If, when you were small, your existing repertoire did not fit a new situation, you tended to generate metaphors—or their first cousin, simile. (Both metaphor and simile originate in the ability to perceive similarity in dissimilarity; the difference is that simile has "pointers"—*like* or *as*—to explicitly signal that we are joining logically unjoinable entities. Metaphor dispenses with these pointers, simply asserting a likeness between two unlike things, thus making a metaphor richer, more open-ended, more resonant.) In *Language and Learning*, British scholar James Britton gives an account of how this works. Presented with the first strawberries of her life, his two-and-a-half-year-old daughter examined them and said: "They are like cherries." As she tasted them, she said, "They are just like sweeties [candies]." Then she summed it up: "They are like red ladybirds." To bring novel experience into meaningful focus, she borrowed qualities already familiar to her—qualities of redness, sweetness, roundness, and spottedness, from cherries, candies, and lady bugs—and applied them to strawberries. For this child, new meaning emerged with this metaphoric play.

Thus children in the stage of the innocent eye, ear, and hand make metaphors because they don't as yet have sufficient fixed and literal terms for all the ideas they want to express; they substitute words and concepts they do know. Once when I was playing gin rummy with my five-year-old, Suzi, she asked in all seriousness, "Mom, in a run, do all the cards have to be the same sex?" In due time she learned the proper—albeit less imaginative—word *suit*.

In my own study of children's metaphoric abilities, I found not only the metaphoric responses came easily and naturally but that these responses were derived primarily from the shapes of the images they conjured up. Four-year-old Simone, for example, readily answered questions metaphorically as each object was pointed out to her:

What is that star like?	It's like a flower without a stem.
What is the moon like?	It's like a smiling mouth.
What is your shoe like?	It's like a little boat.
What is your nose like?	It's like a tiny, tiny hill.
What are my eyebrows like?	They're like two bridges over two swimming pools.

In contrast, children in the stage of the conventional eye, ear, and hand created virtually no metaphors. As the following examples from nine- to eleven-year-olds show, they tend to respond either with rudimentary definitions or the overly familiar.

What is this book like?	It's like reading about something: a lot of words.
What is this TV like?	A movie screen that is close up.
What is this mirror like?	A weird piece of glass; something that makes another of you.
What is this star like?	A light in the distance.
What is the sun like?	A big ball of fire burning in the sky.
What is the moon like?	A shining piece of something in the atmosphere; a big glowing thing in the sky.

As our repertoire of fixed and reliable Sign-mind categories increases, our metaphoric power seems to diminish and we readily observe the boundaries imposed by the literal-minded and formal education. And perhaps necessarily so, for we have to learn to function in a world in which shared and conventional Sign-mind systems are the prime means of communication and expression. The sad and limiting thing is to get stuck there without the tools necessary to move into the third stage—the cultivated eye, ear, and hand of the natural writer.

Yet, even though our metaphor-making has been somewhat eclipsed by constant exposure to the literal use of language, none of us is purely literal-minded. When we dream, we naturally make metaphors. In my dreams, for example, the house images that have recurred again and again seem to be metaphors for my life and perhaps, even more specifically, for my psyche; the unfamiliar rooms I opened with curiosity and wonder were parts of me I was just discovering.

When we are stuck for words to describe accurately what we mean, we say, "You know, it's like . . ." or "Well, it's as if . . ." or "It feels as though. . . ." Not finding in our Sign mind what we need to express a thought or feeling, we shift to Design-mind images to help us out and, in articulating them, we make metaphors.

This tiny poem by W. S. Merwin creates an unforgettable metaphor that requires little commentary.

Absence
Your absence has gone through me
Like thread through a needle.
Everything I do is stitched with its color.

The expressive power of natural writing lies in the ability to reawaken our talent for metaphor-making. If we speak and write with only our left brain, without this reawakening, we tend to sound like Northrop Frye's insistently literal scholar.

As you relearn a feel for the more playful Design-mind connection, you will come to realize that any word, any idea, any subject can be processed literally or nonliterally. Recall Peter, the right-brain damaged patient described in Chapter 4 who verbalized fluently with his intact left hemisphere, but only as long as the demands made on him required literal language. As soon as he was asked to respond to the meaning of the proverb "Too many cooks spoil the broth," he was unable, without his Design-mind skills, to go beyond the literal in order to perceive implied meanings.

But for those whose brains are intact, success with images and metaphors depends on whether the Design mind is allowed to get into the act. Clustering, once again, is the key to effect a conscious shift to nonliteral Design-mind processing. Get past the literal and your Design mind will produce images that can be transformed into metaphor.

. . . listening to a speech by a high authority in the field, I know him to be a good scholar, a dedicated servant of society, and an admirable person. Yet his speech is a muddy river of clichés. . . . The content of the speech does not do justice to his mind: what it does reflect is the state of his literary education. . . . He has never been trained to visualize his abstractions, to subordinate logic and sequence to the insights of metaphor and simile, to realize that figures of speech are not ornaments of language, but the elements of both language and thought. . . . Once again, nothing can now be done for him: there are no courses in remedial metaphor.

Northrop Frye,
The Educated Imagination

WEDDING
WORD TO IMAGE:
METAPHOR

Before you direct your own hand in writing metaphoric vignettes, let's practice by using the simplest, most natural way of developing metaphoric insight: perceiving similarity between shapes.

Seeing Shapes into Things

Seeing an animal shape in a fluffy cloud has shown you the pleasure and illumination of metaphoric insight. The secret of metaphor lies in letting the quality of your attention shift from Sign- to Design-mind processes. Sign mind says: "Yes, a cloud—cumulus, I think," while the Design mind sees a profile of Abraham Lincoln.

As already noted, the visible trigger to the shift lies in the little words "like" or "as." As soon as we say one thing is *like* another, we are letting go of Sign-mind insistence on the literal; it gives us license to compare apparently unlike things. For example, in this phrase by poet Nils Peterson—"our bodies wait patient *as* horses"—*as* tends to block the bossy, logical Sign-mind policeman to give metaphoric insights a chance to surface. True metaphor dispenses with these signposts, further extending and deepening the potency of an image projected on a thing or idea, as in another Peterson line: "Those masters gone they turn,/nuzzle, and flank to flank speak to each other." In simile, bodies are compared to horses; in metaphor those bodies have *become* horses.

Now read Nils Peterson's poem and see how he extends his initial simile into a sustained metaphor.

> *Bedtime*
>   —for Judith—
> If we have quarreled our bodies wait
> patient as horses for their owners' huffy
> departure. Those masters gone they turn,
> nuzzle, and flank to flank speak
> to each other all night long
> the eloquent touching language of the dumb.

For our purposes, we will make no further distinction between simile and metaphor. Both figures of speech serve the same end—to shift to nonliteral ways of seeing, thus giving our writing richer texture and greater expressive power.

Directing Your Hand

Let's see what happens when you are confronted with an object your Sign mind cannot readily identify.

1. Look at the object in Figure 9–4, designed by Glenda Bogen.

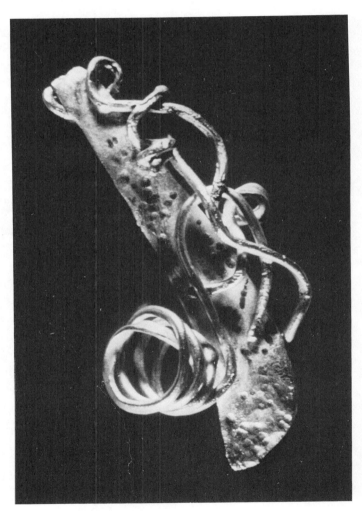

Figure 9–4   GLENDA BOGEN, *UNTITLED*, COURTESY OF THE SCULPTOR.

2. First, name it literally if you can: call it a "thing" or an "object" or a "pendant" or a "sculpture," or whatever you think it *literally* is. Jot down this Sign-mind response in your writer's notebook.

3. Now cluster this literal name, adding "like," as the nucleus: THIS OBJECT IS LIKE . . .

4. Take three to five minutes to scrutinize the object and jot down any insights as to what it is *like*. Don't censor. Let yourself play, even be outrageous to the point that some of your associations might seem absurd; you don't need to claim those later. Right now simply be curious to find out what your Design mind sees in that shape. Squint at it; look at it sideways, say aloud to yourself, "That thing is like a _____." Something will come, and that something will make other associations come. Sooner or later your will have generated a number of metaphoric responses, several of which are sure to give you pleasure and satisfaction.

After Writing

To see how individual an act metaphor-making is, you might try this exercise with friends to see what they come up with. In one of my classes, one student insisted he could never create a metaphor. To demonstrate to him—and the class—that metaphor-making was within reach of *everyone,* I took off the pendant you have just clustered. Each student handled it, and then we clustered on the board with the following composite results.

The pendant is like:

· the cross of the lives of two snakes and the path of fate upon which they are meeting.
· a man's tie whose owner had been eating spaghetti, spilling it all over himself.
· a snake coiled around a woman.
· a woman wrapped in a feather boa.
· a sword cutting an octopus.
· a very old sword that has been found on the beach, entangled in seaweed.
· a saxophone which seems to vibrate and come alive like the music that comes out of it.
· an oar with the water from a lake swirling against it and around it.

- a broken ski with the ski bindings coming apart after a downhill race.
- an overstressed person in need of an Alka Seltzer.
- a hurricane hitting the coast of Florida.
- a baseball pitcher about to toss the ball to first base; the bound-up wire is the dust rising up after the runner ran to first base.
- a toothless comb snagged in hair.
- a treble clef on a musical staff line.

Which of these metaphors especially lights a flare of recognition in you? Recognizing a metaphor enables you to leap beyond the essential privacy of the experiential process. If any of the metaphors listed above struck you enough to say "That's right! It *does* resemble a _____," your Design mind has made that leap of recognition only it is uniquely capable of.

The next step in involving your Design mind is to create multiple metaphors within one sentence.

Metaphor Madness

If one metaphor packs punch because it delivers a potent image in a new context, several metaphors piled on top of each other can intensify this effect. Let the humorous sentence from Raymond Chandler serve as a model for your own series of likenesses.

Each of the images Chandler uses communicates something about the dreadful state the "I" of the sentence is in and yet, because of the series of unlikely comparisons, the total impact makes us laugh.

Directing Your Hand

Using Chandler's sentence as a model, play with multiple metaphors to make a humorous point. Record it in your writer's notebook.

1. Quick-cluster, using one of the phrases in Figure 9–5 or make up your own nucleus phrase along similar lines.

I was dizzy as a dervish, as weak as a worn-out washer, as low as a badger's belly, as timid as a titmouse, and as unlikely to succeed as a ballet dancer with a wooden leg.

Raymond Chandler,
The Little Sister

Figure 9–5

2. Play. Let go. Don't censor. Remember, a cluster is not cast in concrete—you can always eliminate the silly-sounding, the trite, or the clichéd when it is time to put your similes together according to the model sentence. You might play with images resulting from an activity you know well: carpentry, horseback riding, jogging, dancing, cooking. And don't forget the possibility of recurring sounds and language rhythms. Your cluster will give you choices from which you can select the most effective. Stop quick-clustering when you've come up with enough images to make fresh rather than hackneyed connections.

3. Now put your sentence together from your quick-clustered images. Choose whatever feels right, is comfortable, and fits the whole.

4. Read the results aloud and make any changes that will make the language more humorous or more evocative.

After Writing

Below are examples of my students' modeling using Raymond Chandler's sentence to develop their own focus.

Life was as touchy as a step-mother, as unwanted as a wart, as dull as a dorm during winter recess, as frustrating as impotence, and as unrewarding as an investment in the People's Temple.

My brain was as dead as a used battery, naked as a plucked chicken, dormant as a dried pea, and as empty as Old Mother Hubbard's cupboard when I searched it for the answers to the exam.

She was as ugly as a bullfrog, as clumsy as a pregnant cow, as skinny as a hemp thread, as colorless as an aged newspaper, and as uninteresting as a cadaver with an ingrown toenail.

I felt as faded as the paint job, as dented as the bumpers, as flat as the tire, as empty as the gas tank, and as cooperative as the ignition which refused to do anything but groan.

I was as timid as the trembling aspen, as shrinking as a violet, as bashful as a pansy, as retiring as a forget-me-not, and as likely to be noticed as a daisy in a patch of daffodils.

I was as witty as Lewis Carroll, as crazy as the Mad Hatter, as transient as the Cheshire Cat, as hurried as the White Rabbit, and as completely perplexed as Alice in Wonderland.

I was as happy as a cat in a cream pitcher, as smug as a rat in a delicatessen, as silly as a penguin playing the piano, and as unlikely to succeed as a rooster with laryngitis.

I was as fierce as a fiend, as sardonic as Scrooge, as bloodthirsty as a vampire, as abrasive as a scrap of sandpaper, and as callous as a cannibal about to devour his children.

I was as frazzled as an old shoe lace, as frayed as a worn toothbrush, as ragged as a flag in a hurricane, as fizzled as a bottle of champagne, and as unlikely to succeed as a traveling salesman in a wheelchair.

If you explore the images in each of these sentences, you will notice that the writers used different connecting strategies to achieve wholeness. For example, one writer concentrated on images from *Alice in Wonderland* as a focus; another discovered variations on flowers for hers; yet another played with car images for his; several others focused on animal resemblances; the last few focused on an appeal to the ear through recurrences of alliteration. All of them, however, had a distinctly discernible language rhythm based on parallel form that echoed the original model's emphasis on "dizzy as," "weak as," "low as," "timid as," and "unlikely as," having the cumulative effect of a tightly knit whole.

Metaphoric Transformations

As we've seen, metaphor makes nonordinary, nonlogical connections: the psychological with the physical—"Her voice is full of money"; the familiar with the unfamiliar—"that star is like a flower without a stem"; the strange with the commonplace—absence pierces "like thread through a needle." Each new connection has its source in the image-making Design mind but then draws on the Sign mind to articulate and perhaps analyze the connection.

Every time we think of ourselves as an oak tree rooted forever to one spot (a Design-mind image), we expand the truth of what we are in literal, classifiable reality. I am a teacher, a woman, a taxpayer, a mother, a writer, among other things. But how do I express something of the qualitative aspects of myself that are not contained in the literal description of what I am? Well, I might express myself metaphorically through qualities I see myself having in common with nature—an oak tree—or with an animal, such as a cat.

Metaphoric connections with animals are familiar to us from childhood. We surround our children with stuffed animals, tell animal stories, give animal nicknames: Tiger, Kitten, Little Bear. We give our children "horsie rides" and carry them "piggyback." At root, animal metaphors are fundamental images linking qualitative aspects of the human and animal domains, thereby enabling us to learn—as well as to express—something about ourselves. Writing metaphorically about yourself enhances your creative and imaginative powers and makes your writing more graceful, incisive, and memorable.

Directing Your Hand

I recently heard of a San Francisco executive whose key question to prospective employees at the management level consisted of asking them, "If you had the chance of becoming an animal, which animal would you choose to be?" The choice, he maintains, was a better indicator of that person's potential within the company than were all the details of a conventional résumé.

You suddenly have the option of becoming an animal in a second life. Write about yourself in the context of that choice.

1. In your writer's notebook, precluster ⟨ANIMAL⟩ , allowing you to discover all the options your Design mind spills out.

2. Now cluster the animal of your choice, spilling as many associations as you can, including qualities you associate with it (for example, fierceness, timidity) as well as its physical aspects; don't forget possible references to proverbs, stories, lines of songs, whatever comes.

3. In order to clarify this animal's relationship to yourself, do a second cluster with ⟨ME⟩ as nucleus. Focus on associations about yourself, keeping the animal cluster in mind. Continue to cluster until you experience the trial-web shift, which will probably occur with some sudden connective insight relating your chosen animal to your personality; you will experience a kind of metaphoric leap.

4. Record two or three focusing statements, initiating the shift to Sign-mind participation. Then choose the one statement that is most meaningful for you to develop.

5. As you begin writing, use the first person—that is, *be* the animal. Do not write "If I were . . ."; write "I am. . . ." Your objective is to write the vignette as though you *are* the animal while still letting relevant aspects of your personality show through.

6. As you write, keep in mind such Design-mind processes as coming full circle (how do you begin and end?). Reach for recurrences (what is going to be your dominant thread? A word? A phrase? An aspect of your animal?). Also keep in mind parallel rhythms, alliteration, and images in all their multisensory aspects.

7. Now read aloud what you've written with a sense of the whole in mind. Cross out whatever doesn't fit and rewrite anything that jars your aesthetic sense. When you're satisfied, you may wish to recopy the vignette.

After Writing

This exercise is meant to be a discovery process. Chances are that writing metaphorically about yourself as an animal gave you some surprising glimpses you don't ordinarily see of yourself—aspects both positive and negative. A human being is variable and highly complex, but an animal is thought of as stable in terms of its positive and negative qualities. According to Jung, an animal stands for the unconscious areas of the human psyche. Your Design-mind thinking can easily accommodate the ambiguous, the paradoxical, layers of counterpoint in meaning. Identifying yourself with an animal represents an integration of the unconscious with the conscious, affording you new insight into your personality.

With respect to the Design-mind strategies developed in this book, by now you should always be conscious of them as options; that is, all the techniques you have learned don't have to appear in each vignette, but some of them should find their way into your writing every time. They make your writing more rhythmic, more focused, more intensely sensuous, more direct and honest.

If you felt the metaphoric transformation into an animal shape valuable, perhaps exhilarating, try additional variations. For example, become an object such as a mirror or an electron; become a vegetable such as a potato or a cauliflower; become an object in nature—a stream or wind; become a utensil—a pot or a knife; or become an instrument related to your profession—a pen or a piano or a trowel. Play with these metaphorical transformations, surprise yourself into unexpected insights—and discover new dimensions of your inner writer.

Figure 9–6 is a beginning writer's metaphoric vignette. From the self-organizing process inherent in clustering, a pattern emerges around three qualities of the animal of this writer's choosing.

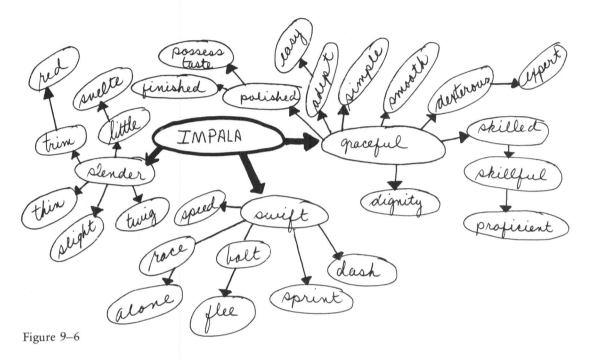

Figure 9–6

Content to Be Alone

I am an impala: slender, graceful, fast. Effortlessly, I glide about the plains and leap among the perilous rocks; powerful my stride, smooth my every maneuver, elegant the carriage of my svelte frame.

My slenderness enables me to move quickly, quietly, qualmlessly. I exhibit a nobility which could not be shown by a more fleshy animal.

I outrace, out-dash, outsprint all my fellow inhabitants of the heights or plains. I enjoy the freedom of flying with the din at my back. I am in a world of my own. I enjoy companionship, but I don't need it. My goals keep me occupied and content. I am lithe, adept, reaching: I am a racer—and a loner.

Jeremy Adams

The writing of this student is spare and to the point, using parallel rhythms almost to excess. But in making this metaphoric relation between himself and something he is not, he reveals an interesting psychological truth about himself and sheds light on the qualities of the animal as well. We perceive both more clearly as a result of the metaphor.

Making Feelings Tangible Through Metaphor

The next step in developing your metaphoric capacities involves making the elusive world of feelings tangible through Design-mind participation. Metaphoric equivalences of a state of mind can often make feelings come to life. Take "sadness," for instance. It encompasses a multitude of sensations, all qualitatively different for each of us. The dictionary tells us sadness is "a melancholy state of mind," but that Sign-mind definition does not tell us much about the different nuances and flavors of each individual's experience of it. Accordingly, a lot of us reach for clichés—metaphors or similes that have lost their impact from indiscriminate overuse: broken-hearted, blue, down in the dumps, in a funk, at sea, mad at the world; we have all seen these in bad novels. But fresh perceptions of a state of sadness will make us sit up and take notice because they flash a flare of recognition in us.

Read poet Al Young's "There Is a Sadness." He uses metaphoric equivalances to re-create for us his perception of sadness, immeasurably enriching our own perceptions of that feeling.

> *There Is a Sadness*
> There is a sadness to this world
> There is a grimness
> a nastiness in the throat
> a foulness of breath
> a slackening of the penis into sorrow
> a chill in the bloodstream that hurts
> —limitations of fleshhood!
>   pain of becoming!
> In a spasm of forgetfulness
> the seed is sown
> There is a ragged edge of my life
> a shabby contour
> rounding down into nowhere,
> the rainyness of wanting
> I might well have known
> wrestling by the woodstove
> in Red Clay Mississippi

There is a tumbling
from noplace to noplace
& there is a crumbling
from nothing to zero,
a journey from germ to germ again
in which the soul travels nowhere
There is such thing as soul,
I have felt it & can feel it moving
within myself & others
in spite of ourselves,
the stolen landscapes we frequent
the caverns of doubt in which we hide
There is such thing as life &
it is not this bleak intermission
during which I scurry for bread & lodging
or judge myself by my failures

O there is a shadowy side of my house
where old dreams harbor
where longings go up in smoke
where a cold & ugly opposite of love
is burning under the sun.

Sadness, for Al Young, is not the pale shadow of the dictionary definition, but a painful litany of events so rich that occasionally we draw in a sudden breath of recognition from his powerful use of images-made-metaphors of sadness: the "shadowy side of my house/where longings go up in smoke. Metaphor and image lead to writing that comes from the depths. Try it for yourself.

Directing Your Hand

In your writer's notebook, you're going to make a feeling come alive through metaphor.

1. Quickly precluster ⟨FEELINGS⟩ to bring into your immediate awareness the range of feelings we can experience. It is always interesting to see what feelings are spilled first—negative or positive, or a mixture of both.

2. Now choose the feeling that beckons you to explore it. Write down COURAGE IS . . . , for example, and then cluster whatever comes, particularly focusing on images of how that feeling looks, tastes, sounds, feels, smells. If you experience difficulty, don't give up; remember your link into metaphor: think of what courage is *like.*

3. Model the poem you are going to write on Al Young's poem, so simply cluster until you think you have enough metaphoric equivalences to shape a poem about half the length of Young's. When you think you have enough options, or you experience the trial-web shift to a sense of direction, begin writing.

4. Begin the poem with "There is a _____ to this _____" or "There is _____ in this _____," and shape your metaphors into an aesthetic whole. Remember to consider other strategies of natural writing: we have stressed recurrences, language rhythms, and especially images, for images lead you to the force-fit of similarity in dissimilarity that is metaphor: sadness is not literally a shadowy house nor is it literally a slackening penis, and yet these images become metaphors of how sadness affects the poet.

Look at Al Young's poem again and notice that the whole is composed of a series of metaphoric equivalences expressed in specific rhythms and peppered with recurrences in such a way that taking away even one word would detract from its aesthetic wholeness. This is the effect you're after.

After Writing

If you are dissatisfied with your first attempts, shift your metaphors around until the poem sounds right and whole when you read it aloud. This exercise is invaluable not only for the ability it offers you to create metaphors but, even more, for the intensity of expression you can generate using metaphors. Metaphor creates tension and drama in perceiving new relationships, and often expresses a truth we neither recognized nor had words for in our literal repertoire.

Modeling a Body Metaphor

Question
*Body my house
my horse my hound
what will I do
when you are fallen*

*Where will I sleep
How will I ride
What will I hunt*

*Where can I go
without my mount
all eager and quick
How will I know
in thicket ahead
is danger or treasure
when Body my good
bright dog is dead*

*How will it be
to lie in the sky
without roof or door
and wind for an eye*

*Without cloud for shift
how will I hide?*

                                    May Swenson

Whether we are aware of it or not, most of us think about our bodies metaphorically. For some, the body is a doormat, to be used and abused until it finally wears out; for others, the body is an adversary, always causing aches and pains and embarrassment—poet Delmore Schwartz saw his body as "this heavy bear that walks with me," always getting in the way of higher spiritual motives; for still others, the body is a friend to be cherished and treated gently. This sense of caring is expressed by May Swenson in her poem "Question."

This body—which is the poet's house, her horse, her hound—is loved so much that the overwhelming speculation at losing it simply trails off into a question: "How will I hide?"

How different are these metaphors from the flat clichés about the body and its sensations in commercial fiction: "my heart thumped in my chest"; "my stomach knotted in fear"; "my hands were clammy with anticipation."

The images you generate in thinking about your body will lead you to a metaphor that expresses your relationship with your body. Read, for example, this student vignette, modeled on Swenson's poem (Figure 9–7).

*Bon Voyage
My body, my berth,
my 3-masted bark,
sailing across the
sea of experience
lit by the beacon
of consciousness;
dependable vessel,
home of my spirit,
buffeted by the
high winds of time,
obedient to will—
A votre santé!*

                                    —Virginia Yauman

"My body" is a "3-masted bark"; the rest of the poem is devoted to telling us how that is so: it sails across the "sea of experience"; it is "lit by the beacon of consciousness"; the speaker feels affection for her body, for it is a "dependable vessel,/home of my

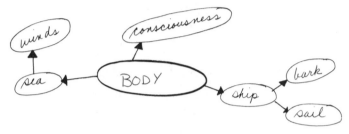

Figure 9–7

spirit." Even though the high winds of time "buffet" it as it ages, it nevertheless is "obedient to will." The final line—"to your health"—indicates an easy, supportive relationship between body and spirit, between the vessel and the owner of the vessel. The ship metaphor is even supported by the poem's title, "Bon Voyage": because the vessel is viewed as a friend, the trip through life on the sea of experience is perceived as highly positive. The upbeat language rhythms with its parallel forms support this friendly frame of mind.

Directing Your Hand

1. Precluster ⬭BODY⬭ for all the possible metaphors and images that might apply to the relationship you have with your body.
2. Choose one of those metaphors (or two or three complementary ones, as May Swenson did) and cluster it for more associations and detail until you experience the trial-web shift that will give you your sense of direction on how to approach this vignette.
3. Articulate your relationship with your body in a focusing statement that includes the metaphor you wish to develop.
4. Now write your vignette/poem, beginning with "Body, my . . ." or "My body, my. . . ." Toy with all the images related to the metaphor you wish to develop. Periodically reread the model poem.
5. When you have finished, read your vignette aloud. Rework it until you are satisfied with the developed metaphor and its rhythms.

After Writing

For some students this exercise is a revelation because they have never really thought about their relationship to their bodies in just such a way. The metaphors they create help to illuminate this relationship and provide them with a whole new way of seeing themselves with respect to their bodies.

A Last Word and Heading On

In this chapter you have enriched your latent potential for metaphor-making by drawing on the power of Design-mind images to perceive an aspect of your world in a new way and to articulate that perception through the awareness of similarity in dissimilarity. Each metaphor springs as a composite image from the Design mind's predilection for seeing pattern: when you walk in a forest, come across a burl of wood, and see it as a face, your Design mind has made a vital metaphoric association. What remains now is for your Sign mind to give it a name. In this way your language resources are infinitely extended and amplified and your writing will take on the dimensions of naturalness: power, clarity, grace, intensity, authenticity. Making metaphor is a highly creative act.

Without the insights of the cultivated eye, ear, and hand, our perceptions tend to be shaped and limited by familiar, everyday, conventional reality. Image and metaphor extend our world and let us see commonplace things in new ways, thus freeing our creative potential for writing naturally.

Just as metaphor opens up new and unexpected dimensions for natural writing, so does creative tension—the subject of Chapter 10—expand our options for drawing out our inner writer.

CHAPTER 10/ *Push/Pull: Creative Tension*

Philosopher Peter Koestenbaum insists that only when we accept the "dynamic tensions" of life can we mold this protean world into a meaning we can actually grasp:

> Each idea and each conviction gives rise to the truth of its opposite idea, belief, and conviction. That is because reality is polarized, is paradoxical, and contradictory. . . . All life oscillates, vibrates, and is symmetrical, with a right and a left side. All life is confrontation and the stress of opposites. If you want conflict removed, you are asking for the unnatural. . . . The conflict of polarity is the weight that moves the ocean's waves and the oceans' tides. Polarity is the cycles of the planets and of the seasons; it is the alternation between night and day, sleep and waking, tension and relaxation. You deal with polarity not by choosing between opposites but by riding and rocking with the swing of the cosmic dialectic. Reality, and life within it, is a dance, a conversation, a series of echoes; that is the meaning of being alive instead of dead. Your heart, as it pumps, knows that.

In this chapter we will explore ways to generate the simultaneous push and pull of creative tension in writing through the use of polarity, paradox, contraries, similar word pairs, and dialogue. Polarity, the father of creative tension, is a philosophical concept that literature, religion, art, and science have been obsessed with for centuries. Paradox, the child of polarity, is a linguistic construct by which we give expression to our polarized human existence. Through the exercises in this chapter, you will extend your awareness of life's polarities and learn to generate the creative tension that gives vitality to natural writing.

"Tension" does not refer to the anxiety you might feel when writing an essay exam or being interviewed for a job. The word comes from the Latin, *tensio,* meaning "stretched," as in "extension," a stretching out, a reaching for ways to join images, connect new patterns, reconcile opposites. Thus when I speak of creative tension, I mean the tensions you produce in your writing through oppositions, juxtapositions, and resolutions of seemingly contradictory ideas or feelings. The purpose of fostering creative tension is to evoke in you a kind of conceptual elasticity that will generate new combinations, not only to lend intensity and surprise to natural writing but also to help you regard seemingly irreconcilable opposites in a new light. In so doing, you will avail yourself of the possibility of new and unexpected patterns by taking from each opposite what is useful and reconciling it in your writing.

Albert Rothenberg, a psychiatrist and student of the creative process, calls the simultaneous recognition of opposites "Janusian thinking," after the Roman god Janus, whose two faces point in opposite directions. In Janusian thinking two or more opposites are conceived simultaneously as equally operative and valid. The study of physics shows us that, depending on how we look at it, light can appear sometimes as electromagnetic waves, sometimes as particles. This paradox was the thrust that led to the formulation of quantum theory, the basis of modern physics. The apparent contradiction between particle and wave images was solved in a completely unexpected way, which called into question the very foundation of the traditional mechanistic world view.

In written paradox—the deliberate statement of seeming impossibility—there is an emphasis on apparent absurdity that leads us to another way of seeing and thus to another level of truth. When Juliet calls Romeo "beautiful tyrant," logically we see the contradiction, but in the tension between the two words we understand Juliet's state of mind. On a deep level, such irreconcilable terms contain a common element of truth that demonstrates something more profound.

Prophets such as Christ frequently spoke in paradox to show

that truth is not obvious. The principal Christian paradox is that Christ died so that humankind might live. Professor David Pichaske defines paradox as the "schizophrenic presentation" of two or more possibilities, each of which has an equal claim to validity. In leaving us hanging, a paradox forces us into a confrontation and a shift to Design-mind consciousness in order to resolve it, since it cannot be resolved by logic.

I have purposely placed this particular Design-mind skill toward the end of the course because—with your Design mind now awakened and developed, enabling you to write naturally—you will find tension acceptable and will be able to work with it and through it, thus energizing your writing. Moreover, creative tension allows you to utilize the other elements of natural writing in new and unexpected ways: you can generate surprise, create clashes that turn into insight, bring in juxtapositions that catapult both you and your reader into illuminating perceptions.

Since your Design mind is not constituted to see things as one way *or* the other, its predilection is always toward patterns; it focuses on complementarity rather than contradiction, on possible ways to connect opposites, to unify meaning. Thus it rejects the categories of either/or and accepts and plays with both/and. This notion of complementarity is essential to Chinese thought, as seen in the yin yang symbol (Figure 10–1).

A recent book by psychiatrist Harold Bloomfield and Robert B. Kory, gives a perspective on these two seemingly opposed ways of seeing our lives by coining a new word for an old difficulty—*anhedonia*, the inability to experience pleasure from within. In the resolution of these opposites lies growth and maturity.

In natural writing the tension between opposing forces becomes a creative principle because it stimulates fundamental and surprising innovations. Creative tension brings new lifeblood into seeing and writing, producing effective surprise and reflecting connectedness. To the Sign mind a polarity is the presence of two irreconcilable opposites. To the Design mind a polarity represents the ends of a single, indivisible whole. The focus is different, that's all, for it is the simultaneous recognition of opposites as equally valid.

Writers use paradox to express this unifying focus, as poet Theodore Roethke has:

In a dark time, the eye begins to see . . .

And in broad day the midnight come again!

Anhedonic perception is either/or thinking; the world and the self appear fragmented, dichotomized, polarized. The shift to inner joy is also a shift away from this dichotomized perception toward a unified frame. You'll find it possible to accept yourself and others as selfish and unselfish, compassionate and indifferent, individual and social, rational and irrational. From the either/or vantage point, the polarities in the world and in the self appear to struggle toward release of tension and finally death. From the vantage point of inner joy, the tension between opposing forces produces energy for growth.

Harold Bloomfield, M.D. and Robert B. Kory,
Inner Joy

Figure 10–1

Literally, the eye cannot see "in a dark time," and literally the midnight cannot come "in broad day." Yet our Design mind moves beyond logic to a different awareness, one that sees the possibility of both as valid on a new level of meaning.

As noted in Chapter 4, right-hemisphere-damaged Peter, who could respond to "too many cooks spoil the broth" only on a literal level, would reject outright both these paradoxical statements as nonsense because his literal left brain would argue that there cannot possibly be midnight in broad day, and that would be the end of it. But those of us with intact right hemispheres might struggle with this contradiction and explore it until we realized that, in times of deepest crisis, we become receptive to new ways of perceiving we wouldn't ordinarily have been open to.

The function of creative tension in writing is precisely to reflect the profound truth of the both/and, rather than only the either/or, nature of life. We can perceive both ways because we have two brains, which process the flux of the world in radically different ways. Our Sign mind tends to focus on the either/or, crisply and clearly cataloguing, making judgments, establishing rules. Our Design mind tends to focus on the both/and, with its ambiguities, its malleability, its flow. Again using the terminology of physics, we might say that our Sign mind thinks in terms of fission, the act or process of splitting into parts, while our design mind thinks in terms of fusion, the act of liquefying or melting together by heat. Fission separates out; fusion merges. Fission focuses on particles—a drop of energy; fusion, on waves—a sea of energy.

In Robert Newton Peck's starkly beautiful *A Day No Pigs Would Die,* the climax of the novel focuses on the adolescent Robert's dramatic epiphany of the both/and aspects of human experience. His father has just killed Robert's beloved pet pig because the pig is barren, but we learn that the father had to kill the pet so that his family could survive. The killing hand is thus also the loving, protecting hand, and this reconciling of a terrible contradiction alters Robert's view of life forever.

I felt his big hand touch my face, and it wasn't the hand that killed hogs. It was almost as sweet as Mama's. His hand was rough and cold, and as I opened my eyes to look at it, I could see that his knuckles were dripping with pig blood. It was the hand that just butchered Pinky. He did it. Because he had to. Hated to and had to. And he knew that he'd never have to say to me that he was sorry. His hand against my face, trying to wipe away my tears, said it all. His cruel pig-sticking fist with its thick fingers so lightly on my cheek.

I couldn't help it. I took his hand to my mouth and held it against my lips and kissed it. Pig blood and all. I kissed his hand again and again, with all its stink and fatty slime of dead pork. So he'd understand that I'd forgive him even if he killed me.

Without the paradox the story would be at best a sentimental tale of a young boy's pet pig and at worst a story of senseless brutality. Instead, it is a sensitive portrayal of one of life's realities, and both protagonist and the reader are immeasurably enriched by this insight.

Childhood Origins of Creative Tension

When we are very young, our logical Sign-mind categories are still limited, and so the conventional way of splitting the world into either/or is not yet our way. In the stage of the innocent eye, ear, and hand, the world is a kaleidoscope of possibility, a mosaic in which everything is potentially related. In childhood we revel in this delicious both/and-ness, in its seamless whole. We play with language, juxtapose improbable elements, invent unlikely events, juggle semantic nonsense, all the while maneuvering in a natural sea of creative tension.

In *From Two to Five* Kornei Chukovsky, Russia's most popular children's storyteller as well as an expert on the speech and learning patterns of children, has observed that, at the earliest stages, children think of words in pairs of opposites. Already, at around the age of three, they naturally look for the polar complement of a word they have just learned. The child, says Chukovsky, "assumes that every word has a "twin"—an opposite in meaning or quality." In the process of discovering these other words, he tells us, children make many mistakes, such as

Young children possess the ability to cut across the customary categories . . . to appreciate usually undiscerned links among realms, to respond affectively in a parallel manner to events which are usually categorized differently, and to capture these original conceptions in words.

Howard Gardner,
Artful Scribbles

"Yesterday it was raw outside," someone remarked.
"And today—it is cooked?" a child wanted to know.

or:

"This is running water."
"Is there sitting water?"

Because children's Sign-mind reasoning powers are not developed, they respond naturally to the creative principle of tension inherent in a both/and awareness of life. Because their repertoires of well-routinized sequences are as yet relatively sparse, most of their encounters with the world are filtered through the Design mind, which is superior to the left at handling new and logically contradictory tasks. By the stage of the conventional eye, ear, and hand this natural both/and orientation is lost in favor of either/or awareness.

Take the following story by my daughter Simone, written before she was six. Observe the tension of the large logical gaps and the effortless way in which she reconciles physical impossibility: there is a marriage of ladybugs, but suddenly the scene shifts to a radical discontinuity; a human hand appears and the two ladybugs become a ring on a finger of the hand. The tension exists between animate and inanimate; at first the ladybugs behave like humans, and then they become an inanimate ring on a real human being's finger. Simone had no trouble reconciling these two events in her narrative.

The Little Ladybug
Once-apon-a time there was a little boy ladybug. He met a girl ladybug. So he asked her if she and him wanted to get mired. So she said o k so they got mired. Then they found a hand so they asked the person if they could be there. So she said o k so they climbed on her finger and pertended to be a ring. The end

As we become socially habituated into a left-brain view of the world, logical categories begin to play a primary role, and we tend to start seeing the world in absolute terms. For example, things can never be both animate and inanimate, and we reject the possibility that the world can be both/and, depending on how we look at it. As

*All of us collect fortunes when we
are children—a fortune of colors,
of lights and darkness, of movements, of tensions. Some of us have
the fantastic chance to go back to
his fortune when grown up.*
            Ingmar Bergman,
            quoted in Time,
            December 29, 1980

our left-hemisphere categories are strengthened by schooling, we develop the unreflective certainty that our everyday perception brings
us into untrammeled contact with the Real World. Because this literal outlook prevents us from entertaining contradictory notions, the
creative tension that can produce insight and illumination in writing
is buried under conventional wisdom and exclusive categories.

In the stage of the cultivated eye, ear, and hand, however, we
get in touch once more with the feelings and knowledge we had as a
child, resulting in an elevation of our adult perceptions.

Now let's develop your awareness of creative tension. As always, clustering is the fundamental tool that will enable you to bring
the tension inherent in image or event into awareness. Once accessible, this tension will find its way into your writing. Moving from the
simple to the complex, the vehicles we will use to explore tension in
writing are word pairs, "contraries," dialogue, and, finally, the most
fundamental of all, polarities themselves.

Creative Tension Through Similar Word Pairs

A word pair—related terms clustered as a double nucleus, such as
look/see—confronts us with obvious likenesses. *Look,* the dictionary
tells us, is "to employ one's eyes in seeing," while *see* is "to perceive
with the eye." But as clustering engages the Design mind and blocks
the input of the literal, conventional Sign mind, we become aware of
subtle shades and nuances of these words and a tension is created
between them. The resonance set up by these two closely related
words has a peculiar generative power. Were you to cluster each
word singly, there would be no tension, but when the Design mind
processes them *in relationship* to one another, you go beyond the
given and discover unexpected perceptions.

Focus on them gently, let associations flow, and allow your Design mind to play with them until you experience a trial-web shift
that will focus your writing on a fresh perception. Let's explore one
student writer's vignette, using the nucleus TOUCH/FEEL , for the
creative tension it exhibits (Figure 10–2).

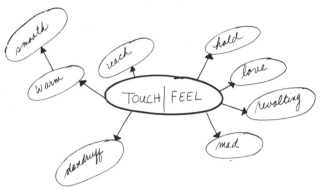

Figure 10–2

I couldn't touch you today. The gesture had to come from you, love rekindled from your feel. I am exhausted by the tension between us, yet I know, to feel, to touch, is not the appropriate release. Today there is no release, no change to be made in our defensive stances. I nurture my anger another day.

Jillian Milligan

Touch rekindles love and release, but touch denied sustains defensive stances. Here is the source of the creative tension that catches our eye and emotions as we read. The language rhythms alternate between short staccato sentences at beginning and end—five and six words, respectively—and long, flowing sentences in between. The rest of the language is spare, with few images, no metaphors—and we know the emotional climate articulated by the writer is highly tension-charged: "exhausted by tension," "no release," "no change," "defensive stances," "nurture my anger." The *feeling* is too wrong for *touch* to occur.

Directing Your Hand

Explore your own word pairs now by letting your Design mind discover your own perspective in relation to a word pair.

1. In your writer's notebook, cluster the word pair of your choice from Figure 10–3. Let the clustering take any shape it wants to. You may discover you are clustering first one nucleic twin, then the other (first "look," then "see," for example). On the other

hand, you may find you are clustering both of them simultaneously, not in the least fussy about what goes where. You may cluster similarities and in the process perhaps discover differences you had never thought about, a friction that may need to be resolved in the writing. You may even discover unconventional perceptions as the words rub against one another. Whatever you come up with, don't censor. The play of clustering lies in giving yourself freedom to associate.

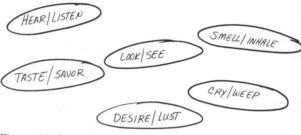

Figure 10–3

2. Associations may appear random at first, but you will soon perceive emerging patterns. That is your Design mind reaching for a trial-web shift. Let it happen.

3. When you experience the trial-web shift and with it a sense of focus, articulate it by writing one or more focusing statements, thus bringing your Sign mind into participation in the creative process. Choose the statement that seems most promising and begin writing your vignette. Write for about ten minutes.

4. When you have finished, read what you have written aloud, giving attention to coming full circle, recurrences, language rhythms, images, metaphors, and, of course, ways to make tension work for you in creative ways.

5. Now reshape anything that still doesn't satisfy your aesthetic sense. The clustering process is not static; even as you reshape, your Design mind will make associations that hone and refine the trial web and, by extension, your vignette.

After Writing

Explore your own process. At some point you probably uncovered some friction in the word pair you chose, which may have triggered the trial-web shift that allowed you to begin writing. The writing very likely was an expression of the friction and its possible resolution. In articulating the friction you will have achieved creative tension.

Creative Tension Through "Contraries"

William Blake wrote, "Without contraries there's no progression," and the sixteenth-century English poet Ben Jonson wrote, "All concord's born of contraries."

Practice with contraries lets you prepare yourself for the ultimate form of creative tension, that of polarities. Contraries, like polarities, contain paradox. When Romeo says "Parting is such sweet sorrow," he suggests that even though parting between lovers brings sorrow, it also has an element of sweetness, for in parting lies the hope of reunion; thus in parting the experience of loving is painfully intensified.

When Juliet discovers that Romeo has killed Tybalt, she rails in a frenzy of tension between contraries:

O serpent heart, hid with a flowering face.
Did ever dragon keep so fair a cave?
Beautiful tyrant, fiend angelical,
Dove-feathered raven, wolvish-ravening lamb!
Despised substance of divinest show,
Just opposite to what thou justly seemst—
A damned saint, an honorable villain!
O nature, what hadst thou to do in hell
When thou didst bower the spirit of a fiend
In mortal paradise of such sweet flesh?
Was ever book containing such vile matter
So fairly bound? O that deceit should dwell
In such a gorgeous palace!

In Juliet's eyes, Romeo is suddenly both/and: "beautiful tyrant," "fiend angelical," "dove-feathered raven," "damned saint," "honorable villain," and so forth. Shakespeare's use of contraries tells us much about the state of Juliet's mind: she is in an agonizing double bind, experiencing both love *and* shock, attraction *and* revulsion, tenderness *and* outrage.

What is literally impossible to the Sign mind strikes the Design mind as highly interesting and unusually moving. It is more vital than ordinary description. It tells us more about the quality of what is being said. Confronted with such contraries, the Sign mind bristles: "No way. That doesn't even make sense!" Even the Greeks called these contradictions "oxymorons"—*oxy,* meaning "pointed," and *moron,* meaning "foolish"; thus, pointedly foolish—and this is exactly how such word combinations must appear to the Sign mind.

It is otherwise with the Design mind. The tension produced by such jarring inconsistency is music to its inner ear. When you cluster, it will immediately set about to search for creative ways to resolve the contradiction, and the resulting vignette will represent an intensely satisfying working out of the opposing sense. See for yourself.

Directing Your Hand

1. In your writer's notebook, choose one of the contraries in Figure 10–4 and cluster it.

Figure 10–4

Let go; invite all associations; don't censor. You can cluster any way you wish. Perhaps you will be attracted first to one word in the pair, then to the other, or perhaps associations will spring from both simultaneously—your Design mind can do several things at once. Soon you will rub up against the contradiction inherent in them and a sudden illumination will show you how to solve it. That is the trial-web vision. Just let your Design mind take charge and trust it for the time being.

2. Cluster until you experience the trial-web shift, which, when experimenting with contraries, may be delayed until you have done considerable clustering to give yourself many options.

3. Having discovered a focus, write a clear focusing statement, which will bring your Sign mind into the act, drawing on what your Design mind has made accessible to it.
4. Now write as fast as you can, using your insight as focus and your cluster as reference. Remember, as you write, that reaching for a metaphor can be a powerful means of expressing a Design-mind insight, that recurrences can unify, that language rhythms create aesthetic quality, and that coming full circle brings wholeness.
5. When you have finished writing your vignette, read it aloud and rework it until the whole feels right, sounds right, looks right.

After Writing

You were probably surprised at the way your writing resolved the paradox inherent in the contraries, despite the fact that it may have all seemed quite puzzling before you clustered them. Because your Sign mind's resistance was blocked through clustering, your Design mind responded to the creative tension inherent in the seeming contradiction of the words.

The student examples that follow (Figures 10–5 and 10–6) show how the explicit awareness of creative tension and the other techniques of natural writing result in the writers' discovering their own authentic subject matter and voice.

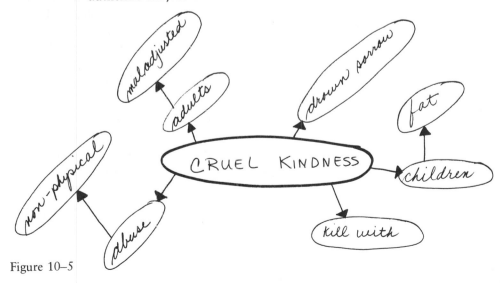

Figure 10–5

You tell me there is no such thing as cruel kindness. I tell you there is, indeed! When the baby fell down, she was picked up and cuddled by mother and offered a bottle as comfort. When the preschooler scraped her knee and ran into the house in tears, mother treated the wound and gave her a cookie. When the ten-year-old fell from her bike and went home all banged, scraped, and bruised, mother tended her needs and cut her a piece of chocolate cake. When the teenager was jilted by her first boyfriend, mother cried with her and they had a hot fudge sundae.

This adult now comforts herself with food when her life gets difficult. She is overweight, unhappy, and unable to cope. Now, tell me there is no such thing as cruel kindness!

The tension is established in the opening two sentences: denial and affirmation. Without explanation, this writer moves to example after example. The clear focus of each image is on food: hurt baby gets a bottle; scraped preschooler gets a cookie; bruised ten-year-old gets chocolate cake; jilted teenager gets hot fudge sundae. All are acts of kindness, but they are also cruel, as we discover in the concluding paragraph with the resolution of the contradiction: food has become the same palliative in adulthood, producing overweight and unhappiness.

Other qualities of natural writing abound: language rhythms take the form of parallelisms beginning with "when," and there are others: "banged, scraped, and bruised" and "overweight, unhappy, and unable to cope." Certain rhythms are the result of balance: "You tell me there is no . . ." and "I tell you there is . . . ." Full-circle wholeness reflects the emphatic tone of the writer: "You tell me . . . I tell you . . ." at the beginning, and "Now, tell me . . ." at the end. This also constitutes recurrence.

Another student vignette plays on the opposition of feeling, as implied in the title "Cold Burn." Written by a nurse in one of my creative writing courses, this moving and powerful poem contains graphic and contrasting images and metaphors illustrating the tension between neutral professional efficiency and profound emotional response.

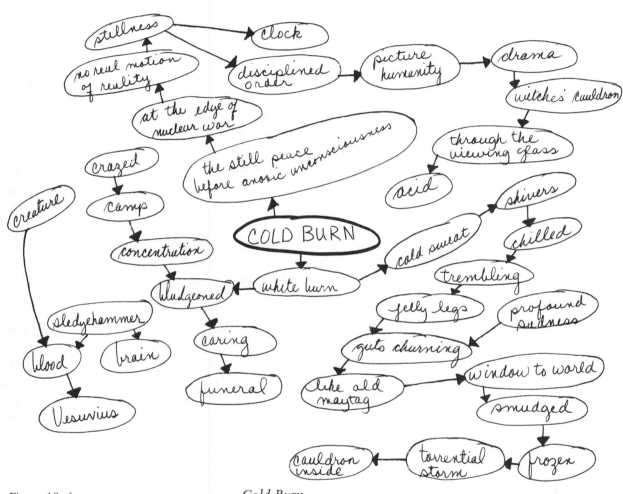

Figure 10–6

Cold Burn
I know the cold burn of disallowed anger.
Like the still peace before anoxic unconsciousness,
it allows me to carry on
the perfunctory essentials of my work.

I see humanity striding:
Granite neurosurgeon bearing
a God-made body gently in his arms.
Tears wash his cheek:
Blood flowing. Brain showing. Bludgeoned
by a concentration camp-crazed creature
called husband.

I see? No, I look. I am distanced
by a me: a built-in viewing glass
looking at war two continents away.

My ministrations done, I sit. Then,
I feel.
I feel the cold of a Himalayan avalanche envelop me.
I feel the clammy river flowing from my pits.
My clothes are wet. My eyes won't see.
I shiver. My gut is snared on meat hooks.
I feel sick.
I feel the cold burn.

Jane Crum

The writer not only creates tension between two opposing emotional states, but she uses all the other techniques she has learned in the course: coming full circle ("I know the cold burn . . . I feel the cold burn"); vivid images ("Tears wash his cheek," "blood flowing," "brain showing," and so forth); metaphor/simile (cold burn is "like the still peace before anoxic unconsciousness," "granite neurosurgeon," "cold of a Himalayan avalanche," and "my gut is snared on meat hooks"); recurrences ("I see . . . I see?," "I feel . . . I feel . . . I feel . . . I feel . . . I feel," "Blood . . . Brain . . . Bludgeoned," and "concentration camp-crazed creature/called"); language rhythms, especially parallel forms ("I know . . . I see?" and "I look . . . I sit . . . I feel").

Should you wish more contraries to explore, here are several pairs: slow haste, living death, relaxed attention, muddied illumination. You will come across others in books and magazines, popular songs, book and movie titles, and, often, poetry. Shakespeare, especially, abounds in them.

Creative Tension Through Dialogue

Inventing dialogue is another natural way to produce creative tension in writing. Dialogue—two people conversing—often portrays the conflicting desires, needs, wishes, or perceptions of the participants. There is also an inherent tension in the format of statement/response. In practice, my students find that dialogue is a relatively easy way to experience creative tension. Dialogue allows response, contradiction, repartee, and negation of what was said before, as well as affirmation. They are sometimes surprised when they realize that both voices have come from the same eye, ear, hand, and brain!

In a segment of the poem "Elegy for My Father" by poet Mark Strand, we encounter a dialogue between a son and his dead father; in it the tension of paradox is almost unbearable because each question is answered twice and in diametrically opposed ways.

2. Answers

Why did you travel?
BECAUSE THE HOUSE WAS COLD.
Why did you travel?
BECAUSE IT IS WHAT I HAVE ALWAYS DONE BETWEEN
    SUNSET AND SUNRISE.
What did you wear?
I WORE A BLUE SUIT, A WHITE SHIRT, YELLOW TIE, AND
    YELLOW SOCKS.
What did you wear?
I WORE NOTHING. A SCARF OF PAIN KEPT ME WARM.
Who did you sleep with?
I SLEPT WITH A DIFFERENT WOMAN EACH NIGHT.
Who did you sleep with?
I SLEPT ALONE. I HAVE ALWAYS SLEPT ALONE.
Why did you lie to me?
I ALWAYS THOUGHT I TOLD THE TRUTH.
Why did you lie to me?
BECAUSE THE TRUTH LIES LIKE NOTHING ELSE AND I
    LOVE THE TRUTH.
Why are you going?
BECAUSE NOTHING MEANS MUCH TO ME ANYMORE.
Why are you going?
I DON'T KNOW. I HAVE NEVER KNOWN.
How long shall I wait for you?
DO NOT WAIT FOR ME. I AM TIRED AND I WANT TO
    LIE DOWN.
Are you tired and do you want to lie down?
YES, I AM TIRED AND I WANT TO LIE DOWN.

In this poem we not only see the tension that is the basis of all dialogue, but we see this tension elevated to a series of paradoxes that cannot be resolved by logic. As we read the poem, we see not only contradiction but reflection, conflict, counterpoint. The paradoxes have, in the last question and answer, led to the stillness of forces in momentary equilibrium, as the father's statement, the son's question, and the father's restatement are all the same. The paradoxes have been resolved into a synthesis within a system of wider scope than logic can encompass.

The impetus for a dialogue-vignette comes from clustering related or conflicting word pairs or from clustering two characters you know—real or imagined—who have something to say to each other.

Directing Your Hand

In your writer's notebook, experiment with creative tension by writing a vignette composed of dialogue.

1. Begin by closing your eyes and vividly imaging two people you know—two strangers; a relative, friend, or enemy and yourself; two characters from history or art; a person and an object; two sides of yourself—the possibilities are infinite. The dialogue can be serious or humorous, or both, or somewhere in between. It is *your* creation.

2. Sustain these two people firmly in your mind's eye as you cluster their names. Think of the words they say, their tones of voice, their attitudes, their physical differences, and so forth. Be alert for the trial-web shift from randomness to sense of direction.

3. Write your dialogue from your cluster. As you write, keep in mind the possibilities of image power, metaphor, language rhythms, recurrences, full-circle wholeness, and, above all, creative tension.

4. When you have finished, read your dialogue aloud. Listen to the "voices" and how they express themselves. Change anything that would enrich your envisioned whole.

After Writing

After they cluster and write their dialogues, my students frequently express amazement that their feelings ran so deep, especially in "encounters" with parents or siblings; that conflicts surfaced which had been long suppressed; that their emotional investment in expressing these conflicts—as though the writer were actually two people—generated a positive creative tension that brought their writing to a level of intensity they had not experienced before.

However, dialogue can also produce lightness and humor, as the writer of Figure 10–7 demonstrates. In this delightfully tongue-in-cheek vignette based on Italian sculptor Antonio Canova's marble of Napoleon (Figure 10–8) we see two megalomaniacs pitted against each other, with Canova outwitting the grand Napoleon. The tension arose from his clustering of ⬭ARTIST/SUBJECT⬭ . If you explore the cluster, you will see that the bit of dialogue found there—"I am my own creation"—came to serve as the focus of the entire vignette.

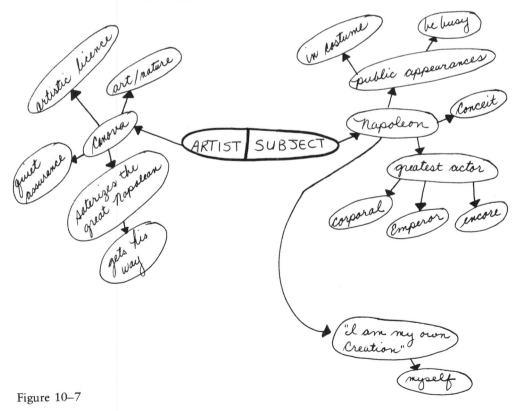

Figure 10–7

Figure 10–8

ANTONIO CANOVA, *NAPOLEON*, COURTESY OF
THE WELLINGTON MUSEUM, LONDON.

Napoleon According to Canova

"I was not meant to be naked!" cried Napoleon, emperor. "I perform my acts in public clothed! I am not a naked vision of Praxiteles! I am my own creation! I appear as myself! I am the greatest actor in the universe. Yesterday, a Little Corporal! Today, an Emperor! Tomorrow, an encore! I cannot appear in public without a costume, not even as a statue! I must always look busy, even in stone!

"Precisely so," assured Canova, admired Italian sculptor. "That is why I have given you something to do with your hands. An orb for your right hand. A staff for your left. Voilà! But use them wisely, mon Emperor. I mean, don't let them droop. Now leave the rest to me. It is up to the artist to render unto Nature what is Art's, to render unto Caesar what is Caesar's."

"Be sure that Nature through Art renders unto Caesar a fig leaf," responded Napoleon.

"I am like him," said an admiring bourgeois of the statue. "I am my own creation."

"Naked, you look like a gouty pig," smirked his less-than-admiring wife. "You are the creation of sauces, cheese, and pastry. Thank God for fig leaves."

—George Russell

The most immediately apparent tension is between the egomaniacal tone of the subject, Napoleon, and the dry, tongue-in-cheek, conciliatory tone of the artist, Canova. Instead of giving in to Napoleon's demand for a costume, Canova cleverly sidetracks him by giving him something for his hands: "An orb for your right hand. A staff for your left." He follows this sleight of hand with an injunction to "use them wisely," followed again by a grandiosely ambiguous statement about the artist's function, which resolves the tension as Napoleon meekly submits, almost humbly requesting only a fig leaf.

The final bit of dialogue between the museum viewer and his sarcastic wife generates additional creative tension as the reader shifts to another time in which a "bourgeois" compares himself to the statue of Napoleon, ironically echoing Napoleon's "I am my own creation." The wife deals him several heavy-handed sarcastic blows: "You are the creation of sauces, cheese, and pastry." The resolution of the tension comes through laughter, and the whole comes full circle through the second reference to fig leaves. Recurrences reinforce Napoleon's megalomaniac attitude: "I was . . . I perform . . . I am . . . I am . . . I am . . . I must. . . ."

Creative Tension Through Awareness of Polarities

And so we come full circle with our opening: polarities. The powerful concept of polarities represents a deliberate shift from seeing opposites as antagonists to appreciating their relatedness as necessary extremes of a single continuum, a way of seeing rarely permitted by the either/or classifications of the Sign mind.

Artists and writers prize their awareness of polarities, for it stimulates their creative activity. British sculptor Henry Moore and German painter Josef Albers praise it.

Polarity is complement rather than opposition, and is a basic quality of all natural processes insofar as it comprises two sides of the same coin. No single absolute can ever represent a complete reality, only a partial one. Each form has its polar counterpart; a total vision embraces both in a synthesis. Think of waxing/waning, day/night, systole/diastole, inhale/exhale, creation/destruction, conscious/unconscious, movement/rest, right/left, sun/moon.

Reconciling polarities has traditionally governed entire schools of philosophy and religion. In *The Two Hands of God*, philosopher Alan Watts takes on one of the most irreconcilable of opposites in most people's minds and, in so doing, enables us to perceive the "polarities" of life and death as Eastern religions do:

> . . . life and death are not so much alternative as alternatives, poles of a single process which may be called life-and-death. Not only is it obvious that living organisms thrive upon dead organisms; it is also only a little less obvious that the very living of any one organism is a perpetual birth, death, and elimination of its own cells. Moreover, death provides for the constant renewal of life by setting limits to accumulations—of population, of property, of memories—which, beyond a certain point, tend to become static and to clog the flow of life—that is, to die. It is thus that accumulation, the building up of some relatively permanent pattern or system, is both life-and-death.

To know one thing, you must know the opposite. . . . Just as much, else you don't know that one thing.

Henry Moore,
British sculptor

I start from experiences and read . . . always between polarities— loud and no-loud, young and old, spring and winter. If I can make black and white behave together instead of shooting at each other only, I feel proud.

Josef Albers,
painter

Poet Alastair Reid addresses the polarities of permanence and change in love and thereby illuminates a profound and painful truth for all of us who seek and cherish it:

In Such a Poise Is Love
Why should a hint of winter
shadow the window while the insects enter,
or a feel of snowfall, taking corners off
the rough wall and the roof,
while the sun, hanging in the sky,
hotly deny its contrary?

. . . .

In such a poise is love. But who
can keep the balance true,
can stay in the day's surprise, moving
between twin fears, of losing and of having?
Who has not, in love's fever,
insisted on the fatal vow, "forever,"
and sensed, before the words are gone,
the doom in them dawn?

As my students reawaken and develop their awareness of the relationship between polarities, they invariably expand their range of seeing with a dramatic increase of creative tension in their writing.

Now it is your turn to discover the creative tension generated by polarities in your writing.

Directing Your Hand

Begin by choosing one of the sets of polarities in Figure 10–9. They remain mere opposites only until you bring them into some kind of relationship with each other through the involvement of your Design mind.

1. Cluster the polarities of your choice. Clustering them as a pair will color your associations quite differently than if you were to cluster them as single nucleus words. Clustering the pair tends to evoke a sense of relatedness rather than pure opposition. Cluster whatever comes: associations, images, metaphors, lines of poems, songs, proverbs—anything that comes your way. Cluster until you experience the trial-web shift of relationship between the two concepts.

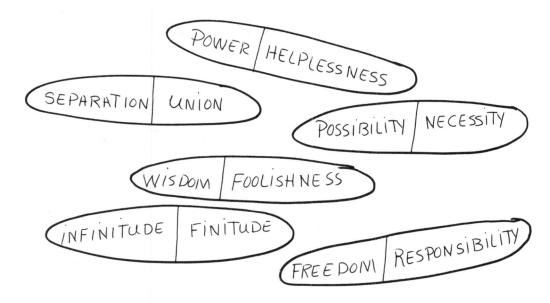

Figure 10–9

2. Make that relationship your focus. Clarify it for yourself by writing a focusing statement, bringing your Sign mind into participation.

3. Now work it out in a vignette, writing as rapidly as you can. Scan your cluster periodically to keep sight of your associations. Let your thoughts flow. Don't stop to correct errors. Do consider using all the appropriate elements of natural writing.

4. Once you have your thoughts down, reread what you have written and do some pruning and shaping until your total design feels right.

After Writing

As you clustered, you very likely experienced some sort of illumination that pointed to the both/and nature of some aspect of life that you suddenly knew you'd like to explore. For many of my students, writing a focusing statement incorporating the both/and quality of the polarities they had just clustered represents the first time they have consciously allowed apparent opposites to connect. Many of them are surprised to see aspects of both as valid and applicable.

Students also note that, in order to express both/and, they find themselves reaching for metaphors, images, and recurrences to express their new way of seeing, for literal language is limited in its ability to explain such unaccustomed perceptions.

This exercise served as a catalyst for the poignant and powerful student writing that follows. The creative tension (Figure 10–10) revolves around the polarities of union/separation, which in his cluster and poem emerge as GOOD MORNING/GOODBYE . Throughout the poem there is a tension between the aliveness of the morning and the "stark sadness" of the speaker. Read the poem aloud, noting the constant polarities.

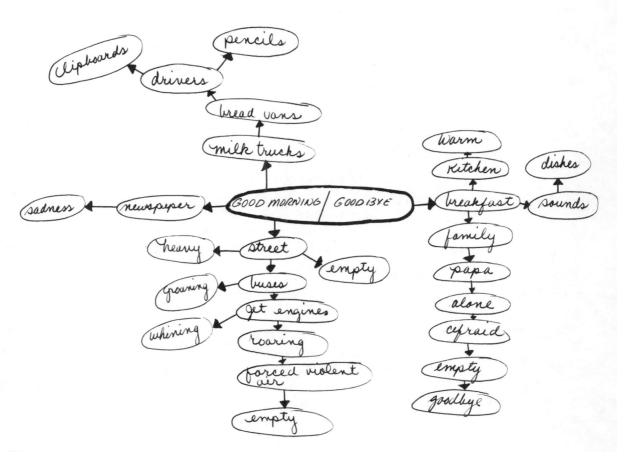

Figure 10–10

Good Morning
The day is early with milk trucks
and bread vans with warm doors,
idling in the brassy light of dawn
beside bright shopping carts,
like gilded hedgerows,
broken where the animals and boys slip through.
The trucks disgorge themselves
for men with clipboards,
men with brief and hungry pencils
tucked behind their ears.
I turn into the street
and it is empty, but for me.
The street is heavy on the earth.
I cannot concentrate. The street
is empty.
Faintly, in the neighborhood
I hear the thump and rustle
of the morning paper, sadly,
and remember I am not concerned
for news.
I have stark sadness of my own
to print, but still
I love the sound the world makes,
thumping once on all those bolted doors.
Kitchens hum and rattle
with the click of bowls and plates
and small sea sounds of running water.
Men in crisp shirts brush
and shave and spit,
and search the mirrors
for kind portraits
of their lives. They wonder
at their dullness,
at the slowness of their wives,
and then dismiss it.
Fountains in the business district stir
with artificial life,

and I have pity for the tired water
pumped into the sky. I feel
like water falling, filtered,
gathered up and thrown against
the sky, but always falling.
Buses roll on cool tires,
hissing at the stoplights,
squealing every hundred-fifty yards.
Street lights wink out in a line.
Buses lurch by, groaning
with their glass throats
full of quarters.
Over at the airport,
engines whine, then roar.
Their throats are full of forced
and violent air. I have no will.
Not like the engines.
Turning down your street,
I know you stir by instinct.
Falling out of sleep,
somehow your body knows
my thin, stiff knuckles
in their Monday gloves
are poised before your door.
And I am thinking
of the way you say good morning.
You are dreaming of the way
I say goodbye.

Robin Nelson

Wonderful images of morning fill the poem: "milk trucks/and bread vans with warm doors"; "the thump and rustle of the morning paper"; "kitchens hum and rattle"; "small sea sounds of running water"; "men in crisp shirts brush/and shave and spit"; "fountains stir with artificial life"; "buses roll on cool tires."

Other Design-mind techniques intensify the creative tension just delineated: recurrences—the "street" is repeated several times, the setting for this little drama of good morning/goodbye; sound recurrences: "I feel/like water falling, filtered" and "small sea sounds." Coming full circle occurs with the good morning of the title and the goodbye of the last line. Beyond recurrences are distinct language rhythms that we can divide into euphonious and cacophonous. The euphonious rhythms imitate the joyful sounds of a world waking: "I love the sound the world makes"; "idling in the brassy light of dawn"; "the click of bowls and plates"; "street lights wink out in a line." These lines are pleasantly musical, and their sound echoes the sense; you can hear the shift to cacophony as the writer moves from positive to negative: "stark sadness," "stiff knuckles," "Monday gloves," "I have no will." Metaphors intensify the whole: "shopping carts,/like gilded hedgerows" and "buses . . . groaning/with their glass throats/ full of quarters." Read the poem again and look for the less obvious ones.

But there are even more contrasts, indicating trouble in this morning paradise: "the street . . . is empty"; "I cannot concentrate"; "and remember I am not concerned/for news"; "I have stark sadness of my own/to print"; "I feel/like water falling"; "I have no will," as if to tell us which way the dice will roll. The poem ends with "I say goodbye."

A Last Word and Heading On

Generating creative tension brings new lifeblood into seeing and writing. The broad philosophical concept of polarities shows us that all life can be viewed through one thing or its opposite—or a reconciliation of both. Paradox and contraries are linguistic constructs by which you can give expression to your polarized existence. In putting your awareness of polarities to use through such strategies as dialogue and word pairs, you are able to develop creative tension in your writing, naturally. In so doing, you increasingly move away from simplistic, either/or modes of perception and expression into seeing more complex relationships, resulting in more vital forms of written expressiveness.

By now you have reached a high level of cultivation in writing naturally. In Chapter 11 we will return to the important Design-mind strategy with which we began: the emphasis on wholeness of vision, in which you discover a focus to guide you before you begin writing and use this focusing vision in revision—the means we use to bring the vignette into greater alignment with the original trial web. The emphasis is on paring down so that every word tells.

CHAPTER 11/ *Re-Vision: Less Is More*

In writing naturally, as in modern architecture, "less is more." This was the paradoxical doctrine of the famous Bauhaus architect Mies van der Rohe, whose aesthetic philosophy of austere elegance, clean lines and clarity, elimination of extraneous decoration or applied ornament, designs of great refinement, visual simplicity, and jewel-like precision speaks powerfully to the revision phase of natural writing. The renowned grammarian William Strunk might well have been influenced by the Bauhaus philosophy in his insistence that "every word tell."

Strunk's prescription reflects the techniques you have been practicing in this book: that the focus be clear, recurrences meaningful, images sharp, the language pleasingly rhythmic and evocative, the tension dynamic. Throughout the book we have concentrated on becoming aware of and developing these techniques of natural writing. Now it is time to look at our writing more critically than we have done up to now, using the detail-oriented talents of the Sign mind yet at the same time checking the detail against the global vision of the Design mind, which ultimately dictates all major decisions. Thus true revision becomes an intensely cooperative process between the hemispheres, a process of continual modification toward some envisioned whole.

Actually, in the writing of your vignettes, you have been learning to do this all along. All natural writing begins with an awareness of a tentative configuration that gives a sense of direction to the left

A sentence should contain no unnecessary words, a paragraph no unnecessary sentences, for the same reason that a drawing should have no unnecessary lines and a machine no unnecessary parts. This requires not that the writer make all his sentences short or that he avoid all detail . . . but that every word tell.
Williams Strunk,
Elements of Style

brain as it begins to sequence the trial web. The very act of sequencing, as I have already pointed out, is a sorting, selecting, grouping process, guided by the trial web. From configuration to detail is like a camera zooming in, making the features of blurred shapes clearer. When you have come to the end of the writing, you have read your work aloud and made any changes that produced a more satisfying vignette. In a sense, you have been revising all along. In this chapter we make the revision process more explicit.

Take some time to skim through the filled pages in your writer's notebook. However satisfying, however surprising your products, each entry is still technically "first draft" material. Now that you have learned to trust your inner writer by producing abundantly and with relative ease and genuine pleasure—with a host of Design-mind strategies at your fingertips—it is time to move from immersion in the process to perspective.

Revision (literally, re-vision, seeing again) is second sight; it is recalling the original vision, comparing it with the writing you achieved the first time around, and then paring it through one or more successive drafts until you have truly achieved an aesthetic whole. Children writing in the innocent stage never revise; to them their first product is beautiful as it stands. Writers in the cultivated stage almost always revise, for in that second sight they hone and sharpen, bringing the specialized talents of both Design and Sign minds into the creative act.

Second sight lets you re-evaluate the whole and then begin the process of paring for greater economy and attention to craftsmanship. Every artistic endeavor or creative act involves two broad phases—the generative phase during which the original vision is discovered and roughly expressed, and the paring and polishing phase during which the ideas are reworked and refined, and finally regarded critically to ensure that the expression aligns with the original vision.

Painters do it; composers do it. And all great writers are especially aware of the necessity for revision. D. H. Lawrence, for example, rewrote *Lady Chatterley's Lover* three times, and Dylan Thomas has affirmed the necessity for re-vision.

American poet Laura Chester beautifully describes how this process works in discussing her poem, "Pavanne for the Passing of a Child":

When I first begin writing a poem, the words come quickly and I don't try to censor myself. Then I immediately type up what I have, regaining control for gradual revision, pressuring the poem while trying not to lose that initial blood beat. I type draft after draft almost obsessively until that first soft clay shapes itself into the poem it has become. . . . When I rewrite I have to retrieve that original urge, otherwise it becomes mere correction and something vital is lost. True revision can be as exciting and "creative" as the first attempt. I love to feel the poem as a malleable substance that I can push and reshape on the page.

Hemingway was no stranger to rewriting, as he explained in a *Paris Review* interview:

INTERVIEWER: How much rewriting do you do?

HEMINGWAY: It depends. I rewrote the ending of *A Farewell to Arms,* the last page of it, thirty-nine times before I was satisfied with it.

INTERVIEWER: Was there some technical problem there? What was it that had stumped you?

HEMINGWAY: Getting the words right.

"Getting the words right" does not mean "mere correction," as Laura Chester put it, but refers to the *relationship* the words have to one another and to the overall meaning a writer strives for; it refers to a qualitative fitting together, to the aesthetic totality a writer has fashioned. In this sense, getting the words right is more a Design-mind phenomenon than a Sign-mind phenomenon.

The case of composer Maurice Ravel is interesting evidence of right-brain processing of aesthetic wholes. A stroke produced severe left-hemisphere damage, rendering Ravel aphasic—that is, unable to express himself in words. Other left-brain skills were also destroyed: he could no longer play the piano, nor could he read music, a left-hemisphere skill. However, the composer's neurosurgeon discovered, to his surprise, that Ravel's incapacity did not seem to affect his aesthetic judgment; in fact, the reverse seemed to be true. He angrily noted errors in the performance of his own works, particularly in regard to pacing, rhythm, omissions, and wrong notes. Ravel's intact Design mind knew when the performance was out of alignment with his sense of the total form. In another experiment, his neurosurgeon had Ravel's work played on a piano that was deliberately out of

What I like to do is to treat words as a craftsman does his wood or stone or what-have-you, to hew, carve, mould, coil, polish, and plane them into patterns, sequences, sculptures, fugues of sound expressing some lyrical impulse, some spiritual doubt or conviction, some dimly realized truth I must try to reach and realize.

Dylan Thomas

tune. The resulting disharmony—processed by the right brain—caused the composer to fly into a rage. It disturbed his aesthetic sensibility, which was "contained" in his intact Design mind.

Similarly, in the initial stage of revision, your Design mind sweeps across the total form of your vignette just as you might scan a face, keeping the whole in mind. This strategy will prevent you from a premature shift to such Sign-mind activities as correcting grammar, spelling, or punctuation. Your critical Sign mind is particularly eager to dominate this stage of the writing process, since there are words on paper it can analyze, but it is too soon. Resist it as you reread, focusing on the forest, for the time being ignoring the trees. Your Sign-mind skills will be called upon soon enough.

The Design mind, oblivious to grammatical or syntactical error correction, knows, deep down, when "getting the words right" has still not been achieved. That is why you sometimes remain uneasy, dissatisfied with what you have written. In the natural writing process, redesigning the aesthetic whole must occur before detailed error correction.

Appropriately, poet and professor Diane Middlebrook defines revision as making a poem more true to its own terms. In *Worlds into Words,* she uses one of her own poems to demonstrate. The poet tells us that the poem originated in a dream out of which she woke full of anxiety, sleeping in a house that stood near a large forest; her grief at losing a person close to her is embodied in the images of emptiness: denuded trees and the sound of an axe falling. Her first draft reads as follows:

> Winter; the woods
> Empty; the axe
> Buried in a stump
> Its fall become a sob in the sleep
> Of the dreamer waking, calling out
> Where am I? Who is there?

In this earliest version, the poet explains, the line endings were arbitrary, sometimes coinciding with units of syntax, sometimes not. Then she decided on the syllabic form—four syllables to a line, except for the last line.

> The demands of the syllabic form, once I decided on it, helped me purge the poem of dead language: "become," "in," "the," "out." "Buried" became "sunk," discarding a syllable and gain-

The spoken or the written word
Should be as clean as is a bone,
As clear as is the light,
As firm as is a stone.
Two words will never serve
As well as one alone.

Anonymous

The written word
Is clean as bone,
Clear as light,
Firm as stone.
Two words are not
As good as one.

ing force in the process; "become" was exchanged for "startling." The rhythm produced by shortening the lines enhanced the feeling in the poem of being suddenly awakened into a terrible sort of questioning clarity. Here is her final version, purged of dead language.

Writing a Poem in Syllabics—Losing You
Winter; the woods
empty; the axe
sunk in a stump;
its thud a sob
startling the sleep
of the dreamer
waking, calling
Where am I? Who
is there?

You will be doing much the same kind of paring. Take time now to look at "dead language" in a little anonymous poem.

Cut to a mere twenty-one words from thirty-six, the central impact, message, and meaning come through. The excess verbiage of the first version buries the essence of the poem, whereas the words in the second version practice what they preach: not one superfluous word. In short, it is an aesthetic whole.

In this chapter you will learn some strategies for redesigning first-draft vignettes, a necessary step as we prepare for longer writing. We will explore the value of reclustering to achieve a tighter focus, follow a student's progress in revising a whole through several exploratory rewritings, and experiment with word painting to achieve economy of language. Finally, our redesign strategies will culminate in modeling a highly evocative and compressed poem.

Redesign Through Reclustering

In any aesthetic activity, of which natural writing is one, consciousness is heavily dependent on Design-mind processing. Your first insight into the form your writing would take came with the trial-web shift; you saw a focus and your vignette flowed from that. The first writing, however, may not have been as clear as you wanted to make it. Reclustering not only refines the focus but provides an additional burst of images and associations, reimmersing you in the totality of the vision, an important first step in revision.

Let's follow a beginning writer, a freshman in college, through an assignment from preclustering to clustering to writing to reclustering to rewriting again and again until she experienced the sense of "getting the words right." The assignment was to precluster the nucleus word (CIRCLE) for whatever possibilities would emerge. Figure 11–1 shows her discovered options.

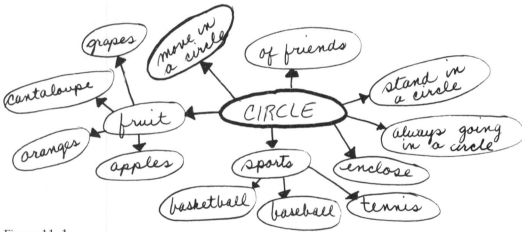

Figure 11–1

The options seemed random until she wrote "circle—of friends," at which moment she experienced a trial-web shift. She immediately clustered (CIRCLE OF FRIENDS) (Figure 11–2), which became the new—and far more focused—nucleus. This cluster produced associ-

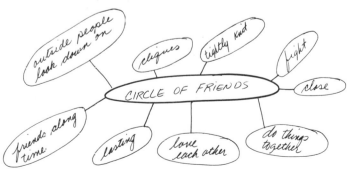

Figure 11–2

ations that related exclusively to her notion of what a circle of friends was and did and meant to her.

Part of the idea of this assignment was to experiment with the visual form of the circle, so I asked students to draw a large circle on a sheet of paper as a form of limitation and to write the vignette within it. Having drawn on Design-mind associations and experienced the trial-web shift, this student began to write her vignette. The resulting draft began with a negative, "no/you can't/be a part of our/group." which in turn led to an affirmation of what a tightly knit circle of friends is all about. An interesting metaphor holds the whole together: "bound like/a favorite old/pair of levis."

no
you can't
be a part of our
group: our circle of
friends. Years have sewn
us together, tightly.
We are bound like
a favorite old
pair of levis
we cannot
part with.
Friendships
are the
same.

Rereading her work at this stage, this writer felt the whole to be too wordy, too negative, the final sentence too "lame": "Friendships are the same." She felt two metaphors conflict: "years have sewn us together" and "like . . . levis we cannot part with." She saw too many words that did not contribute powerfully enough: "group," "tightly," "friendships." She wanted to explore more options, more images, better metaphors, so she reclustered the word "friendships" (Figure 11–3).

The deliberate return to Design-mind patterning through reclustering, even after she had already written her first draft, gave this student additional perspective, new options to choose from, vivid detail in support of her vision of friendship.

At this point we will stop—even though this writer's revision play is far from complete—to give you the opportunity to experience redesign through reclustering.

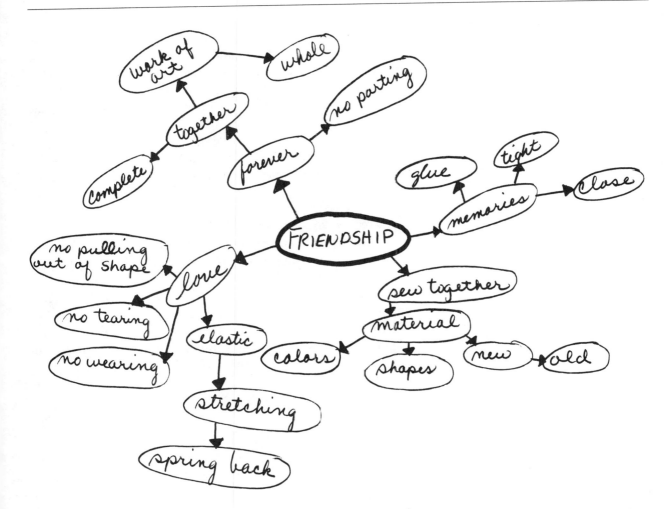

Figure 11–3

Directing Your Hand

The movement from preclustering for discovering a focus to clustering for a trial web, then to writing a rapid first draft and reclustering for additional options and clearer focus, encourages the cooperation of both sides of the brain in achieving natural writing.

1.   In your writer's notebook precluster the word ⬭CIRCLE⬭ , keeping in mind that circles are archetypal—that is, a frequently recurring image in human experience. A circle encompasses natural cycles such as birth and death, the changing seasons, night and day. It is also a natural image for completion, enclosing, shutting in as well as shutting out (which is evident in the first

draft of the student's circle poem). Moreover, variations of the circle shape make up the natural world—think of oranges, eggs, mangoes, tree trunks, the sun—whereas the man-made world is almost exclusively angular: look at the houses we build, the windows we look out of, the tile on the floor, the rectangular rooms we live and work in, the cribs we're put into as babies, the caskets we're buried in. The natural qualities of circle forms attract us powerfully. Filter this word through your own experiential sieve and see what associations unique to you emerge in your cluster.

2. When you experience the trial-web shift, ask yourself "What triggered it? What in my precluster led to a sense of design, vision, something to write about?" The shift represents your own discovered focus and becomes the nucleus for clustering proper. Record the new focus in a statement in your notebook below the precluster, and cluster it for images, associations, detail, lines of songs, poems, whatever will come.

3. When you experience a second trial-web shift, draw a large circle in the center of a fresh piece of paper and begin writing your vignette within that circle. That circle as frame not only imposes its own limitations regarding the length of what you will write but will influence your design and placement of words. Keep in mind the Design-mind strategies of natural writing: a clear focus, recurrences, language rhythms, images, metaphor, creative tension, coming full circle.

This vignette will become your first draft, a preliminary piece of writing that will be refined into a polished, final product. Put it aside while we look at the next step in redesign.

Redesigning: The Relationship Among Words and Ideas

Go back to the first draft of the sample "circle of friends" vignette and read it aloud. Now examine the reclustering of "friendship" done when the first draft didn't satisfy this student writer. Note a host of new images and expansions on old ones. This recluster led the writer to explore the spontaneous associations in the five disciplined redesignings that appear below, until she was finally satisfied with the

*Memories
sew us together,
years being the thread.
We will never part; our love
is elastic—stretching, yet
pulling us forever back,
keeping us together—
a circle of friends.*

*Memories
sew us together,
years being the thread.
We hold together, love
being the glue, tight, close,
us, a circle of friends
never to be pulled
out of shape.*

*Memories
sew us together,
different pieces of material,
different colors, different shapes,
years being the thread.
A piece of artwork—
we are completed.
New material,
no thread.
We are
a circle
of friends—
clique.*

*Memories
sew us together,
years being the thread.
We cannot be torn, worn
apart. Forever—
our circle of
friends*

sixth version. Here we see Sign- and Design-mind cooperation at work as the writer moves between larger design and detail, between the tentative vision and experimental sequences, until her economy of words reaches a stage where the "less is more" maxim becomes truly applicable.

The first redesigning immediately after reclustering omits the negative opening of the first draft; since she is talking about friendship, the negative "no, you can't be . . ." sounded foot-stampingly childish and slightly hypocritical.

Now "memories" has become the focus and a sewing metaphor is apparent; however, the metaphor shifts to a rubberband: "stretching, yet/pulling us forever back." "Keeping us together" and "a circle of friends" are somewhat redundant, repeating what the two metaphors have already expressed. The writer is not yet satisfied, and redesigns.

She drops the "rubber-band" metaphor and experiments with a "glue" metaphor: "love being the glue," taken from her reclustering. But the "never to be pulled/out of shape" seems to be a remnant from the "levis" metaphor of the first draft. The words still don't express what she wants to convey about friendship. She is not yet satisfied, and redesigns once more.

The first two lines satisfy her, so they remain. But the "glue" metaphor goes, as does the "levi" metaphor. She scanned her reclustering and experimented with the "art" metaphor she found there. The "sewing" metaphor still stays, although she has introduced a new aspect of sewing—the material. There is some confusion with "new material,/no thread." She goes back to a line from the first draft: "we are/a circle/of friends" and adds "clique." As you can see, there is a constant shift from Design-mind vision of friendship and Sign-mind sequencing to make that vision clear. The words on the page muddle the vision of friendship. She is not yet satisfied, and redesigns yet another time.

Here is drastic pruning. The first three lines are stable since the second redesigning. Dropped is the "material" as too general; dropped is "a piece of artwork" as too wordy; dropped is "clique" as having negative connotations. The "sewing" metaphor is strengthened by "we cannot be torn, worn apart." "Forever" is added. But the approximation of the vision does not yet ring true on the page. She is still not satisfied, and redesigns a final time.

*Circle of Friends
Memories
sew us together,
years being the
needle, love
the thread.
Paula Mangin*

True to the principle of "less is more," this writer has striven to put the essence of her vision of friendship into words. "Circle of Friends" is dropped from the body of the vignette and becomes the title. What is left is the sewing metaphor expanded to include "love/the thread." Memories and love, for this writer, are the essence of friendship. She is satisfied.

In redesigning again and again, shifting from whole to part, from vision to sequence and back, this writer became sensitized to word economy, paring her poem to a most exquisite simplicity. With this last attempt she experienced deep satisfaction and stopped. To her cultivated eye, ear, and hand, her poem was an unalterable aesthetic whole.

Let's return to your own emerging circle vignette.

Directing Your Hand

Read the first draft of your circle vignette aloud. Let your Design mind sweep over the whole, hear its rhythms, feel the fit of its images, recurrences, full-circle wholeness.

1. Give yourself more options for experimentation by reclustering your focus from the first draft. You might even wish to shift focus at this point; that is fine, too.
2. Cluster until you experience the trial-web shift, which may be quite similar to your first vision or may move in a radically different direction.
3. Either way, clarify your focus by writing a focusing statement.
4. Now write the second draft of your circle poem, again within a circle shape, which is a reminder of your limitations of length and form.
5. Once more, let your Design mind take in the whole, hear its rhythms, feel the appropriateness of its images, recurrences, full-circle wholeness. Then shift to a critical Sign-mind attitude and closely look at parts and syntax, the appropriateness of a word or phrase. Ask: Do the images and metaphors get my meaning across effectively? (Only the Design mind can generate a metaphor, but the Sign mind can analyze it.) Do any recurring words serve their purpose? What words need to go? Is there creative tension in the writing—a problem and resolution? Do I come full circle in a graceful, satisfying way?

6. Now go through at least three or four more redesignings (more if you wish), each time writing in a circle frame; each time pruning, adding, shifting, tightening, selecting; each time reading the whole, then examining and clarifying its parts, and then shifting back to a more clearly delineated whole. Do this until your poem feels aesthetically unalterable.

After Writing

You have played with your language and images and striven for wholeness to such a degree that even one word removed or added would impair or destroy the whole. You continued until you had a feeling of completion, satisfaction, the sense that tells you the whole is right. Imagine a painter looking at a completed canvas and adding splashes of color here and there, painting over a partial image and re-creating it elsewhere for better composition, working on the background until the whole is pleasing to him. This is the experience of holistic redesigning. Anything you write deserves this kind of attention before you engage your Sign mind exclusively in correcting spelling, grammar, punctuation, and careful proofreading for careless errors after typing your final draft.

Most authors go through many such redesignings of their work, as we saw at the beginning of this chapter. In his own writing, Dylan Thomas, expresses the necessity for being consciously selective.

One of the arts of the poet is to make comprehensible and articulate what might emerge from subconscious sources; one of the great main uses of the intellect is to select, from the amorphous mass of subconscious images, those that will best further his imaginative purpose.

Dylan Thomas,
Notes on the Art of Poetry

Word Painting: Evocative Versus Explanatory Language

Another way of practicing redesigning is to do what I call word painting, which is the deliberate shift from prose to poetic form.

The two extremes of language use might be characterized as primarily *explanatory,* or conveying information, and *evocative,* or stimulating feelings. The former tends to be linear, logical, and unambiguous, thus largely influenced by the Sign mind. The latter tends to be highly compressed, amalgamating images, using rhythm and sound, evoking an overall feeling, thus heavily influenced by the Design mind. Word painting is the almost exclusive use of evocative language.

Most prose is a mixture of the two; sometimes we want and need explanatory components, at other times we strive almost exclusively for evocative language. Word painting helps us recognize the difference between them and achieve the shift away from tedious explanatory expression toward natural writing.

The student examples below illustrate both shift and differences. Asked to respond to a painting by Hiroshige (Figure 11–4), this budding inner writer began by recording his dominant impression as nucleus and then clustered his observations and associations around it (Figure 11–5).

Figure 11–4

HIROSHIGE, *EVENING SNOW A KAMBARA*, COURTESY OF HEIBONSHA, LTD., TOKYO.

He wrote the first-draft vignette in prose, which contained many observant explanatory components. But he felt the result was flat, conveying information but doing it in a fairly uninteresting way.

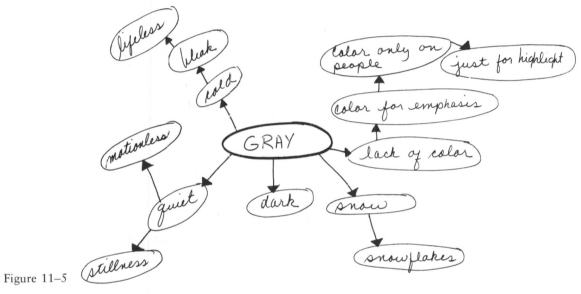

Figure 11–5

Hiroshige's *Kambara*

It is all done in shades of gray. Only the living figures have color. All else is gray. Hiroshige used the tones of gray and the absence of color to portray vividly a winter scene. The sky goes from light gray near the horizon to black at the top of the frame. The gently varied shades of gray in the foreground give a sense of depth. The black undersides of the tree's branches are very realistic, even though they are not drawn in great detail. The realism comes from the use of the tones. The thatch-roofed houses are also devoid of color. Drawn in high contrast, they are white and snow-covered on the roofs, dark gray, almost black underneath.

Only the living figures have color, emphasizing the fact that they are living. Hunched over and covered with snow, the figures are not full of life, but rather clinging to life.

The expert use of the shades of gray and the sparing use of color make this point striking—and one of the most unique and valuable of all of Hiroshige's works.

Steve Sano

The rich detail of the vignette turns primarily on an exploration of the painting's colors or lack thereof. We also find a number of interpretive comments: the branches are "realistic"; the "varied shades of gray in the foreground give a sense of depth"; the human figures "are not full of life, but rather clinging to life." Clearly, this writer is intrigued by the painting, and his interest is reflected in the sensitively written response, despite its fairly dry, explanatory quality.

Once students had described and analyzed the painting, I asked them to redesign their writing through word painting—that is, to compress their language until it was highly evocative, being conscious of rhythm, sound, and recurrences and eliminating all explanatory components in favor of creating an overall feeling. I asked them to recast their vignette in poetic form.

With these instructions, this student writer reread his vignette and became aware that the vision of "grayness" triggering his dominant impression did not quite align with his written form. He wanted something more—and at the same time something less. How to reproduce the feeling of the painting rather than just talk about it? How to compress? How to intensify in words the effect this painting had on him? How to repaint the painting in words? The aim of word painting is to evoke more, explain less, so:

1. He focused on a dominant impression, decided he still liked "grayness," and used it as his recurring unifying thread.
2. He began to pare all deadwood—words that didn't add anything to the whole.
3. He began to cut explanatory phrases.
4. He looked at what he had left, refocused on his original trial vision, rescanned the painting, and then reshaped the remaining words. As shown in the circle poem, he reshaped two or three times until he felt he had re-created the painting in words.

His redesign took on highly evocative dimensions through the deliberate use of word painting. Read it aloud for full flavor.

Kambara
Gray,
Shades of black.
The lack of color
Is cold.
Only the figures have color,
Only the color has warmth,
Only warmth has life.
The life moves ankle-deep
Through gray powder.
The same powder covers
Living backs,
The mountains, trees,
And the thatched roofs
Of dark houses.
Look at the sky:
one shade of gray
Except far on the horizon
Where it is black,
One shade of gray
With gray powder falling,
Cold,
Bleak,
Forever
Gray

Steve Sano

From his first vignette, the writer has eliminated all explanatory efforts and almost anything that does not draw a vivid picture, such as "it is all done with"; "portray vividly a winter scene"; "top of the frame"; "gently varied"; "sense of depth"; "the black undersides of the tree's branches are very realistic even though they are not drawn in great detail"; "the realism comes from the use of tones"; "are also devoid of color"; "emphasizing the fact that they are living"; and "one of the most unique and valuable of all of Hiroshige's works." What is left in the second vignette is highly compressed meaning. The first vignette explains; the second re-creates in words.

Now it is time for you to experience the distinction between evocative and explanatory prose in your own writing.

Directing Your Hand

Experience the dictum "less is more" in natural writing. Learn to evoke as well as to explain, thereby learning to be sensitive to word overload by becoming a word painter.

1. Give your Design mind the opportunity to scan the picture of the untitled sculpture by Ole Langerhorst (Figure 11–6). Record your dominant impression in a circle. It can take the form of a polarity or a "contrary" if you wish.

Figure 11–6   OLE LANGERHORST, *UNTITLED,* COURTESY OF THE SCULPTOR.

2. Now cluster around it whatever you see, whatever you feel as your eyes explore the figures and your Design mind responds with associations.

3. Stay alert for the trial-web shift that will spur your urge to write. When it comes, hold it fast in a focusing statement.

4. Now write your vignette, using whatever pertains from your cluster. Remember, clustering gives you choices; there is no need to try to squeeze in everything just because it's there. Choose from the rich array your Design mind has made available to your Sign mind to work in integrated fashion.

5. Read your vignette aloud, listening for rhythms, images, metaphors, recurrences, tension, full-circle wholeness—all the elements of natural writing.

6. Now focus again on your dominant impression (in the Hiroshige example, it was "gray"). This should be your point of reference for redesigning. Everything in your revised vignette should contribute to this central idea. Begin your word painting by cutting as much explanatory language as you can; strengthen your evocative language through recurrences, images, metaphors, and language rhythms. Cultivate tension. Come full circle.

7. Read your new vignette aloud. Your ear will tell you what still doesn't sound right. Listen and respond by making any changes that will pare it down and intensify the feeling you have created.

8. Now that you have produced your evocative whole, deliberately shift to a Sign-mind bias and read only to correct spelling, punctuation, and grammatical and typographical errors. If you have a tendency not to see these, try reading your vignette backward, which will enable you to catch errors you might not otherwise notice.

After Writing

Count the words of your first vignette and compare it to the count of the second. Very likely the compression of the evocative vignette yielded fewer words, much tighter compression, and far greater intensity. The point is now how many words you use, however, but how effectively you use language. Every word should tell.

Expect Nothing
*Expect nothing. Live frugally
On surprise.
Become a stranger
To need of pity
Or, if compassion be freely
Given out
Take only enough.
Stop short of the urge to plead
Then purge away the need.*

*Wish for nothing larger
Than your own small heart
Or greater than a star;
Tame wild disappointment
With caress unmoved and cold.
Make of it a parka
for your soul.*

*Discover the reason why
So tiny human midget
Exists at all
So scared unwise.
But expect nothing. Live frugally
On surprise.*

Alice Walker

Modeling Evocative Writing

Studying and modeling the evocative writing of others intensifies your ability to manipulate language for evocative purposes. American poet Alice Walker holds explanatory language to a minimum in this "advice" poem without sacrificing clarity of meaning. Read it aloud.

She offers no explanation—no who, where, when, how—yet we can infer that the poet is giving advice on authentic living. The focus is on the *what,* or content, of wise advice, and that content is communicated through twelve parallel statements of command: "expect nothing," "live frugally," "become a stranger," "take only," "stop short," "purge away," "wish for," "tame," "make of it," "discover the reason," "expect nothing," "live frugally." This directness gives the feeling that this writer knows through experience deeper than words whereof she speaks.

In the first stanza we learn that pity and compassion are dangerous. In the second we learn that wishes can encompass the tiny as well as the enormous, and that wishing is permissible if we know how to "tame wild disappointment." Implicit in this advice is the assumption that wild disappointments are inevitable. In the third stanza we learn that to spend time wondering about human existence is a worthwhile endeavor. But most important is the injunction to "expect nothing," for then we are sustained by the unexpected surprises life brings to our doorstep. The antithetical notions of expectation and surprise begin and end the poem, reconciling the tension between the scared unwise "human midget" and his unrealistic expectations, which bring only disappointment.

Directing Your Hand

Now it's your turn to give some advice while striving to achieve your own highly compressed, highly evocative language. Go back to Alice Walker's poem and read it aloud.

1. In your writer's notebook precluster the nucleus word ⟨ADVICE⟩ . Do so to garner a great many options, until you experience the trial-web shift signifying that one of these options resonates with deep meaning for you.

2. Cast your trial-web vision in a word or phrase and cluster it for all the associations, feelings, details you can muster. Don't forget about the possibility of lines of poetry, songs, advice from plays (such as Polonius's from Shakespeare's *Hamlet*: "This above all: to thine own self be true/and it must follow, as the night the day/Thou canst not then be false to any man").

3. Now quickly write your vignette on advice that is genuinely important to you. Mean the advice you give. Write it in prose first, if you wish, and then turn it into a word painting on the second go-round. Pay little attention to form at this stage. As always, just get your thoughts on paper.

4. Now begin to redesign: compress, tighten, prune, shift, experiment. Leave only language that is evocative; omit explanation. You may want to let it run through several redesignings before you are satisfied.

5. Remember to let that which is significant recur, to be sensitive to language rhythms and especially to parallel forms, to strive for metaphor, to create images, to play with opposites for creative tension. Let every word tell.

6. Read your "advice" aloud. Make any other changes you wish, and then proofread for grammar, spelling, and punctuation.

After Writing

In writing your advice poem you probably wrote several drafts to "get the words right." With each draft you found yourself tightening, compressing, cutting deadwood, shifting bits of advice for sound, rhythm, image, and meaning. Some of you may have written a first draft, found it wanting, and reclustered for better images and metaphors to approximate your original vision—perhaps you even changed to a thought that struck a stronger emotional chord in you. Whatever course your writing took, you probably found that with each revision your focus became clearer and more finely honed.

Let's look at a student writer's advice poem that hinges on the metaphor of making a "deal" with life for security's sake (Figure 11–7). But we learn the enormous price of such a deal is ultimately to "ignore the quintessential/Substance of your soul."

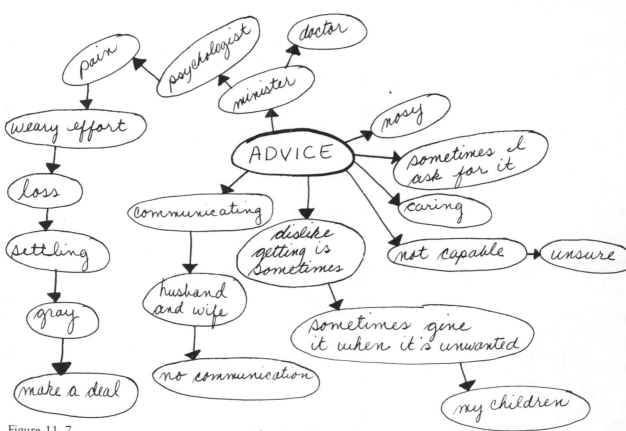

Figure 11–7

The Way You Make a Deal with Life
Listen, life is lean, reality disappointing.
So consume your hope like body fat, draw in.
Fill chasms of despair with nonessentials.
Be ashamed of hunger, and, denying need,
Learn to counterfeit a satisfaction.
Put your trust in shades of gray.
Bank on security—be sensible.
Ignore the quintessential
Substance of your soul.

Having made your deal with life, it's certain
Then, when evening comes,
Having lived your life in twilight,
You'll be content to sleep.

Lavelle Leahey

You have just read the final revision of the six drafts this advice poem went through. To give you a sense of where this writer began, I reproduce her first draft after clustering.

The way you make a deal with life
                    hope like body fat
Is to consume ~~withdraw~~ draw in

Forget the dreams you never believed ~~in~~ them anyway

The way you make a deal with life

~~Is to~~ fill up chasms with the trivial

Remember life is lean ~~it's lean~~

"Real" disappointing

The way you make a deal with life

~~Is to~~ forget the needs that made you hungry

Find a substitute, counterfeit a satisfaction.

The way you make a deal with life.
       disbelieve in   prospects
~~Is to forget a~~ golden ending
Put your trust in
~~Learn to study~~ shades of gray

The way to make a deal with life

~~Is to~~ mature until your dreams are sensible

Then anesthetize the pain by forgetting
        trade in security; ignore the loss
Then settle ~~the pain of loss~~

Because she was modeling the already highly evocative language of Alice Walker's advice poem, this writer's first draft is already relatively compressed for a first writing. Yet she went on to revise it five more times before she felt she "got the words right." In the course of these revisions the seventeen lines and one hundred thirty-five words of the first draft were pared to thirteen lines and seventy-five words.

Even in the first draft you can already see that she is cutting dead language: she crosses out "is to" four times. The first line, "The way to make a deal with life," repeated five times, becomes the title of the final draft. At the same time, even in her first draft, we have a sense of the original trial-web vision preserved in her final draft: making a deal with life may bring security, but it robs one of the joy of being an authentic human being.

The most evocative lines in the first draft also make their appearance in the final draft: "consume hope like body fat, draw in"; "chasms of despair"; "needs that make you hungry" becomes "be ashamed of hunger, and, denying need"; "counterfeit a satisfaction"; "trade in security" becomes "bank on security"; "until your dreams are sensible" becomes "be sensible"

Yet the first draft seems unfinished, as indeed it must have been, for in the progressive revisions there emerges the important twilight/sleep metaphor: "Having made your deal with life, it's certain/Then, when evening comes,/Having lived your life in twilight,/You'll be content to sleep." These last lines of the final draft imply that those who make that "deal" for security have little cause to "rage, rage against the dying of the light," to use Dylan Thomas's famous line, because they never lived in the full light of their full human potential in the first place.

The final draft uses the language rhythms of parallel forms for directness and power: "listen," "consume," "draw in," "fill," "be ashamed," "learn," "put," "bank," "be," "ignore." The advice drips with the tension of heavy irony. We get her message.

A Last Word and Heading On

In this chapter you have had opportunity to redesign, striving for the principle of word economy that "less is more." Perhaps the best way to sum up the process is to let two writing specialists comment on the value of revision. The first is Jacques Barzun, in *Simple and Direct;* the second is William Irmscher, in *Teaching Expository Writing.*

*One great aim of revision is to cut
out. In the exuberance of composition it is natural to throw in—as
one does in speaking—a number of
small words that add nothing to
meaning but keep up the flow and
rhythm of thought. In writing, not
only does this surplusage not add
to meaning, it subtracts from it.
Read and revise, reread and revise,
keeping reading and revising until
your text seems adequate to your
thought.*

Jacques Barzun,

*In an art form like film-making, we
know that editing and revising cannot be dismissed as superfluous, for
they are an integral part of the
whole process. In fact, what we
eventually see on the screen is not
what was filmed, but what was edited.*

William Irmscher

These quotes underscore what we have stressed throughout this chapter: the active interplay of Sign and Design minds in the writing process, reflecting the two sides of your nature working in harmony. Cooperation and orchestration between the creative and the critical, between generating and refining your ideas, are the keys to natural writing.

You are now on the threshold of applying all the techniques you have learned to a longer, more sustained piece of writing. Let's stop for a moment to evaluate how far you've come.

In reclaiming the natural writer within you and in cultivating your eye, ear, and hand, you have learned to draw on your Design mind's sensitivity to images, to patterns and wholeness through clustering; you have learned to discover a guiding vision for a vignette by becoming aware of the trial-web shift; you have learned to look, listen for, and utilize recurrences, images, metaphor, and language rhythms; you have learned to recognize, and experiment with, creative tension.

Finally, in this chapter, you have learned to hone and compress language until it becomes more evocative than explanatory. You also learned that redesigning requires the realignment of your writing with your original vision until the writing feels right—and what's "right" lies not outside you but within your Design mind's ability to focus on a whole, complex vision.

All this you have accomplished by writing vignettes—mini-wholes characterized by their spontaneous, playful nature. Now you are ready to expand and put it all together in the final chapter of this book.

CHAPTER 12/ *Coming Full Circle*

In Chapter 1, I described a *vignette* as a mini-whole. One meaning of the word, the dictionary tells us, is "a tendril-sized vine." A vignette contains all the attributes of the mature vine, just as a molecule of DNA contains the genetic code for the entire human body, and just as a vignette in natural writing contains all the stylistic and conceptual attributes of a short story, a poem, an essay, a novel, or a play. As a mini-whole, a vignette has a structure and a content that can stand alone, as well as the distinctive voice of the writer who generated it. By concentrating on vignettes throughout this course, you have experienced the shaping of a coherent whole again and again.

The secret of sustained longer writing lies precisely in vignette writing, since longer writing is merely a series of mini-wholes woven together by a larger vision. An inner writer intent on creating an essay, a short story, a business proposal, an academic dissertation, a novel, or a play first generates the larger vision that will guide him throughout the long process of writing. Then, as he begins writing, he generates a mini-whole, which generates another mini-whole, which in turn suggests the next, until the larger vision is realized. All coherent writing is structured in this fashion whether the writer is aware of it or not, and regardless of what it is called. In an essay, a vignette might be a paragraph; in a novel, a chapter or an episode; in a poem, a stanza; in a play, a scene or an act.

The point is that by now you have to hand all the skills necessary to expand your vignettes into a more sustained and developed

260

piece of writing. And you will discover how extensive your skills are through writing a "family portrait," a series of interlocking vignettes that become a voyage of self-discovery.

Designing a Family Portrait

Creative acts most readily arise from the things closest and most profoundly meaningful to us. The subject of "family," for example, generally stimulates complex feelings—enriching or devastating—in all of us and therefore has great inspirational potential for natural writing. The influences of your family are part of your being, thinking, feeling, behavior. By recognizing and interpreting these influences through clustering, you can discover the powerful intangibles that have shaped your life and your personality. Moreover, family portraits are an apt way to get from vignettes to longer writing, since you tend to remember your life within the family unit in terms of brief episodes or vignettes, of acts, interludes, individual characters in a real-life drama.

There is something inherently compelling to writers in considering family relationships. The practice is as old as the Greek family tragedies, such as *Antigone, Oedipus Rex,* and *Electra*. In the nineteenth century it was John Galsworthy's trilogy, *The Forsyte Saga*. In this century many great writers have used families as the basis for their most compelling works: Thomas Mann in *Buddenbrooks,* Dostoevsky in *The Brothers Karamazov,* John Steinbeck in *The Grapes of Wrath,* John Cheever in *The Wapshot Chronicles,* John Irving in *Hotel New Hampshire,* to mention a few. The reason for this is clear: our families are the stuff life is made of. Giving aesthetic shape to our own experience elevates it to something beyond mere experience; it becomes a profoundly creative act.

Discover what influences your unique family experience has had on you. The form your writing takes will emerge organically as you cluster. Trust your inner writer.

The confessional poem [poems of family relationships], then, is like a lens that magnifies and organizes particulars, a mirror that for an instant frames an identity . . . . It is an act of disclosure, in which experience is always richer than any ideas about it expressed in examples, conventions, or stereotypes.
Diane Middlebrook,
Worlds into Words

First, by way of illustration, let's examine two quite different family portraits, both triggered by the same set of instructions. I directed my students to precluster (FAMILY) either in terms of names or of qualities family members exhibited, such as loyalty, quarrelsomeness, and so forth. Then I told them to choose a point of view—of an adult either looking at the past or looking at the present; or of a child looking at an adult world; or of an adult looking back over a span of generations—whatever suited the writer's purpose. On separate sheets of paper they were to cluster each family member or each chosen quality characterizing the family or its members.

Then they were to write a separate, self-contained vignette for each cluster, embodying the strategies of natural writing learned throughout this book. I asked them to recluster for a dominant thread if that thread had not yet appeared in the earlier clustering or in the vignettes themselves. This dominant thread was to be stitched through each vignette to give the whole unity and focus. They were to rework the vignettes to include the dominant thread in order to make the larger whole cohesive, and they were to prune until every word told and until the commonplaces of a single family with its joys and problems became something more than merely commonplace through the presentation. In short, they were to experience the tremendous cumulative effect that using all the strategies of natural writing has on a piece of writing.

They were either to leave the vignettes separate as stanzas unified by a dominant thread or to work them into an indivisible whole. Finally, they were to type and proofread carefully for errors in punctuation, spelling, and grammar (the final Sign-mind task that Professor John Trimble likens to the quality-control stage at the end of the assembly line).

The first family portrait, entitled simply "Family Portraits," was written by a beginning writer whose "before" and "after" work you have already seen in Chapter 1. Over three and a half months in a course that met twice a week, she grew from a stifled, fearful writer into someone enormously willing to trust her Design-mind processes and to risk emotional vulnerability in her writing. Each of her vignettes is a self-contained whole, yet they were all skillfully woven together by the "dinner-table" image that constitutes her unifying thread, the hub around which she explores each family member's personality and the relationship of each to her.

Family Portraits
The Striver
Swedish blonde to my dark, her years were
steadfast on sturdy young legs in corrective shoes,
a child only needing glasses to complete
a large intellectual capacity.
Strive, Jann. Strive for logic, for reason,
for science, for strength. Strive for success.
Forget havoc of emotion, the insecurity of life.
Sit at the dinner table creating a greenhouse
of goals and personal achievements to view
the world as your stepping stone from.
Sullenly lift your nose out of your heavy books
to sneer at a simple complaint
or to reach for more rare beef.

The Psycho-Dabbler
Green eyes dredged in coal lashes
brighten her sharp, inquisitive face.
With intent she drinks our quiet guilt for breakfast,
defecates daily a friend's death,
sleeps on the blunder of an unknown love affair.
She wanders asking everyone about the closeness
we are all silently looking for,
as she seeks the enduring beauty
of every unresolved conflict.
Mother sits at the dinner table each evening
with grave concern pasted on her pale lips.
She suggests creative answers to all her
creative problems; she asks how you are,
to hear how you are not, to hear how you are not.

The General
Family communication finds him buried
in the evening news,
until questions arise at the dinner table.
Provoked, he peers over his horn rims at us:
"There is no God," he announces,
suddenly subjecting our digestion to his roar.
No one asks, but the deep answers to all eternity
are fiercely offered for want,
lest there be intellectual quiet in his house!
Humiliated by his voice as big as thousands,
his demands for agreement taut as barbed wire,
we withdraw into our books, our insights,
our lives, my fears.

And Me
In my small heart it is always winter
and my dinner is always cold.
Freezing tears pour in loneliness as I quietly
absorb dinnertable differences.
I pain for my sister's determination.
She succeeds by will at great cost
to her emotional fiber.
She is eternally mature.
        I will never reach her.
I yearn for a motherly soul,
while mommy rushes aimlessly about
in a profusion of feelings belonging
to another family named Humanity.
She is strapped to a raft,
lost in an emotional sea.
        I will never find her.
I hope for fatherly comfort
when his hands squeeze mine too tightly.
I scream fear at the angle of his sailboat,
and he abruptly rights the vessel, sending me
into fits of capsized agony and anger.

There was no calm with daddy at the helm.
His bold uniqueness constantly threatened,
all questions were followed by question
after question, after question.
I never received a simple, reliable answer.
    I will never trust him.
Like wood shrinking in the drying cold,
we have shrunk from each other,
carefully hiding our lives' memories away
in a warm safe deposit box of emotion
and swallowing the key.
My dinner is cold; there is a
great winter storm of
bitter flurries in me, even today.

                                        Jillian Milligan

Each vignette has its own structure, its own unity, even its own
title. However, these vignettes cohere into a larger whole precisely
through the recurrence of images drawn from the dinner table. For
example, in the vignette characterizing the sister, we have "sit at the
dinner table creating a greenhouse/of goals" and "Sullenly lift your
nose out of your heavy books/to sneer at a simple complaint/or to
reach for more rare beef." In the second vignette, characterizing the
mother, "she drinks our quiet guilt for breakfast"; she "sits at the
dinner table . . ./with grave concern pasted on her pale lips"; "she
asks you how you are,/to hear how you are not, to hear how you are
not." In the third, characterizing the father, we find him "buried/in
the evening news,/until questions arise at the dinner table." He subjects "our digestion to his roar" and "peers over his horn rims at
us."

    And in the last stanza, characterizing herself, the poet writes that
"my dinner is always cold" and that she experiences "loneliness as I
quietly/absorb dinnertable differences." She comes full circle by repeating the image, and in so doing underscores the profound effect
her family has had on her life: "My dinner is cold; there is a/great
winter storm of/bitter flurries in me, even today."

The power of this portrait lies in its insights into human relationships in a family that, unlike many today, at least has its meals together and whose parents talk to their children. But the creative tension builds when we see that the talk is either superficial or autocratic, revealing the pain and vulnerability of the writer. In choosing the dinner-table setting—ironically signifying "togetherness"—as her unifying thread, we gradually perceive the profound separateness that yawns like an unbridgeable chasm for the writer.

Design-mind strategies are apparent throughout this family portrait:

Wholeness

The dinner table and all its ramifications, seen through the personalities of the eaters, unifies each vignette with the larger whole, which demonstrates a terrible separateness under the convention of togetherness. As discussed above, the dominant image pattern of dinner-table references engender this sense of unity among the four vignettes.

Images

"sturdy young legs," "sullenly lifting her nose," "green eyes dredged in coal lashes," "pale lips," "freezing tears,"
    "winter," "cold"

Language rhythms

Parallel forms: "Strive for logic, for reason,/for science, for strength"; "she drinks . . . , defecates . . . , sleeps"; "we withdraw into our books, our insights,/our lives, my fears"; "I will never reach her/ . . . I will never find her . . . I will never trust him."

Balanced forms: "Strive for success./Forget havoc of emotion"; "she asks how you are,/to hear how you are not."

Metaphors

"greenhouse/of goals"; "drinks our quiet guilt for breakfast"; "mommy . . . strapped to a raft,/. . . in an emotional sea"; father as stern captain of sailboat; "demands . . . taut as barbed wire"; "wood shrinking in the drying cold"; "safe deposit box of emotion"; "winter storm of/bitter flurries"

Recurrences

"dinnertable difference . . . determination"; "steadfast on sturdy young legs"; "pasted on her pale lips"; "agony and anger"; "provoked . . . peers"; "question/after question, after question"; "creative answers . . . creative problems"; "how you are . . . how you are not"; "I will never reach . . . find . . . trust"; "our books, our insights,/our lives"

Creative tension

mother's emotional sea versus father's stern, commanding intellectuality; sister's sturdy strength versus "my" emotional vulnerability; group versus loneliness, isolation; comfort versus pain and fear

The effect of these techniques on the content is profound, for we are inexorably drawn into this little drama by the nuances and subtleties of language—from image to metaphor to recurrences and so forth—that appeal to our aesthetically sensitive Design mind. From a Sign-mind perspective this scenario is commonplace enough not to merit much attention; after all, no one was beaten or maimed or murdered. Recorded in Sign-mind language it would be downright dull: sister is an intellectual snob; mother is a wishy-washy do-gooder; father is an intellectual bully; "I" am alienated from them all. So what?

But because of the use of Design-mind strategies, this family portrait unfolds as a rich tapestry of human lives, sadly flawed, sadly doing what they perceive to be their best, and sadly missing the boat. We are left with resonating feelings of pity but also with empathy and insight, because this particular family drama is also a universal one: we can all tell stories of small successes and large failures in our own families, and we admire the courage it took to risk telling the story as this writer perceived it. Natural writing encourages such risks

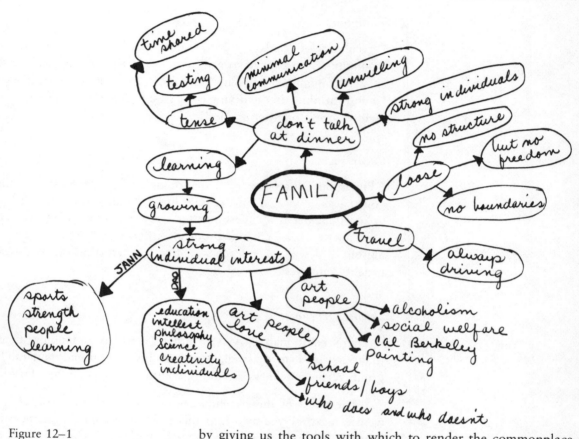

Figure 12–1

by giving us the tools with which to render the commonplace aesthetically, and thereby enrich and clarify our view of humanity.

Now let us briefly look at one of the clusters that spawned this writing, remembering that a cluster is the Design mind's shorthand, thus very private and not meant to be comprehensible until the cooperative effort of both hemispheres make the private vision public.

A brief glance at the precluster (Figure 12–1) reflects memories of the entire family structure. Yet it is already here that we see the unifying thread—"don't talk at dinner"—emerging, the thread that will bring unity to the whole. Here we also can see the incipient form the entire family portrait will take, for "strong individual interests" results in thumbnail clusters for each member of the family. The subsequent 3 clusters (not shown) represent a deepening of the exploration of each individual in the family structure, allowing this writer to discover what is important to *her,* with the result that certain qualities and events emerge unchecked by the critical censorship of the Sign mind.

The second family portrait, entitled "Lines of Descent," is quite different in approach. It contains no specific delineation of individuals in the family, only a "woman" and a "husband" and several unspecified children. The recurrence of "Once there was . . ." creates an air of false detachment, almost as if this poem were a fairy tale, but underneath volcanic feelings are seething and simmering.

The structure consists of six distinct vignettes, the first five beginning with the fairy-tale-like "Once there was. . . ." The last begins with "Now there is this woman who is 23"—and that is all, as though the history of this woman, the writer, is as yet unwritten because it must first unfold as experience. Also implied by the shift from "Once there was . . ." to "Now there is . . ." is the certainty of a change from the child who "learned to turn the other cheek" and to build walls "as some children must," to the woman "who was tired of turning the other cheek," and finally to a woman who is gradually achieving self-realization. Each "once there was . . ." vignette represents a progression of events, adding a new dimension of understanding of why and how "this woman who is 23" arrived at where she is now.

> *Lines of Descent*
> Once there was this woman who was pregnant
> who didn't want to be pregnant,
> who didn't want a baby.
> She already had one baby.
> One was enough. More than enough.
> She thought about abortion;
> Someone talked her out of it.
> Someone wanted the baby.
> So she bore this baby
> who was born in the spring,
> who was born a girl,
> who started small and grew larger and older as all babies do.
>
> Once there was this woman with a boy and a girl and a husband,
> A husband who worked hard and drank a lot,
> A husband who had a bum leg and a lot of war memories,
> Who had a bike and a lot of biker friends,
> Who had a boy and a girl and a wife who was pregnant again.

Once there was this woman who was 21,
Who had a boy and three girls and a husband,
Who had a job and a taste for alcohol and a penchant for the
     arts,

Who hated her life and her oldest daughter and herself.
One child had been enough. More than enough.
Once, goaded by her circumstance and her anger and her alco-
     hol,
she hit her oldest daughter.
She hit her hard many times.
She might have killed her daughter, but her husband saw
               and stopped her.
So this daughter, who had started small, grew taller and
               older as all children do.
And she learned to come when she was called,
               and fetch when she was bid
               and never, never raise her hand or her voice
               or her eyes to her elders.
She learned to turn the other cheek and to catch herself
               when she fell.
She learned to wash dishes and pack lunches and fix the
               other girls for school.
And she built castles and fantasies as all children do.
And walls, as some children must.

Once there was this woman and her husband who decided they'd
               had enough. More than enough.
Who decided that this separation would be the final one.
Who had been together 17 years and had a boy and three girls.
And the boy, who had mostly been with relatives, joined the
               men who joined the army,
And the woman found a new husband who took her and the
               three girls away, leaving
A husband who had an ex-wife and a lot of memories,
Who had a bike and a lot of biker friends,
Who worked hard and drank a lot.

Once there was this daughter who decided she'd had enough,
Who was tired of turning the other cheek and catching herself
               when she fell,

Who had a choice to make and a father to run to,
A father who had an extra bed and a girlfriend,
Who had open arms and a mending heart.

Now there is this woman who is 23.

Donna Ducarme

The power of this piece comes from the anonymity of the characters, giving the writing the universal quality of the story of all
abused children. This universality is sustained by the recurrence of
"who" and "and" and the anonymous "someone." The story is re-
lentless in its third-person voice. It is also like a fairy tale, beginning
with "Once there was . . . ," and this fairy-tale quality is implicit
in the telescoping of events that happened over many years and in
the description of the "oldest daughter" who "learned to come when
she was called,/and fetch when she was bid/and never, never raise her
hand or her voice/or her eyes to her elders." She also learned to "wash
dishes and pack lunches and fix the/other girls for school."

The image of Cinderella floats before us as we read. Like Cinderella, "she built castles and fantasies." Like Cinderella she "learned
to turn the other cheek" in the face of abuse. And this veiled allusion
adds to the sense of hopelessness and helplessness of a child who is
hated but doesn't know why. Only the prince does not come to res-
cue this modern Cinderella; rather, she herself "decided she'd had
enough, . . . was tired of turning the other cheek." She "had a choice
to make" and she makes it, growing into independence so that instead of the impotent *child,* "Now there is this *woman* who is 23."

Numerous other Design-mind strategies play a part in creating
this fairy-tale/real-life drama of a child's growth from helplessness to
independence:

Wholeness

· Wholeness is achieved by the strategy of recurrence, already discussed, gradually shifting the story from hopelessness to determination.

Images

· There are only a few, kept simple and understated to the barest
  outlines so as not to interfere with the universal fairy-tale quality
  the writer was striving for: "bum leg," "biker friends."

Metaphors

·   These are also sparing: "build walls" (referring to psychic walls built by those who must protect themselves from a hostile environment), "mending heart."

Language rhythms

·   The heavy use of "who . . ." focuses on a rhythmic repetition of terrible inevitability, giving the whole story a sense of fatalism and despair: "who worked hard," "who did not want to be pregnant," "who didn't want a baby," "who hated her life and her oldest daughter and herself."

Coming full circle

·   "Once there was this woman who was pregnant [with the child who is] now . . . this woman who is 23," and the teller of this tale.

Creative tension

·   There is tension between acquiescence and taking a stand: "Once there was . . . Now there is . . ."; between stasis and change; between staying and leaving; between falling and standing; between all children who build fantasies and some children who *must* build walls.

As in the previous example, the content taken at face value is quite simple. The Sign mind might tell it as the story of a child whose mother really didn't want her and therefore didn't treat her very well, which left her with numerous emotional difficulties to be resolved in adulthood. But the *how* of the writing—its evocative style and insight—elevates it to the status of an aesthetic whole in which the nuances and subtleties of the language evoke a complexity of feeling within us as we read. In developing this story through the Design-mind strategies she had learned, this writer's grim tale is not one of judgment against mother—who, after all, "didn't want to be pregnant" and was "goaded by her circumstance"—but a subtle tale of emotional stunting and victory over adversity. The tale is bitter-sweet; to paraphrase Diane Middlebrook, it is an act of self-disclosure richer than any ideas about it expressed in conventions or stereotypes.

Again, analyzing this writer's Design-mind shorthand, we see that the first precluster (Figure 12–2) of "Lines of Descent" is exploratory, laying bare some of the negative emotional components that

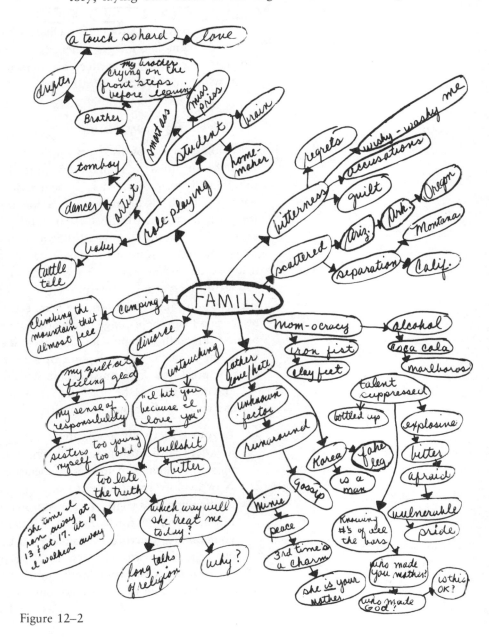

Figure 12–2

come to underlie the vignettes. The next three clusters (not shown) examine these emotional components in greater depth as qualities and emotions characterizing this family unit:

(SEPARATENESS) , (TOUCH) , (CRY) .

Altogether, the progressive clusters show much activity. Many of the thoughts and images generated did not find their way into the portrait, but this inner writer gave herself an abundance of choices from which to select the most fitting.

Directing Your Hand

Take a voyage of discovery into your own family circle. Use your fertile history to write a qualitative portrait of yourself in relation to other family members. As is evident from the family portraits you have just read, all of us live out a lifelong drama of relationships that, when evoked by the Design mind, allow often surprising insights and patterns to emerge. Begin with a vignette, and then another, and another, until you have created an evocative longer whole, using all the techniques you have learned for natural writing.

Consider your vantage point (point of view) as you write. It suggests your angle of vision, the perspective you establish. You may be writing from the vantage point of a six-year-old; from the vantage point of an adult longingly looking back at something that will never be again; from the vantage point of a teenager torn by family conflicts or pressures. You must decide whether to use the first-person "I," the third-person "he" or "she," or some other angle from which to observe and reflect on your family.

1. In your writer's notebook precluster (FAMILY) to gain access to a variety of pictures in your Design mind. Work toward filling a page. This invites memories, associations, feelings, images.
2. Now explore your cluster to see what emerged—particular family members and some of their personality characteristics, events, feelings, and so forth. Focus on qualities that seem to reflect your family structure. A "quality" is definable as a distinguishing aspect, feature, characteristic, or property of a phenomenon—in this case, your family unit and the members within it. You may come up with emotions or persons, or with a word that describes the whole, such as loyalty, or divisiveness, or independence.

Cluster several (at least four) of the most telling qualities, or cluster the individuals making up your family, each on a separate sheet of paper. If you find yourself clustering qualities, you will notice that certain qualities point to a particular family member; if you cluster a family member, you will notice that qualities emerge in the cluster to fit that person. Where you start can be determined by either your preference or where your pre-cluster is nudging you.

3. For each of the clusters write a tentative focusing statement, or experiment with several. The focusing statements are tentative because you are now doing more extended writing and you may find the focus of each subsequent vignette shifting as your family portrait begins to emerge. After you have written the focusing statements for each vignette, write an overall focusing statement for the entire portrait to give you a sense of direction. Many students discover a title for their family portrait in their overall focusing statement.

4. Now experiment with form. You may wish to write prose or you may prefer free-verse poetry; you may experiment with dialogue; you may want to cast your vignettes in the form of letters. Whatever shape your writing takes, begin by creating four or more separate vignettes, in keeping with our emphasis on mini-wholes. Each will be a self-contained unit that you will ultimately tie together with a unifying thread. The vignettes, of course, will result from the four or more clusters you have done.

5. Write an exploratory rough draft based on the first "quality" or "person" cluster; then go on to write the others. *Allow* the writing to emerge naturally, using your clusters as guides. Don't censor. When you revise later, you can trim. Ideally, it would be best if you could put these first-draft vignettes aside for a day or two to let them simmer. Letting some time pass between each revision may give your Design mind a chance to ruminate on these emerging portraits and so discover a way to unify them into the larger vision necessary for the sustained whole.

6. When you have completed the vignettes, read them aloud. Look for a dominant thread. It may be a phrase, an action, an object, an event, a symbol, a feeling, a behavior pattern, a central person. Recall the dinner table as a microcosm of life interactions in the first sample family portrait, the vague fairy-tale focus of the second. If no dominant thread has surfaced for you (although that is unlikely), recluster for DOMINANT IMAGE, scanning your clusters for ideas. Something will come up.

7. Begin your revision by working your unifying thread into each one of your vignettes. If you find that you wrote purely chronological history (although it is unlikely that this happened) it is time for you to redesign; following a temporal sequence represents Sign-mind organization since the Design mind does not organize its thoughts sequentially. As you begin your revision, stay focused on the qualitative whole and rework your vignettes with the following in mind:

· Allow the unifying thread to make its appearance in several places throughout the whole; consider its relevance for your title.

· Coming full circle. Strive to make your ending in some way reach back toward your beginning so that your writing will have a sense of unity and wholeness reflecting your Design-mind vision.

· Recurrences. Recurrences help to unify, emphasize, and pattern your writing for significance.

· Language rhythms. This includes word flow, parallel forms, balanced sentences, rhythms that reflect content and meaning—smooth or choppy language, slow or animated, depending on what you are trying to communicate. Language rhythm also means the sound of the words as they are read aloud—the implied sound of a human voice telling a story. That voice registers on the inner ear and tells us things about the writer and the writing, and about the story being told. Read your work aloud for the sound of it before you consider it finished.

· Creative tension. You will have feelings, ideas, polarities that conflict and resolve. For example, a father or a mother can be simultaneously caring and cruel, weak and strong, involved and detached.

· Images. Sensory images bring the writing to life. Allow your words to make images in the reader's head.

- **Metaphor.** Use it to express the logically inexpressible, to paint shades of meaning, to arrest attention, to surprise.
- **Title.** Test any tentative titles you have given your portrait; it should express something about the whole you have shaped. A title acts as an advance organizer, helping to guide the reader, suggesting tone, attitude, point of view. A title really is a metaphor or an image for the whole creation.

8. Make several drafts until you are satisfied with your work. Then edit for mechanical errors and spelling, proofreading carefully. Retype it on clean paper and then proofread again for typographical errors.

After Writing

Receptive once more to the innocence of eye and ear we had as children, as adults we can cultivate a freshness of perception and expression that articulates our thoughts in ways that are soul-satisfying to us and to others. In writing naturally, you are engaging in a creative act that is fulfilling in a way you probably do not expect writing to be. If you continue to tap your inner writer as you have been doing throughout this book, you will grow ever more deeply into the possibilities of seeing with the cultivated eye, listening with the cultivated ear, writing with the cultivated hand.

Language has been yours since you were very small. Reclaim the innocent delight in words and your natural creative potential by orchestrating your Design- and Sign-mind talents. Cereamicist/poet/ educator M. C. Richards displays a clear sense of natural writing. Given Richards's sentence to model, a student writer expressed her feelings about writing as follows:

> What is writing if it is not the discovery of our inward selves: sorrowful, precious, persistent, what we need and desire, fear for, how it is born within us, grows larger or smaller as we do, presses itself against the boundaries of our understanding, and finally flows itself through our minds, our fingertips, our ink pens.
>
> Nancy Wambach

What is writing, if it is not the countenance of our daily experience: sensuous, contemplative, imaginary, what we see and hear, dream of, how it strikes us, hôw it comes into us, travels through us, and emerges in some language hopefully useful to others.

M. C. Richards,
Poetry, Pottery, and the Person

Now that you've gone through the exercises of this book, I invite you, as I do all my students, to cluster the word (WRITE) so you can actually see how your experience with and feelings about writing have changed. When you have finished your vignette, check it against the first entry in your writer's notebook, in which you also wrote about writing. The difference will be illuminating.

I close with a vignette triggered by the nucleus (WRITE) (Figure 12–3). As you read this writer's serious and witty, yet profoundly affirmative response to what writing has come to mean to her, let her affirmation spur you onto ever more fulfilling natural writing experiences.

Figure 12–3

Writing transcends the mundane, fills my skies with light, mind-light, with poetry and music, a mosaic of thought, spread out on a page, all mine to give.

To write the unwriteable wrong is to be a journalist; to write feelings—a poet; to write songs and suns and moons and stars—a living being. For the soul of one human being to touch the soul of another with words is glory—a God-given glory, and I celebrate it. I sing myself, I celebrate you, we communicate.

Communication and response; teaching and learning; giving, giving, writing is giving. Writing is joy; writing is finding things inside you you didn't know were there. Writing is mind-light for others to see.

Linda Pierce

Creativity has not only made the human race unique in Nature: what is more important for the individual, it gives value and purpose to human existence. Creativity requires more than technical skills and logical thought; it also needs the cultivation and collaboration of the appositional [Design] mind.

Joseph E. and Glenda M. Bogen,
"The Other Side of the Brain III:
The Corpus Callosum and
Creativity"

Coming Full Circle

As one by one you rediscovered the natural writing strategies presented in this book, you increasingly developed your cultivated inner writer. Creative cultivation orchestrates both hemispheres of the brain, as surgeon Joseph Bogen has insisted.

Now, as you continue to tap your natural writer with an attitude of wonder and an impulse to story your experience, you will grow even more deeply into the possibilities of seeing with the cultivated eye, listening with the cultivated ear, writing with the cultivated hand. Continue to trust your Design mind as source.

Bibliography

Alajouanine, Th. "Aphasia and Artistic Realization." *Brain* 71, 1948.

Barzun, Jacques. *Simple and Direct.* NY: Harper & Row, Publishers, 1976.

Bertelson, P., "The Nature of Hemispheric Specialization: Why Should There Be a Single Principle?" *The Behavioral and Brain Sciences,* 4:63–64, 1981.

Black, Max. *Models and Metaphors: Studies in Language and Philosophy.* Ithaca, N.Y.: Cornell University Press, 1962.

Bloomfield, Harold H. and Robert B. Kory, "Inner Joy," New York: *Playboy Paperbacks,* 1980.

Bogen, Joseph E. "Some Educational Aspects of Hemispheric Specialization." *UCLA Educator,* Spring 1975. Also in: *Dromenon,* February 1978; *The Human Brain,* Merle Wittrock, ed. (Englewood Cliffs, N.J.: Prentice-Hall), 1977; *Allos,* K. Gabino, ed. (La Jolla, Calif.: Lingua Press), 1980.

———. "The Callosal Syndrome." *Clinical Neuropsychology,* K. Heilman and J. Valenstein, eds. London: Oxford University Press, 1978.

———. "Cerebral Duality and Hemispheric Specialization." *Behavioral and Brain Sciences.* (in press).

Bogen, Joseph E. and Glenda M. Bogen. "The Other Side of the Brain III: The Corpus Callosum and Creativity." In *The Nature of Human Consciousness.* Robert Ornstein, ed., San Francisco: W. H. Freeman & Co., 1973.

Brain/Mind Bulletin. Interface Press. P.O. Box 4211, Los Angeles, CA 90042.

Brande, Dorothea. *On Becoming a Writer.* Los Angeles: Tarcher, 1981.

Britton, James. *Language and Learning.* Miami: University of Miami Press, 1970.

Broudy, Harry. "Impression and Expression in Artistic Development." *The Arts, Human Development, and Education,* Elliot Eisner, ed. Berkeley, Calif.: McCutcheon, 1976.

Brown, Jason, and Jaffe, Joseph. "Hypothesis on Cerebral Dominance." *Neuropsychologia* 13:1, 1975.

Bruner, Jerome S. *On Knowing: Essays for the Left Hand.* Cambridge, Mass.: Harvard University Press, 1962.

Buzan, Tony. *Use Both Sides of Your Brain.* New York: Dutton, 1976.

Chomsky, Noam. *Reflections on Language.* NY: Pantheon, 1975.

Chukovsky, Kornei. *From Two to Five.* Berkeley: University of California Press, 1963.

Corballis, M. C., "Toward an Evolutionary Perspective on Hemispheric Specialization." *The Behavioral and Brain Sciences,* 4:69–70, 1981.

Dewey, John. *Art As Experience.* New York: Capricorn Books, 1934.

Didion, Joan. "On Keeping a Notebook." *Slouching Towards Bethlehem.* New York: Dell, 1968.

Dromenon: A Journal of New Wave of Being. G.P.O. Box 2244, New York, NY 10001.

Edwards, Betty. *Drawing on the Right Side of the Brain.* Los Angeles: Tarcher, 1979.

Ehrenzweig, Anton. *The Hidden Order of Art.* Berkeley: University of California Press, 1971.

Eisner, Elliot. *Educating Artistic Vision.* New York: Macmillan, 1972.

Elbow, Peter. *Writing Without Teachers.* London: Oxford University Press, 1973.

————. *Writing with Power.* London: Oxford University Press, 1981.

Emig, Janet. "Children and Metaphor." *Research in the Teaching of English* 6:2, 1972.

Ferguson, Marilyn. *The Aquarian Conspiracy.* Los Angeles: Tarcher, 1980.

Foss, Martin. *Symbol and Metaphor in Human Experience.* Lincoln: University of Nebraska Press, 1949.

Frye, Northrop. *The Educated Imagination.* Bloomington: Indiana University Press, 1964.

Fuller, Renée. *In Search of the IQ Correlation.* Stony Brook, N.Y.: Ball-Stick-Bird Publications, 1977.

Galin, David. "Implications for Psychiatry of Left and Right Cerebral Specialization." *Archives of General Psychiatry* 31, 1974, pp. 572–583.

Gardner, John. from "Foreword." in Dorothea Brande, *On Becoming a Writer.* Los Angeles: Tarcher, 1934.

Gardner, Howard. *Artful Scribbles.* New York: Basic Books, 1980.

————. *The Shattered Mind.* New York: Knopf, 1975.

Gardner and Winner, Ellen. "The Child Is Father to the Metaphor." *Psychology Today,* May 1979.

Gazzaniga, Michael and LeDawe, G. E. *The Integrated Mind.* New York: Plenum Press, 1978.

Gendlin, Eugene. *Focusing.* New York: Everest House, 1978.

Gerard, R. W. "The Biology of the Imagination." in *The Creative Process,* Brewster Ghiselin, ed. New York: Mentor, 1952.

Ghiselin, Brewster. *The Creative Process.* Berkeley: University of California Press, 1952.

Goldberg, Elkhonon, and Costa, Louis D. "Hemispheric Differences in the Acquisition and Use of Descriptive Systems." *Brain and Language* 14:144–173 1981.

Gordon, W. J. J. *The Metaphorical Way of Knowing and Learning.* Mass.: Synectics Education Press, 1960.

Gray, James. "Understanding Creative Thought Processes: An Early Formulation of Emotional-Cognitive Structure Theory." *Man-Environment Systems* 9:1, 1980.

Grether, Tobias, *Homochronos: Evolution and Development of Consciousness* (unpublished ms.). Camarillo, CA.

Harnad, Stevan R. "Creativity, Lateral Saccades, and the Non-Dominant Hemisphere." *Perceptual and Motor Skills* 34, 1972.

Irmscher, William. *Teaching Expository Writing.* New York: Holt, Rinehart & Winston, 1979.

Jones, Richard M. *Fantasy and Feeling in Education.* New York: Harper & Row, 1968.

Keen, Sam. *Apology for Wonder.* New York: Harper & Row, 1969.

Kepes, Gyorgy, ed. *Sign, Image, Symbol.* New York: Braziller, 1966.

Kinsbourne, M. "The Neuropsychological Analysis of Cognitive Deficit." *Biological Foundations of Psychiatry,* R. G. Grenell and S. Gabay, eds. New York: Raven Press, 1976.

Koch, Kenneth. *Wishes, Lies, and Dreams.* New York: Vintage Books, 1970.

Koestenbaum, Peter. *The New Image of the Person.* Westport, Conn.: Greenwood Press, 1978.

Koestler, Arthur. *The Act of Creation.* New York: Macmillan, 1964.

Langer, Susanne. *Problems of Art.* New York: Scribner's, 1957.

La Violette, Paul. "Thoughts about Thoughts about Thoughts: the Emotional-Perceptive Cycle Theory." *Man-Environment Systems* 9:1, 1980.

La Violette, Paul. "The Thermodynamics of the "Aha" Experience." presented at the 24th Annual North American Meeting of the Society for General Systems Research, San Francisco, California Ja.; 1980.

Leondar, Barbara. "Metaphor and Infant Cognition." *Poetics* 4, 1975.

Levy, Jerry; Nebes, Robert D.; and Sperry, R. W. "Expressive Language in the Surgically Separated Minor Hemisphere." *Cortex* 1:1, 1971.

Lewis, C. Day. *The Poetic Image.* London: Oxford University Press, 1948.

Lhermitte, François. "Mysteries of the Intelligence." *Réalités,* May 1976.

Lucas, F. L. *Style.* New York: Collier Books, 1955.

MacLean, Paul D. "On the Evolution of Three Mentalities." *New Dimensions in Psychiatry: A World View,* Vol. 2, Silvano Arieti and Gerard Chrzanowski, eds. New York: Wiley, 1977.

Macrorie, Kenneth. *Telling Writing.* Rochelle Park, N.J.: Hayden, 1966.

Maritain, Jacques. *Creative Intuition in Art and Poetry.* New York: New American Library, 1953.

McCluggage, Denise. *The Centered Skier.* Waltham, Mass.: Crossroads Press, 1978.

Mearns, Hughes. *Creative Power.* New York: Dover, 1929.

Middlebrook, Diane Wood. *Worlds into Words.* New York: W. W. Norton & Co., 1980.

Moss, Richard. *The I That Is We.* Millbrae: Celestial Arts, 1981.

Nebes, R. D. "Direct Examination of Cognitive Function in the Right and Left Hemispheres." In *Asymmetrical Functions of the Brain,* M. Kinsbourne, ed. NY: Cambridge University Press, 1978.

———. "Man's So-Called 'Minor' Hemisphere." *The Human Brain,* Merle Wittrock, ed. Englewood Cliffs, N.J.: Prentice-Hall, 1977.

Nin, Anaïs. *The Diary of Anaïs Nin,* V. 5. NY: Harcourt Brace, 1964.

Ortony, Andrew, ed., *Metaphor and Thought.* London: Cambridge U. P., 1979.

Paivio, Alan. *Imagery and Verbal Processes.* New York: Holt, Rinehart & Winston, 1971.

Pearce, Joseph C. *The Bond of Power.* New York: Dutton, 1981.

Piaget, Jean. *The Construction of Reality in the Child.* New York: Basic Books, 1954.

———. *The Language and Thought of a Child.* New York: Meridian, 1955.

Pich, David R. "Beowulf to Beatles and Beyond." New York: Macmillan, 1981.

Polanyi, Michael. *The Tacit Dimension.* New York: Doubleday, 1966.

Ransom, John Crowe. *Poems and Essays,* NY: Vintage Books, 1955.

Richards, M. C. *Centering: Poetry, Pottery, and the Person.* New York: Columbia University Press, 1962.

———. *The Crossing-Point.* Middletown, Conn.: Wesleyan University Press, 1973.

Rico, Gabriele Lusser *Metaphor and Knowing.* Unpublished doctoral dissertation. Stanford University, 1976.

———. "Reading for Non-Literal Meaning." *Reading, the Arts, and the Creation of Meaning,* Elliot Eisner, ed. Reston, Va.: National Art Education Association NAEA, 1978.

——— and Claggett, M. F. *Balancing the Hemispheres: An Exploration of the Implications of Brain Research for the Teaching of Writing.* Berkeley: University of California Bay Area Writer's Project Monograph, 1980.

Ross, Elliot. "Aprodosia." *The Sciences* 22:2, 1982.

Rothenberg, Albert. *The Emerging Goddess: The Creative Process in Art, Science, and Other Fields.* Chicago: University of Chicago Press, 1979.

Samuels, Mike, and Samuels, Nancy. *Seeing with the Mind's Eye.* New York: Random House, 1975.

Sewell, Elizabeth. *The Human Metaphor.* Notre Dame, Ind.: University of Notre Dame Press, 1964.

Sommer, Robert. *The Mind's Eye.* New York: Dell Publishing Co., Inc., 1978.

Sommers, Shula. *Journal of Personality and Social Psychology* 41:3, pp. 553–561. (Psychology Department, University of Massachusetts, Boston, MA 02125).

Spender, Stephen. "The Making of a Poem." in *The Creative Process,* Brewster Ghiselin, ed. NY: New American Library, 1952.

Sperry, R. W. "Hemisphere Disconnection and Unity in Conscious Awareness." *American Psychologist* 23 (2), 1968.

Stafford, William. "A Way of Writing." in *Writing the Australian Crawl.* Michigan: University of Michigan Press, 1977.

Strunk, William, and White, E. B. *Elements of Style.* New York: Macmillan and Co., 1979.

Thomas, Dylan. "Notes on the Art of Poetry." in *Modern Culture and the Arts,* James B. Hall and Barry Ulanov, eds., NY: McGraw-Hill Book Co..

Watts, Alan. *The Two Hands of God.* Canada: Macmillan, 1963.

Whitely, Opal. *Opal.* New York: Macmillan, 1976.

Wyke, M. A. "The Nature of Cerebral Hemispheric Specialization in Man: Quantitative vs. Qualitative Differences." *The Behavioral and Brain Sciences,* 4:78–79, 1981.

Zaidel, Eran. "The Elusive Right Hemisphere of the Brain." *Engineering Science,* September/October 1978.

Zangwill, O. L. "Aphasia and the Concept of Brain Centers." *Psychology and Biology of Language and Thought: Essays in Honor of Eric Lenneberg,* George A. Miller & Elizabeth Lenneberg, eds., New York: Academic Press, 1978.

Index